Global and Multicultural Public Relations

Juan-Carlos Molleda and Sarab Kochhar

WILEY Blackwell

Registered Office
John Wiley & Sons, Inc., 111 River Street, Hoboken, NJ 07030, USA

Editorial Office
101 Station Landing, Medford, MA 02155, USA

For details of our global editorial offices, customer services, and more information about Wiley products visit us at www.wiley.com.

Wiley also publishes its books in a variety of electronic formats and by print-on-demand. Some content that appears in standard print versions of this book may not be available in other formats.

Library of Congress Cataloging-in-Publication Data

Names: Molleda, Juan-Carlos, author. | Kochhar, Sarab, 1982– author.
Title: Global and multicultural public relations / Juan-Carlos Molleda, Sarab Kochhar.
Description: First Edition. | Hoboken : Wiley-Blackwell, 2019. | Includes
    bibliographical references and index. |
Identifiers: LCCN 2019001709 (print) | LCCN 2019005068 (ebook) | ISBN
    9781118673973 (Adobe PDF) | ISBN 9781118673928 (ePub) | ISBN 9781118673966
    (paperback)
Subjects: LCSH: Public relations. | Globalization–Economic aspects. |
    Strategic planning. | BISAC: BUSINESS & ECONOMICS / Advertising &
    Promotion.
Classification: LCC HD59 (ebook) | LCC HD59 .M586 2019 (print) | DDC
    659.2–dc23
LC record available at https://lccn.loc.gov/2019001709

Cover Design: Wiley
Cover Images: © Liu zishan/Shutterstock, © poolarchive/iStock.com

Set in 10/12pt Warnock by SPi Global, Pondicherry, India

Printed and bound in Singapore by Markono Print Media Pte Ltd

10 9 8 7 6 5 4 3 2 1

Global and Multicultural Public Relations

Contents

1

Introduction and Overview of Global and Multicultural Public Relations

Central Themes

- Significant historical events with economic, political, and social implications have determined the evolution, growth, and sophistication of public relations in countries and regions across the world.
- Emergent technologies are dramatically speeding up the development and increasing the reach of organizations, media outlets, citizens, and consumers, facilitating the instantaneous exchange of contents from one location to multiple locations.
- Communication conglomerates, global agencies, and networks of independent agencies are major players and influencers in the public relations industry worldwide.
- Since the 1940s, European and North American professional associations have made significant contributions to modern and strategic public relations as a profession and to the career development of national and international professionals.
- All types of organizations practice global and multicultural public relations, including government and nongovernmental organizations (NGOs), multilateral organizations, multinational corporations (MNCs), and agencies.
- The complexity of public relations programs increases when organizations operate across borders, because of the existence and dynamism of home, host, and transnational stakeholders and publics.

Keywords *multilateral organizations; trade groups; professional associations; communication hubs; evolution; transition; clearinghouse; home, host, transnational, and multinational corporations; global agencies; communication conglomerates; growth*

Global and Multicultural Public Relations, First Edition. Juan-Carlos Molleda and Sarab Kochhar.
© 2019 John Wiley & Sons, Inc. Published 2019 by John Wiley & Sons, Inc.

Introduction

The geographical scope of action and level of specialization of public relations and communications management professionals are expanding rapidly worldwide. All types of organizations face the need to communicate with and engage stakeholders in a multiplicity of national and regional environments. Concerning the need for public relations professionals to spend time overseas, the 2013 Career Guide of *PRWeek* emphasizes:

> This embrace of international experience comes as the industry has become increasingly global. Technology makes it even easier to communicate across the world. The supply chain now stretches across continents; as more companies draw talent, materials, and resources from all corners of the world. These changes require communications pros to speak to a growing range of audiences. (Palmer 2013, p. 25)

This textbook documents and discusses specific practices used by various business, government, and nongovernment sectors to cultivate relationships and develop corporate reputations among foreign and multicultural stakeholders. Overall, the textbook will cover some main questions, like: What are the skills and knowledge required to practice strategic global and multicultural public relations in a specific sector? What are the implications for practice when managing relationships with home, host, transnational, and multicultural stakeholders? Which strategies are considered best practices in each sector?

Understanding global public relations in multicultural environments is essential in an increasingly interconnected world. Organizations constantly face the emergence, expansion, and contraction of markets; better informed and engaged stakeholders and consumers; greater competition; and the availability of communications and media technologies. Technologic platforms and channels blur geographical boundaries and facilitate the coordination, production, implementation, and evaluation of public relations and communications efforts, with the active participation of agency, in-house, and outsourcing teams working from several world locations.

Thus, the primary goal of this textbook is to introduce you to the evolving field of global and multicultural public relations, including its infrastructure, issues and opportunities, and strategies and tactics, through illustrations and case studies.

Forces Driving the Growth of the Practice

Historically, the evolution of public relations can be attributed to the result of social pressures on organizations or the empowerment of public opinion demanding social responsibility and organizational transparency, both locally and globally (Sharpe and Pritchard 2004). Historical events have also impacted the evolution of the practice and field of study. The reconstruction of Western European countries after World War II and the subsequent increase in cross-Atlantic trade led to a significant growth in modern public relations. Similarly, other successive economic, political, social, and sporting events positively impacted the growth and sophistication of public relations and communications management in regions and countries across the world. Examples include the Olympic Games in South Korea in 1988, which stimulated the country's economy and catapulted it on to the world stage as a technology center; the fall of the Berlin Wall and the subsequent collapse of the Soviet Union in 1989, which led to new freedoms for Central and Eastern European nations; and the end of apartheid in South Africa and the subsequent election of Nelson Mandela (1918–2013) – the so-called Father of the New South Africa – as the country's president in 1994, which put into action a reconciliation commission and nation-building plans to unify segregated populations into one national identity. Strategic public relations has contributed to these countries' and regions' ability to plan and communicate their dynamic economic, political, and social transitions.[1]

Previous studies have found at least six major environmental variables affecting the evolution and growth of public relations in many countries.[2] In no specific order, these are: (i) social culture and traditions; (ii) political systems; (iii) the level of economic development; (iv) news media practices and infrastructure; (v) the nature and types of activism or social movements; and (vi) the laws and regulations directly or indirectly impacting the practice of public relations in a given country. International business scholars Christopher Bartlett and Sumantra Ghoshal (2002) explain how **multinational corporations** (MNCs) adapt or react to evolving, challenging contexts:

> Even within particular industries, worldwide companies have developed very different strategic and organizational responses to changes in their environment. While a few players have prospered by turning environmental turmoil to their advantage, many more are merely surviving – struggling to adjust to complex, often contradictory demands. Some large well-established worldwide companies have been forced to take large losses or even to abandon businesses. (Bartlett and Ghoshal 2002, p. 3)

The public relations industry follows historical events closely because such events offer great challenges and opportunities for multinational organizations (MNOs) and the involved societies. For instance, when the outlook is positive, MNCs and global public relations agencies follow the path of economic growth and initiate or expand operations in the growing market. Poland is an example of a Central European country that has benefited from the economic and political changes caused by the dissolution of the Soviet Union. The size and location of the country – next to Germany, surrounded by former Soviet republics, and with a large coast on the Baltic Sea – further contribute to its level of development and geopolitical importance. The middle class has grown, consumers are more demanding, and business competition has increased, which attracts MNCs and public relations agencies to this evolving and expanding market.

Professional Associations

Among the leading players who have catapulted the growth of public relations as a profession are **trade groups or professional associations**, which continue to build, advocate, and strengthen the profession and to support the career development of professionals. European and North American professional associations have influenced the practice since the 1940s (see Table 1.1).

The establishment of public relations associations and institutes progressively continued in the 1950s and 1960s, on every continent. In particular, the UK Chartered Institute of Public Relations (CIPR) and the

Table 1.1 Pioneering European and North American professional associations.

Professional association	Foundation year
The Netherlands Association for Public Contact, renamed first as the Association for Public Relations in the Netherlands and later as the Dutch Association of Communication	1946
Public Relations Society of America	1947
The Canadian Public Relations Society	1948
UK Institute of Public Relations, named the Chartered Institute of Public Relations after obtaining government recognition	1948, 2005
The Norwegian Public Relations Club, later named the Norwegian Public Relations Association and finally the Norwegian Communication Association	1949, 1972, 2000

Public Relations Society of America (PRSA) have been influential in the development of trade groups on various continents. Similarly, the International Public Relations Association (IPRA), founded in 1949, has promoted ethical, professional, and educational standards worldwide. For instance, the IPRA Code of Conduct was adopted in 2011 by consolidating the 1961 Code of Venice, the 1965 Code of Athens, and the 2007 Code of Brussels, and provides global intellectual leadership for the public relations profession.

International and national associations rely on a **clearinghouse organization** to share common interests, concerns, and issues facing the industry. Established by 23 professional organizations at a meeting that followed the 2000 World Public Relations Congress (PRSA and IPRA were the cosponsors) in Chicago, the Global Alliance for Public Relations and Communication Management (GA) unites and represents national professional associations and offers knowledge and programs to help with their development. As a clearinghouse organization, the GA works to set standards for the practice and provide venues and channels for increasing interactions among global professionals. The GA's core offering is that it allows member associations and institutional members to share resources and achieve greater unity by building constructive relationships.

Strategic Communications Hubs

The business of global and multicultural public relations has historically been concentrated in four major world hubs: France (Paris), Japan (Tokyo), the United Kingdom (London), and the United States (New York City). Singapore has emerged as a strategic hub of the South East Asian region. In the same geographical order, the five conglomerates that lead the strategic communications industry today are: Publicis Groupe and Havas (France), Dentsu (Japan), WPP (UK), and Omnicom Group and Interpublic Group (USA).[3] Omnicom and Publicis announced their potential merger in 2013 and again in 2018. We should expect mergers, associations, and the emergence of new conglomerates and agencies in an ever-changing global environment.

In particular, WPP has a group of public relations and public affairs agencies with a great global reach, such as Hill + Knowlton, Ogilvy Public Relations Worldwide, Burson Cohn & Wolfe, and Specialist Public Relations. Edelman Public Relations Worldwide is the biggest global independent agency and not a part of any strategic communication conglomerate. In addition, at least four networks of independent agencies assist organizations in coordinating public relations and communications practices in a matrix of world locations: Iprex, Pinnacle Worldwide, Public Relations Global Network, and Worldcom. Organizations reaching out to home, host, transnational, and multicultural stakeholders combined their in-company public relations and communications departments with global, regional, and national agencies from the strategic communications conglomerates and independent networks. The benefit of these configurations is that they allow MNCs to act and react speedily in multiple world locations with a combination of their own resources and specialized outsourcing capabilities. The extent of the use of agency support by MNCs is determined by their in-house capabilities, the scope of their work, and the complexity of the markets they are trying to reach.

Globalization has redefined global and multicultural public relations and increased the interdependence of countries through an integration of trade, finance, resources, and ideas. The information technology revolution has further helped MNCs, in particular, operate in a world market outside of their national boundaries and attain relative comparative advantage among their global counterparts, leading to growth in global and multicultural public relations. The next section will define strategic global public relations in a multicultural environment – a definition that will guide the viewpoint of this textbook.

Definitions and Outlook

Public relations and communications management professionals practicing in a foreign location must coordinate between the headquarters of their organizations or agencies in one or several world subsidiaries or offices and involve and engage stakeholders at the home, host, and transnational levels. "The important elements in an international program, therefore, boil down to *where the entity is located* and *to which publics it must build relationships*" (Wakefield 2008, p. 141, italics in original). Thus, global and multicultural public relations is a strategic communication function of organizations responsible for relationship-cultivation and reputation-management programs with internal and external stakeholders in multiple world locations. These settings include a variety of home, host, and transnational stakeholders, as well as a diversity of subcultures between and within national boundaries.

Let's first understand the concepts of **home**, **host**, and **transnational** stakeholders. Home stakeholders are those operating in the country where they have their main office or headquarters, host stakeholders are those existing in other countries where a given organization is operating, and transnational stakeholders are a combination of stakeholders in several world locations simultaneously, such as activist networks or global news media. To illustrate this, let us take the example of H&M, an apparel company founded in Sweden in 1947, which as 2015 has more than 132000 employees in 62 markets (see case study). The home stakeholders are in Sweden, and the host stakeholders are in countries including Germany, Canada, and Singapore. An example of a transnational stakeholder is the Agence France Presse, which has published news articles on H&M and many other MNCs.

Illustrations from Various Economic Sectors

Examples from different kinds of organizations practicing global and multicultural public relations are plentiful. In New Zealand, the government has promoted the country's natural landscapes to the world by giving financial incentives to domestic and international film companies. The New Zealand government paid about US$150 million in support of the "Lord of the Rings" trilogy, and an estimated US$117 million for "The Hobbit" trilogy: US$99 million for production costs, US$10 million to help market the movies, and US$8 million to promote New Zealand tourism. Mexico, on the other hand, coordinates the promotion of its tourist destinations through its extensive network of embassies and consulates, with the assistance of advertising, lobbying, and public relations agencies mainly in Europe and North America.

Disneyland Paris plans and executes special events with a European or, more specifically, a French flavor to engage potential and actual visitors with the local offerings of their US-originated theme parks. British firm BP promotes energy alternative projects such as community relations, corporate responsibility, and sustainability programs in all its subsidiaries worldwide.

A Danish-Swedish dairy cooperative, Arla Foods, faced a boycott that affected its business in the Middle East following negative reactions among citizens there to the publication of cartoons depicting the Prophet Muhammad in a Danish newspaper.

How Can Global Public Relations Be Defined?

The evolving nature of public relations as a field of study and practice motivates trade groups, professionals, and scholars to define and redefine domestic and global public relations. Since 2012, PRSA has defined public relations simply as "a strategic communication process that builds mutually beneficial relationships between organizations and their publics." CIPR offers an expanded definition:

> Public relations is about reputation – the result of what you do, what you say and what others say about you.

> Public relations is the discipline which looks after reputation, with the aim of earning understanding and support and influencing opinion and behaviour. It is the planned and sustained effort to establish and maintain goodwill and mutual understanding between an organisation and its publics. (CIPR n.d.)

The core terms in these definitions, among many others that have been crafted worldwide, are "communication," "relationships," "reputation," "understanding," and "goodwill between organizations and publics." When we take the practice and field of study to global and multicultural levels, these definitions need to incorporate a more complex set of publics or stakeholders. The stakeholders at home where the organization is headquartered, host locations where the organization operates in other countries or regions, and the transnational "marketspace" where voices are heard from all geographical directions – that is, a transnational flow of relationships – are all important for an organization. For instance, global public relations has been defined as "the planned and organized effort of a company, institution, or government to establish and build relationships with the publics of other nations" (Wilcox and Cameron 2009, p. 504). Concerning the public in other nations, the multicultural aspect implies relationships and involvement with diverse communities in host locations (other nations). Thus, the definition of global and multicultural public relations that frames the content of this textbook is:

> A strategic and dynamic process that cultivates shared understanding, relationships, and goodwill among organizations and a combination of their culturally heterogeneous home, host, and transnational stakeholders, with the aim of achieving and maintaining a consistent reputation and established legitimation.

With this definition, we would like to emphasize that the diverse stakeholders across the globe dictate the practice of global and multicultural public relations. The definition also encompasses outcomes that help to measure the value and contributions of public relations and communications management to all types of multinational and multilateral organizations.[4]

The Practice of Global Public Relations

The increasing movement of people, commodities, products and services, and financial transactions in the world economy offers attractive opportunities and unavoidable challenges to all types of organizations. Public relations professionals globally experience the difficulty of cultivating and developing strategic relationships between organizations and stakeholders. This complexity exponentially increases when organizations engage stakeholders and consumers in more than one country simultaneously. Governments, corporations, multilateral organizations with membership of and representation in many nations (e.g. the International Monetary Fund, the United Nations and all its agencies, the World Bank), large media operations, nongovernmental organizations (NGOs), and activist networks (e.g. Amnesty International, CorpWatch, Greenpeace) operating in multiple world locations practice global and multicultural public relations.

More than ever before, corporations based in developed or Western economies are sharing international trade with corporations in emergent and developing countries. For instance, Grupo Bimbo of Mexico became the biggest producer and distributer of baked goods in the United States in 2013. Similarly, HTC of Taiwan is ranked a top-three smartphone seller in China, and Chilean LAN Airlines is ranked as the top carrier in South America after buying TAM Airlines of Brazil, also in 2013.

The world economy is becoming more dynamic with the participation of diverse actors. The Boston Consulting Group produces an annual study of the top-100 global challengers from emerging economies. This growing competition for national and regional markets spans many economic sectors. North–South trade has traditionally been dominant globally, but South–South trade is acquiring prominence. The United Nations Development Programme (UNDP) explains that "South–South cooperation is a broad framework for collaboration among countries of the South in the political, social, cultural, environmental and technical domains" (United Nations Office for South–South Cooperation 2014, para. 1). These emerging business giants represent opportunity and growth, as well as high levels of competition and obstacles. For instance, Tata Group of India employs people in the United Kingdom, and the Chinese carmaker Wanxiang employs people in the United States. Emerging multinational business giants engage in internal communication and employee relations that cross geographic borders and time zones.

Moreover, escaping the world's financial crisis of the late 1990s and early 2000s, many countries in Africa, Asia, and Central and South America have experienced economic growth and the subsequent rise of their middle class. This segment of the population is associated with greater consumerism, activism, and plurality of voices in society. The growth of public relations and an increase in sophistication in societies with a significant consumer and civil society base have posed new challenges for the field.

All types of organizations and influential individuals practice global and multicultural public relations, including MNCs, national and local governments, international nongovernmental and nonprofit organizations, multilateral and trade organizations, activist and other interest groups, and an array of celebrities, intellectuals, and experts. MNCs are becoming larger than many national economies. This is important, as their immense resources give them the power to positively and negatively influence entire countries and regions in terms of their economic, social, political, environmental, and technological development. This entails significant corporate responsibilities. For example, General Electric's revenue is larger than New Zealand's GDP. MNCs from developed nations have been dominant in international trade and commerce; however, MNCs from developing nations and emergent economies are successfully competing in increasingly interconnected global and regional marketplaces.

MNCs launch global and regional brands and services that are not limited to just one business offering. They diversify into different industries as part of their business strategy, with the aim of expanding their operations around the world. An example is Al Othman Holding Company, a Saudi Arabian construction company that has established itself as a key international player in several industries, including construction, dairy production, oil and gas supply, steel grating manufacture, industrial material trading, high-quality plastic packaging manufacture, and spun melt nonwoven fabrics production, information technology services, and the hotel industry.

MNCs may develop their own global public relations departments or hire global and national public relations agencies for assistance in coordinating a myriad of projects. They have also introduced modern and strategic public relations practices to countries all over the world. It is common to include the influence of MNCs in historical accounts of the evolution and professionalization of practice in many developing and emergent countries.

National and local governments develop public relations and communication plans to capture the attention of and build relationships with foreign (host and transnational) publics. For example, Mexico launched its "Vive Mexico" campaign to increase tourism, which is its third-largest sector. A country may be promoted holistically or by highlighting specific sectors of its social, political, cultural, or economic structure. The main aims of countries using global public relations are to attract foreign investment, gain political clout, increase the number of tourists visiting their destinations, increase development or social change, and achieve membership in the international community of nations, trading blocs, and regional political alliances.

Individual cities, states, or regions can also design and execute global and multicultural public relations campaigns and programs in order to build understanding with publics in other countries. There may be some coordination between national and local governments during the development of these global public relations efforts. For example, the governor of the US state of Florida, Rick Scott, went to Spain in May of 2012. His delegation encouraged Spanish companies and individuals to develop business in Florida. In particular, Florida Realtors' President Summer Greene presented to Spanish investors the advantages of investing in the state's real estate industry.

International nongovernmental and nonprofit organizations focusing on development practice global public relations to achieve their missions and goals. For example, the World Wide Fund for Nature (WWF), an international NGO working on issues regarding the conservation, research, and restoration of the environment, developed the Earth Hour Campaign. This campaign was launched in Sydney, Australia in 2007 to raise awareness of climate change, encourage energy efficiency, and make a significant contribution toward reducing the global carbon footprint. The symbolic gesture encouraging people to switch off their lights for an hour grew from one city in 2007 to 188 countries in 2018. The Earth Hour is a global call to action to every individual, business, and community throughout the world. It is a call to stand up, to take responsibility, to get involved, and to lead the way toward a sustainable future.

Multilateral and trade organizations, such as the World Health Organization (WHO), World Bank, United Nations International Children's Education Fund (UNICEF), and United Nations Development Program (UNDP), work with multiple governments to address their particular issues, such as public health, education, and poverty. As part of this, they practice global public relations to raise awareness about their campaigns for poverty reduction. The World Bank, for instance, provides a source of financial and technical assistance to developing countries. Established in 1944, it is headquartered in Washington, DC, has more than 100 offices worldwide, and supports governments in attempts to reduce poverty and support development. The organization has 188 member countries, which come together to help reduce poverty in middle-income and poorer countries.

Celebrities use media and public relations extensively to increase their popularity and build their personal reputation in the public eye. For example, "Gangnam Style," the record-breaking single by the South Korean musician Psy, helped promote "hallyu" or the Korean Wave: the increasing popularity of Korean culture in other countries, including pop music, television programs, and film. The South Korean government has supported the movement; the Ministry of Foreign Affairs and Trade announced in 2012 that promoting its culture would be a major aspect of its programs. The South Korean Ministry of Culture, Sports, and Tourism formed a fund of US$10.7 million in order to promote the Korean Wave. Within five months of being posted on YouTube, the "Gangnam Style" video had received 1 billion views. An Australian morning show, "Sunrise," declared a "Psy Day" in October of 2012.

Case Study   A Multinational Crisis that Tested H&M's Commitments

Home and transnational news media, NGOs, politicians, and netizens are increasingly scrutinizing the operations of MNCs in developed, emergent, and developing countries. In October 2012, the Swedish television show *Kalla Fakta*[5] aired a 22-minute segment reporting that workers at Cambodian facilities where H&M[6] clothes were made earned 34 € cents an hour (2.92 Swedish Krona), and at least one employee worked 70 hours a week. This is not the first allegation of issues with facilities in the South East Asian country for H&M. In August 2011, 86 workers became ill at an H&M-related manufacturing facility close to the Cambodian province of Kampong Chhnang. Two days later, 198 workers collapsed. More than 100 were hospitalized overall. This occurred despite the fact that H&M has worked with Better Factories Cambodia since 2005.

Royalty and politics have played a role in the crisis. The Prince of Cambodia, Charin Norodom, lives in Sweden. He said he had requested to meet with H&M executives in October 2012. The MNC did not agree to the meeting. However, in May 2012, H&M's chief executive officer (CEO) Karl-Johan Persson met with Sheikh Hasina, the Prime Minister of Bangladesh, to request an increase of the minimum wage. H&M has been in Bangladesh since 1982.

The garment industry is important in Cambodia. In 2011, it accounted for 85% of total exports and employed about 300 000 people. In February 2012, there was a 2-day tribunal at which more than 200 factory workers spoke about debt, poor living conditions, malnutrition, and other topics. While Adidas and Puma had representatives at the tribunal, H&M and Gap did not attend. The judges, who were from three continents, stated the MNCs needed to take action so that factory workers would not continue to live in poverty.

The tribunal's conclusions and the factories' practices demonstrated the effects of fast fashion. H&M constantly changes its inventory, with clothing that is cheap, to feed customer demand for new designs. In achieving this goal, human labor may be exploited. If so, this would violate one of H&M's seven commitments: "Choose & reward responsible partners" (see www.hm.com). H&M positions itself as one of the leaders in the realm of corporate social responsibility (CSR).

Kalla Fakta posted about the segment on Facebook and Twitter in both Swedish and English, and the segment has English subtitles. H&M has multiple Twitter accounts, but only one, @hmsverige, tweeted about the segment, stating that the program contained incorrect information.

The Accusations

The Swedish television show led a series of online and broadcast accusations that were liked, commented on, shared, retweeted, and selected as favorite by netizens in Sweden and abroad. The series of allegations were generated during four months from October 2012 to February 2013.

The segment aired on October 24. During the show, *Kalla Fakta* invited Karl-Johan Persson to the TV4 Studio via two tweets, which were retweeted for a combined total of 18 times. The same day, the show also tweeted: "For our foreign viewers. This is our story tonight. #Kallafakta." A link led to an article in *The Local* newspaper, the headline of which was: "H&M Slams Claims of 'Low' Cambodian Wages" (*The Local* 2012). Between October 23 and February 28, *Kalla Fakta* posted about H&M on Facebook 45 times on 19 days. Some of the posts contained links to newspapers such as *The Local* and *Expressen*, while others linked to the segment with English subtitles and H&M's response. During the same time period, *Kalla Fakta* tweeted, retweeted, or had a conversation with people that mentioned H&M 55 times on 18 days.

H&M's Responses

H&M went on the offensive even before the segment was aired. Persson said, "We are working with one of the world's leading experts on salaries in countries like Cambodia. We want the salaries to be raised. Furthermore, I was in Bangladesh myself recently and visited the prime minister where I put forward our demands that the wages are raised and that they're increased annually" (*The Local* 2012, pp. 5–6). He accused *Kalla Fakta* of not being an objective news program.

H&M's UK Twitter account, @hmunitedkingdom, made no mention of "Cambodia," "*Kalla Fakta*," or "Scandal." Its "main" Twitter account, @hm, made no mention of the case either. H&M did tweet about *Kalla Fakta* on its Swedish account, @hmsverige. On October 24, it tweeted in Swedish, stating that the program had incorrect information and providing a link to its statement. It did not post anything about the situation on Facebook.

Following a second segment on H&M's Bangladesh manufacturing in December, H&M posted a statement on its website claiming that *Kalla Fakta* was not objective and that therefore its CEO had declined to be interviewed on the show. Persson did answer questions from the *Kalla*

Fakta reporter about conditions in Cambodia before the segment was aired. Given that H&M does not own any factories, he claimed, factory workers are not H&M employees. Consequently, H&M does not directly pay any of the Cambodian workers. Persson reiterated that H&M is not the only company that utilizes these facilities.

In February 2013, H&M was criticized for not properly handling its Facebook account. A 21-year-old woman posted that it should not make a sweatshirt with the face of Tupac Shakur, who was convicted of sexual abuse in 1995. People who disagreed with her wrote comments stating that they hoped she would be raped. One comment included her address. Even though H&M posted that comments with swearwords or unpleasant language would be removed, some remained on its Facebook page for a month (Hansegard 2013).

The MNC announced that it would be collaborating with IF Metal, a Swedish union, to help in Cambodia. The relations between the employers at the factories and the workers were "confrontational," and IF Metal helped facilitate communication between the two groups. Helena Helmersson, the head of sustainability at H&M, met with the ILO/Better Works Cambodia and discussed the conditions for factory workers.

H&M addressed the use of Cambodian facilities. All of the supplier factories in Cambodia where H&M clothes are produced have a trade union. In 2012, the MNC conducted 2541 audits of its "first-tier" factories worldwide. It examined 485 potential factories, and found that 119 failed; 96% of the factories where H&M clothes were manufactured were audited before it agreed to have clothes produced in them. Among the factory workers, 62% were female. The minimum monthly wage for a factory worker in Cambodia was around €63, and the average wage for workers at factories where H&M had contracts was about €68. Four of the seven factories in Cambodia where workers either fainted or felt nauseous produced clothes for H&M.

In April 2013, six months after the segment first aired, H&M published the names of its suppliers in all 23 countries where it had clothes manufactured. The list named 785 suppliers operating in 1798 factories. These suppliers accounted for 95% of all the clothes manufactured for H&M. Out of the 785 suppliers, 148 were "strategic partners," which produced more than 50% of H&M's products.

As of May 2013, 33 factories in Cambodia produced clothes for H&M. In March of that year, an H&M supplier, New Archid, agreed to pay more than €34 000 for workers who were not compensated when a factory closed in December 2012 in Phnom Penh. H&M, along with Walmart, the Cambodian Legal Education Center, New Archid, Saramax, and three government ministries, attended a meeting chaired by the American Center for International Labor Solidarity before the decision was announced.

Governmental Reactions

Hun Sen, the Prime Minister of Cambodia, said that if protests over factory conditions and wages continued, manufacturers would leave the country; he was referring to protests against H&M and Nike. Pia Olsen Dyhr, Minister for Trade and Investment in Denmark, said in November 2012 that she would ask H&M what it was doing to correct the problems in the South East Asian country. The government in Norway also asked to meet with H&M following the segment on *Kalla Fakta*. The Swedish government did not publicly meet with H&M. On May 1, 2013, an increase in minimum wage went into effect in Cambodia.

NGOs Stepping In

NGOs were quick to respond to *Kalla Fakta*'s segment. One was the Clean Clothes Campaign (CCC), established in 1989 and now comprising organizations in 15 countries in Europe. CCC believes companies are responsible for the wellbeing of each worker in their supply chain, even if they do not directly employ them. It works with other organizations with similar goals in Canada, Australia, and the United States. The International Labor Rights Forum, which was established in 1986 under the name International Labor Rights Education & Research Fund, works with CCC in the United States. CCC was involved in planning "fashion mobs" in 10 European countries in December 2012, which helped pressure H&M and other stores into creating a living wage in Cambodia.

In 2013, CCC launched the "No More Excuses" campaign in Europe, demanding that companies increase the wages of Cambodian facility workers. From October 23 to February 28, CCC had nine posts, shares, and photos about H&M and Cambodia. On Twitter, it had 12 tweets, retweets, or links that mentioned H&M and Cambodia. CCC created a petition for people to sign against H&M, Gap, and Zara. Labour Behind the Label (LBL), a branch of CCC in the United Kingdom, has its own Facebook and Twitter accounts. On Facebook, LBL had 10 posts, shares, or mentions of H&M between October 23 and February 28. On Twitter, it tweeted, retweeted, or included links about H&M 55 times.

In response to H&M's announcing that it would be adding a line of clothes to its already existing collection in March 2013, CCC altered an H&M ad with model Vanessa Paradis, adding photos of factory workers to show that they were malnourished. Additionally, a series of cartoons and illustrations designed by the *Humor Chic* blog compared H&M with Adolf Hitler.

What's Next for H&M?

H&M was expected to be in eight new countries between January 2013 and the end of 2014. In 2019, the H&M group, a global fashion and design company is in 47 online markets and stores in72 markets. As H&M expands, the MNC needs to consider governments, NGOs, home and transnational media, netizens, and the consumers that purchase clothes at each of its six brands. Public perceptions of H&M are negative, and it seems that people do not believe what it says. For example, no H&M clothes were found at Rana Plaza, a building that collapsed in Bangladesh, killing more than 1000 people, in 2013. However, Avaaz, a nonprofit organization established in 2007, created an advertisement with a photo of Persson and a survivor from the building collapse. Furthermore, even though H&M stated that it is not a fast-fashion operation, the *Triple Pundit* classified it as such (Kaye 2012).

Given that *Kalla Fakta* provided English subtitles of its 22-minute segment about H&M and Cambodia, one might think that H&M would respond in English on its social media sites. After all, H&M's official Twitter account is in English. However, there is no mention of the crisis. CCC has partnerships with other NGOs that conduct campaigns in predominantly English-speaking countries such as the United States and United Kingdom; H&M has stores in both countries.

However, H&M is due credit; it released the factories that it works with and signed a fire safety agreement (along with the Spanish Inditex and other MNCs) in Bangladesh. Persson met with the Prime Minister of Bangladesh and asked for the minimum wage to be increased. The minimum wage in Cambodia also increased, and H&M did not leave the country.

Lessons Learned

The crisis demonstrated to H&M and other MNCs that they are not immune from criticism and conflict, even if they do not directly employ the workers at the factories they use. It also demonstrated that the public does not "buy" everything that a company says; one article refers to H&M as a "fast-fashion" store, even though H&M states that it is not.

A third lesson following the crisis is that one 22-minute segment has the potential to spark petitions and negative reactions online in numerous countries. Multiple government officials from different countries, and even the Prince of Cambodia, wanted to meet with H&M following *Kalla Fakta*'s segment. H&M had been aware since May 2012 that *Kalla Fakta* was planning on doing a show about the MNC, and it did do some work proactively. Other MNCs, regardless of their home and host countries, learned the need to respond to the crisis in different markets and to manage the message. There were articles in English in the United States, but H&M did not communicate directly to its second-largest market. Consequently, consumers there may have heard the criticism over the problems in Cambodia but not H&M's response.

Summary and Structure of the Book

Planning, executing, and evaluating public relations strategies and tactics across borders challenges the practice and the professional because of the distinctive characteristics of the countries and stakeholders involved. Throughout this book, we hope it will become clear how the complexity of simultaneously or individually engaging home, host, and transnational stakeholders in a variety of national and regional environments determines the sophistication and coordination of public relations in multilateral organizations and MNOs. In-house and agency global teams are active participants in this dynamic.

The book is divided into two main parts: the first focuses on strategy formulation and the second on strategy implementation. Chapter 1 provides a definition of global and multicultural public relations, introduces key industry players, and provides a brief illustration of the different types of organizations using public relations across borders. Chapter 2 explains the strategic process for global and multicultural public relations, the importance of formative and evaluative research unique to the practice, and the measurement and evaluation of programs and campaigns.

Culture, traditions, and other contributing contextual or environmental variables of importance in practicing global public relations are elaborated in Chapter 3. Chapter 4 emphasizes the state of professionalism and ethics integral for professionals practicing global public relations, as well as the skill sets and training necessary for success in international assignments. Chapters 5 and 6 develop the reader's understanding of each organization practicing global and multicultural public relations. Transnational corporations (TNCs), government institutions and agencies, NGOs and multilateral organizations, global public relations agencies, and activist networks are discussed individually to analyze how global public relations is practiced and the opportunities it may provide for professionals.

Chapter 7 discusses coordination and control, and standardization and localization, as ways of managing global public relations campaigns. Chapter 8 describes a crisis situation as handled in an international environment, developing a cross-national conflict-shifting or transnational crisis approach. Chapter 9 highlights the importance of CSR and the role multisector partnerships can play in the strategic management of global campaigns and other communications efforts. Chapter 10 explains how teams work across the globe and how employee relations are streamlined using communication. The emergent technology as an important indicator of success in global public relations practice is developed in Chapter 11. Finally, public diplomacy, corporate foreign policy, and how they can influence nation building and country branding efforts are covered in Chapter 12.

All of the chapters follow the format of explaining the key concepts and illustrating them with case studies to elaborate on the practice of public relations and communications management globally.

Discussion Questions

1 How can we identify the unique challenges of global and multicultural public relations and learn to appreciate them?

2 What dominant forces do you think will further shape the practice of global and multicultural public relations?

3 What role do you think media systems play in defining the practice of global and multicultural public relations?

Class Activity

Students should visit the website of the communication conglomerate WPP and read about its structure and services. The instructor may want to divide the class into small teams and assign each one of WPP's global public relations agencies, asking it to identify the core services that agency offers and where in the world its operations are concentrated. The class then could discuss how much the conglomerate's operations and network of offices overlap and complement one another.

Notes

1 For an extended analysis of transitional public relations and the evolution of public relations, see Ławniczak (2001, 2005, 2007) and Sharpe and Pritchard (2004).

2 Chapter 3 fully describes and illustrates three of the environmental or contextual variables impacting the evolution, growth, and practice of public relations across the world. For a complete exploration of contextualized research, see Sriramesh and Verčič (2009).

3 For more information, see The Global 250 Agency Ranking of the Holmes Report (2018).

4 Measurement and evaluation are core components of Chapter 2.

5 *Kalla Fakta*, which literally translates to "Cold Facts," is similar to the show *Frontline* on PBS and *Panorama* on the BBC. The show started in 1991 and is on TV4. It has won multiple awards, including first place in the History & Society category at the 2012 New York Festivals in Las Vegas.

6 The first H&M store opened in 1947 in Västerås, Sweden, under the name "Hennes." The store only sold apparel for women. Hennes became a multinational corporation in 1964 when a store opened in Norway. Erling Persson, the founder, purchased Mauritz Widforss in 1968, which sold hunting and fishing gear. Later that year, the name of the stores was changed to Hennes & Mauritz (H&M). The clothing store first went on the Stockholm Stock Exchange in 1974, and the first H&M outside of Scandinavia opened in London in 1976. The United States and Spain each welcomed H&M stores in 2000, and stores were opened in Hong Kong and Shanghai in 2007. Today, the company operates in 49 markets; the largest, in order, are: Germany, the United States, the United Kingdom, and France. Hennes & Mauritz AB has six brands, all of which are independent: H&M, COS, Monki, Weekday, Cheap Monday, and & Other Stories. Combined, there are about 2900 stores. Despite its size, H&M only has an in-house public relations department, which handles worldwide communication from its headquarters.

References

Bartlett, C.A. and Ghoshal, S. (2002). *Managing across Borders: The Transnational Solution*, 2e. Boston, MA: Harvard Business School Press.

CIPR. (n.d.). "What is PR?" Retrieved January 10, 2019 from https://www. cipr.co.uk/content/policy/careers-advice/what-pr.

Hansegard, J. (2013). "H&M fumbles on Facebook." *The Wall Street Journal*. Retrieved January 10, 2019 from http://blogs.wsj.com/corporate-intelligence/ 2013/02/07/hm-fumbles-on-facebook.

Holmes Report. (2018). "Global top 250 PR agency ranking 2018." Retrieved January 10, 2019 from https://www.holmesreport.com/ranking-and-data/ global-pr-agency-rankings/2018-pr-agency-rankings/top-250.

Kaye, L. (2012). "H&M, the ethical fast fashion leader?" *Triple Pundit*. Retrieved January 10, 2019 from http://www.triplepundit.com/2012/04/ hm-sustainability-report-2011.

Ławniczak, R. (ed.) (2001). *Public Relations Contribution to Transition in Central and Eastern Europe: Research and Practice.* Poznań: Biuro Usługowo-Handlowe.

Ławniczak, R. (ed.) (2005). *Introducing Market Economy Institutions and Instruments: The Role of Public Relations in Transition Economies.* Poznań: Piar Publications.

Ławniczak, R. (2007). Public relations role in a global competition 'to sell' alternative political and socio-economic models of market economy. *Public Relations Review* 33: 377–386.

The Local. (2012). "H&M slams claims of 'low' Cambodian wages." Retrieved January 10, 2019 from http://www.thelocal.se/44016/20121024.

Palmer, A. (2013). Global growth. *PR Week Career Guide* 24–26.

Sharpe, M.L. and Pritchard, B.J. (2004). The historical empowerment of public opinion and its relationship to the emergence of public relations as a profession. In: *Toward the Common Good; Perspectives in International Public Relations* (ed. D.J. Tilson and E.C. Alozie), 14–36. Boston, MA: Allyn and Bacon.

Sriramesh, K. and Verčič, D. (eds.) (2009). *The Global Public Relations Handbook: Theory, Research, and Practice.* New York: Routledge.

United Nations Office for South–South Cooperation. (2014). "What is South–South cooperation?" Retrieved January 10, 2019 from http://www.arab-ecis.unsouthsouth.org/about/what-is-south-south-cooperation/

Wakefield, R.I. (2008). Theory of international public relations, the Internet, and activism: A personal reflection. *Journal of Public Relations Research* 20: 138–157.

Wilcox, D.L. and Cameron, G.T. (2009). *Public Relations Strategies and Tactics*, 9e. Boston, MA: Allyn and Bacon.

2

Research, Measurement, and Evaluation

Central Themes

- Research is an essential part of public relations management, especially on the global stage. Without research, public relations would not be a true management function. It would not be strategic or a part of executive strategic planning within an organization.
- Research makes public relations activities strategic by ensuring that communication is specifically targeted to a variety of stakeholder groups that want, need, or care about the information and, most important, are willing to be involved.
- The purpose of research is to develop strategy in public relations, to define goals and objectives for a campaign, to operate as a part of the strategic management function within an organization, and to measure the success of efforts.
- Designing an international media measurement program is a challenging task, but a very important one for global organizations.
- After a public relations plan has been formulated and put into practice, evaluative research allows an organization to determine whether and to what degree its objectives have been achieved.
- Quantitative and qualitative research methods have complementary and unique strengths. These two research approaches should be used in conjunction whenever possible in public relations management.

Keywords   *measurement; primary research; secondary research; evaluation; quantitative research; qualitative research; media monitoring; outtakes; outcomes; domestic consultancy; internal and external validity; transnational corporation; corporate social responsibility*

Global and Multicultural Public Relations, First Edition. Juan-Carlos Molleda and Sarab Kochhar.
© 2019 John Wiley & Sons, Inc. Published 2019 by John Wiley & Sons, Inc.

Introduction

Let's imagine a scenario where a large consumer-goods corporation with headquarters in the Netherlands and the United Kingdom is in the process of creating a multiple-platform corporate identity campaign to emphasize its contribution to consumer health and wellbeing in South East Asia. A corporate identity campaign focuses on the core values and philosophy of management of an organization, including its visual identity components and the main causes it supports. It is executed in multiple communication platforms and channels, including traditional media and emergent interactive technologies. The corporation requests its global public relations agency and regional headquarters in Singapore to evaluate public perceptions concerning these topics in the region, as well as opinions on the corporation's corporate social performance. In a conference call, the UK marketing-communication team explains the rationale and business goals behind such a request and articulates the specific questions and countries involved in this phase of a global communications effort. With a purpose and goal in mind, the public relations team in Singapore then follows the articulation of overall questions to guide the design of a research methodology. In the case of multinational businesses, research is a systematic process that follows a specific purpose, clear goal, and strict timelines. In public relations, **formative research** is used for data gathering, which helps initiate a strategic plan. This formal and informal data-gathering process is used to develop an analysis of the situation, to define goals and objectives with desired outcomes or effects, to select strategies and tactics, and to outline a timeline for implementation. **Monitoring research** is used for the assessment of the partial impact of the campaign under implementation, and evaluation research focuses on the final results and the measurement of outcomes; that is, the effectiveness of the campaign.

The UK team provides initial arguments and information to support the reasons for the regional campaign, including the emphasis on health and wellbeing, countries involved, and preliminary budget. The team also specifies the role of the global agency, the South East Asian headquarters, and the interplay among the various parties involved. All parties can access and share existing reports and the campaign briefing through a corporate shared-point website. The conference call is an opportunity for the global agency and the office in Singapore to ask pertinent questions and offer regional insights to refine the request and set expectations for the formative research component of the campaign. For instance, how is the campaign's focus related to the business goals of the corporation and to its global operation and the region? How many countries will be involved? What is the timeline and budget for data collection and analysis? Who will be in charge of each stage of the research process? Should primary or secondary research be used? If secondary research will be part of the process, what will be considered reliable sources? If primary research has to be conducted, what will be the ideal research methods? What are the deliverables and when do they need to become available? Will the global agency, the UK office, or the Singaporean office lead the research process? Will data gathering be outsourced to specialized companies? What role will be played by country offices of the corporation, and perhaps of the agency?

These and other questions will allow the multinational virtual team to clearly explain the purpose of the research; to specify its scope; to define responsibilities; and to decide how data will be gathered, analyzed, shared, and presented for easy consumption of the results. A follow-up conversation might focus on the unique challenges the formative research stage of the campaign process may encounter in certain countries, and whether common research methods can be used to allow comparison and contrast among the populations in the various countries involved. Potential public relations problems are often first uncovered during **informal environmental scanning**, while more formal methods are used to confirm and define them.

The public relations strategic process is grounded in organizational vision, values, and overall management philosophy. It starts when a business or organization decides on a public relations campaign and the reasons why it is needed. Top-management leaders dictate the roadmap that the organization will take and how the various organizational units should support business strategies. Public relations, as an organizational unit, works with top management and other units to develop action plans to achieve business goals. This is true in organizations with a domestic reach and in organizations with a global presence.

Going back to the earlier example of the large consumer-goods corporation with headquarters in the Netherlands and the United Kingdom, the business goal, as identified in South East Asia, is to increase the market share of a new line of environmentally friendly and nature-inspired products. The public relations goal will then be to enhance the reputation of the corporation as an industry leader with a clear vision – a reputational attribute that is supported by the quality of its products and its socially driven corporate performance. The merger between business and public relations goals demands coordinated campaigns among marketing, advertising, sales promotion, and strategic public relations. The multiplicity of traditional and emergent communications platforms – such as intranets, websites, shared drives, and cloud – allows for an efficient coordination among these organizational functions.

More specifically, the chosen strategy will guide the articulation of key communications messages, the selection of spokespeople and communications channels and media, and the identification of possible environmental or country-specific aspects that should be considered in programming. For instance, in the earlier example, if the host country is Indonesia and the target stakeholders are middle-class households in the capital city of Jakarta, the strategy will indicate the ways and means of reaching this stakeholder group in order to achieve the desired change in the allotted time. Formative research will allow organizational and agency professionals to understand the target stakeholder group, the way it thinks about health and wellbeing, and the factors that will help it relate to and understand the organization's message. Research before the development of a communication plan or campaign will also help professionals to design strategies for the organization to achieve and evaluate stakeholder reactions and actions during and after the program's implementation.

Moreover, research on the meaning of health and wellbeing for Indonesian families might indicate the following: overweight figures are attractive because they are a symbol of good health (Singh and Luis 1995); and the association between environmental conditions and health seems not to be a priority for this population. If the public relations professional can understand the way the target stakeholders think about the environmental or contextual factors through research, then the choice and articulation of strategies will be precise and meaningful. In addition, research on what might inform the decisions of the target stakeholders, marketing data on the way they behave, and identification of their cultural idiosyncrasies and traditions can help develop and evaluate the success of the campaign. The formative research helps define objectives and goals and to align the public relations unit with the business vision. The acronym ROPES (research, objectives, programming, evaluation, and stewardship) can then be used to plan and execute programs and campaign globally and locally through the research, objectives, planning, evaluation, and stewardship components of the public relations strategic process.

Research Sources and Methods

Leading organizations are always on a quest to manage resources efficiently and achieve organizational goals effectively. They realize that the emphasis of organizational operations and outcomes should be on their internal and external stakeholders, clients, and consumers. These publics confer organizations a license to operate and have the power to contribute to or hinder their organizational success. Organizations that operate in multiple countries must balance internal efficiencies and external effectiveness strategically. This is done by aligning resources to well-informed strategies and pairing these purposive efforts to the characteristics of targeted groups, which maximizes desired impacts. Organizations call public relations to justify strategic choices and provide evidence of the impact of their plans and efforts to the organizational bottom line; in other words, the **return on investment** (ROI).

Stacks and Michaelson (2010) and Stacks (2002) explain the advantages of research for both the public relations function and public relations professionals:

- Gain credibility among top-management members and secure financial and human resources and infrastructure for the function.
- Help define the orientation and purpose of campaigns and communications plans.
- Assist in the articulation of goals, objectives, strategies, and tactics.
- Allow for the writing of measurable and achievable outcomes among stakeholders.
- Facilitate the continuous improvement of the public relations and communications strategies of an organization with the aim to obtain, maintain, and enhance corporate reputation, trust, credibility, and legitimacy.

Primary and Secondary Research

Research in public relations begins any strategic process or campaign. Broom and Dozier (1990, p. 4) define research as "the controlled, objective, and systematic gathering of information for the purposes of describing and understanding." Research is integral to the public relations process. Two steps of the four-step public relations process, developed by Broom (2000), depend on research: defining the public relations problem or opportunity and evaluating the program. Public relations professionals use a variety of research methods and data collection techniques to identify and engage stakeholder groups nationally and internationally. **Primary research** and **secondary research** differ in their concepts and methods.

One of the major differences between primary and secondary research is that primary research is conducted with the help of primary sources, whereas secondary research is conducted on the basis of data collected from someone who themselves obtained it from another source. Let's look at an example to elucidate this difference. If you interview community leaders who live close to a mining operation operated by a Brazilian multinational corporation (MNC) in a town in South Africa and ask them their preferences regarding a water-treatment system in their locality, you are conducting primary research, because you are obtaining data direct from the source. If, on the other hand, you consult reports that have been issued by South African utilities companies or government agencies regarding water-treatment options and their advantages and disadvantages, you are conducting secondary research, because you are using secondary sources to inform your organization's decisions and actions. Ideally, an organization's decisions and subsequent actions will be informed by a variety of data points.

Another important difference between primary and secondary research is that the time taken to conduct primary research is usually long when compared to that taken to conduct secondary research. The Internet has made secondary research a quick and effective tool for gathering information.

One of the main criticisms of secondary research is that the results are not specific to organizational needs and cannot be used to clearly understand the viewpoints of cross-national stakeholder groups.

Qualitative and Quantitative Research

Public relations research provides the foundation for almost everything communicators do, including identifying and understanding key publics, framing important issues, developing public relations and organizational strategy, and measuring results. Using public relations research to develop strategy can involve both informal and formal methods.

There are two main types of public relations research: **qualitative research** and **quantitative research**. Qualitative research captures people's own words, opinions, and views on topics under investigation and uses these responses to identify consensus, disagreements, or perspectives. The purpose of qualitative research is to provide a rich, in-depth understanding of how certain people think or feel about a subject. However, the results cannot be generalized to larger populations. Qualitative research allows public relations practitioners to "discover rather than test" ideas (Broom and Dozier 1990, p. 400).

Quantitative research employs closed-ended questions with specific answer choices, such as in a survey questionnaire, to identify majority or minority opinions through the calculation of responses in groupings. In other words, it "is the controlled, objective, and systematic gathering of data" (Stacks 2002, p. 6), which can be generalized to larger populations. Both types of research are valuable, and both can provide critical insights, especially when used together. For example, a public relations professional might conduct a series of focus group interviews (qualitative research) to identify possible issues that concern employees, then use the information from the focus groups to develop questions for an employee survey (quantitative research).

In a global operation, the country or region of origin may be used as an **independent variable**. The location of a subsidiary or branch (independent variable) might influence the views of employees on certain aspects of their work or issues faced by their business. Knowing the impact of an office's location can help public relations professionals to develop a more effective model of internal communications, with an emphasis on national or regional differences. Moreover, a balance between global and local contents can be used to increase the effectiveness of employee relations programs.

Qualitative methods involve the analysis of language and human behaviors in order to understand social phenomena. Case studies, interviews, focus groups, direct and indirect participant field observations, and ethnography are examples of qualitative research. In contrast, quantitative research methods focus on the articulation of concepts in precise categories to uncover existing patterns among participants' responses. Examples of quantitative research are surveys, content analyses, experiments, and longitudinal studies. How do you decide between quantitative and qualitative research? You should identify and understand the research approach underlying any given study, because the selection of a research approach influences the questions asked, the methods chosen, the statistical analyses used, the inferences made, and the ultimate goal of the research.

Measurement and Evaluation

Through measurement activities, research also helps quantify the value of effective public relations. The measurement and evaluation of public relations effectiveness have long been a major professional and research priority. Public relations practitioners constantly attempt to establish a clear connection between public relations efforts and the bottom line (Michaelson and Stacks 2011). Results of the 2012 Peripheral Vision Study by Ogilvy Public Relations, Australia and the International Association for the Measurement and Evaluation of Communications show a dire need for the quantification of public relations effectiveness if the field is to survive (OPR n.d.). The need for streamlined processes and quantifiable methods has been emphasized by academics and practice. Professionals and scholars have debated whether standardized measures for public relations activities have ever been recognized, but agree that measurement and assessment are important aspects of any successful communication effort (Michaelson and Stacks 2011).

Wilcox and Reber (2013) provide three levels of public relations measurement. Measuring media placements or coverage is the most basic form, followed by comprehension and retention of messages, and finally opinion or behavioral change. Michaelson and Macleod (2007) present a best-practice systems approach to public relations, emphasizing quality research methods that lead to outputs (tactical), outtakes (perceptions), and outcomes (behaviors). Paine (2011) contributes to the understanding of the public relations measurement by categorizing outputs (i.e. physical products of public relations efforts, such as news coverage), outtakes (i.e. awareness and attitudes), and outcomes (i.e. behavior) as distinct approaches to be taken by professionals and scholars.

National and global trade groups and professional organizations have discussed and provided guidelines for research in public relations. For instance, the Global Alliance for Public Relations and Communication Management (GA), the International Communications Consultancy Organisation (ICCO), the Institute for Public Relations (IPR), the Public Relations Society of America (PRSA), and the International Association for the Measurement and Evaluation of Communication (AMEC) sponsored the Barcelona Declaration of Measurement Principles of 2010 (IPR 2010). The Declaration includes seven principles: (i) goal setting and measurement are essential; (ii) measuring the effect on outcomes is preferred to measuring outputs; (iii) the effect on business results can and should be measured where possible; (iv) media measurement requires quantity and quality; (v) advertising equivalencies (AVEs) are not the value of public relations; (vi) social media can and should be measured; and (vii) transparency and replicability are paramount to sound measurement. These principles are discussed and promoted by the sponsoring organizations and other leaders of the sector worldwide annually.

Media Monitoring

Media-monitoring companies offer media measurement specifically tailored for its clients around the world. **Media monitoring** is the process of reading, watching, or listening to the editorial content of media sources on a continuing basis, and identifying, saving, and analyzing that which contains specific keywords or topics. Media-monitoring companies like Cision, Gfk MRI, CyberAlert, and Dow Jones monitor traditional, broadcast, and social media to help organizations measure the efficacy of their public relations efforts and communications programs. They use specific keywords to multisource news about their clients, their competitors, and any events of interest. For example, the media-monitoring company Cision operates in more than 125 countries and provides four services for each of its clients: (i) management of content gathering; (ii) analysis and organization of the content gathered; (iii) provision of reports and performance indicators; and (iv) provision of client recommendations and insights based off the observations. The media coverage or placement is categorized with tags, including for region, competitor, spokesperson, product, and tone. Cision also monitors social media, analyzing the number of blog posts, followers, fans, votes, commenters, and more.

Another media-monitoring company, Dow Jones, offers media monitoring as well as media measurement, industry research, corporate reputation, and business research. Some of its resources include: (i) Factiva, which allows companies and organizations to monitor their competitors, learn about influencers, and learn about industries; (ii) Barron's, which analyzes trends in trading, information about stocks and bonds, and emerging markets; (iii) WSJ.com, which provides news 24/7 about financial information, world events, business, technology, culture, and lifestyle (Dow Jones n.d.).

Media relations continues to be a popular practice in public relations. It has acquired special relevance with the advent of emergent communications technologies like social media. Mike Daniels and Angela Jeffrey offer an international media analysis guide on the IPR website (Daniels and Jeffrey 2012). They argue that the main challenge faced by global public relations professionals in conducting international media analyses is the identification of established news sources and user-generated media sources among the increasingly fragmented global media. The strategy here should be active listening – a primary component of the Melbourne Mandate, which includes the culture of listening, engagement, and reporting (Global Alliance n.d.).

Daniels and Jeffrey outline steps that can help a public relations professional to plan and conduct evaluations of programs and of the specific practices of media relations (Daniel and Jeffrey 2012). The first step is to understand business goals and objectives involved in aligning the communication efforts. The second is to determine suitable measures (i.e. outputs, outtakes, and outcomes) and metrics that will help to identify what success looks like and what is really wanted to be accomplished. The third is to select the media content needed, using parameters such as countries and languages, media sources, and specific contents (i.e. traditional print and broadcast media, traditional monitors, aggregators, social media, client-supplied clips, etc.). The fourth is to decide the type of analysis needed, including artificial intelligence or natural language processing, human analysis (e.g. reading and summarizing contents), or a combination of the two. The fifth is to select a monitoring and analysis provider, considering its international experience, knowledge about local markets, handling of language, and ability to customize solutions, domestic representation, or management. The sixth is to determine language and analysis processes, develop measurement scorecards (i.e. coding sheets or check lists), and select provider services. The seventh is to present the plans to all constituencies and listen to their questions and feedback. Finally, the eighth step is to evaluate the success achieved, explain how the results can be used to improve public relations practices aligned to business objectives, and list the aspects that can be used to maintain and improve the evaluation process.

Media monitoring is just one example of the type of evaluation research that global and multicultural public relations professionals are able to carry out. All other research processes involve similar stages, beginning with: (i) the research questions; followed by (ii) the justification of the qualitative or quantitative research to be used; (iii) the selection of a population and of the segment/sample of that population to study; and (iv) the development of an instrument for data gathering (i.e. interview guide or survey questionnaire); and ending with (v) the actual data-gathering and data-analysis protocols. The presentation and discussion of findings ends the research process; here, the use of the results to inform the decision-making process regarding the formulation, implementation, monitoring, and evaluation of global and multicultural public relations programs and campaigns is critical. The section on "Challenges in International Research" delves into the aspects we need to consider in using specific research methods to gather data in a multiplicity of host countries (see later).

Research Program Stages and Components

In order to explain the challenges of conducting applied research to monitor and evaluate public relations and communications impacts, let's go over the elements of any research program; that is, the selection of the research method, the selection and analysis of the population (universe) and sample, the construction of the research instrument, the protocol for data gathering, and the procedures for data analysis.

Selection of the Research Method

The purpose of the applied research project will determine the selection of the method, which may be qualitative, quantitative, or a combination of the two. As a general rule, qualitative research allows us to gain a deeper understanding of the subject under investigation because it provides access to a specific language to describe an issue or situation and the reasons why people think or act in certain ways. In contrast, well-designed and conducted quantitative studies allow for the generalization of the results from the sample to the entire population. The numbers collected with quantitative research also facilitate cross-national comparisons. However, in some countries or locations within a country, people may not be familiar with closed-ended survey questionnaires. Therefore, qualitative research may be a more appropriate method to employ.

Selection of a research method can be greatly determined by a country's infrastructure, such as Internet penetration or how widespread

Internet access is, the distribution of land and mobile telephone lines, roads and transportation, specialized research services, and so on. In addition to infrastructure, cultural and social habits, norms, and traditions also impact the selection of the method and the other components of the research process (see "Challenges in International Research," later). In terms of cultural characteristics and social orientations, a researcher may have a difficult time trying to obtain honest criticism from an interviewee who lives in a collectivistic and hierarchical society, in which expressing negative views of others, including organizations, is avoided and seen as impolite.

Selection and Analysis of the Population (Universe) and Sample

A public relations objective statement should specify the target stakeholder group that the program or strategy aims to influence or engage. The quality of physical and electronic record keeping, available databases, government statistics, and knowledge of the market will determine the accuracy in analyzing a selected population (e.g. all the members of the target stakeholder groups or pieces of observation in public relations materials or media coverage) and sample (a small segment of the total population). If a comparative evaluation of goal attainment in a region is needed or desired, researchers need to use the same method to select the population and the sample for study. For example, Teléfonica's Department of Institutional Relations requests a comparative analysis of community relations initiatives in several countries of Central America. The challenge is that there may be better record keeping and database or statistics access in Costa Rica than in Nicaragua. This implies that public relations agencies, clients, and in-house departments should develop, communicate, and enforce policies and procedures to maintain efficient and up-to-date record keeping in every country where the multinational client or organization has operations and relates to host stakeholders.

Construction of the Research Instrument

Also guided by the public relations objective, the **research instrument** (e.g. focus group agenda, survey questionnaire) is created to inform the levels of awareness, the types of attitudes, the array of opinions, the levels of knowledge, and perhaps the actual or potential behaviors of members of the target stakeholder group. The questions and statements of the research instrument should consider language use, the previously known level of understanding of the subject matter by the sample group, and all the principles of designing research instruments, including clarity, conciseness, and appropriateness for the aim of the study. We would advise consulting research manuals and textbooks for the principles that guide the construction of instruments for effective data gathering.

If a multinational organization (MNO) or agency needs to conduct comparative research, the data-gathering instrument should be similar in every participating country. However, we do not advise the implementation of word-by-word instruments. Language plays an essential role in writing research instruments and gathering useful data, because respondents or participants understand the meaning of statements or questions in their own context and circumstances. For instance, Teléfonica's global headquarters in Spain may need to assess its corporate reputation (i.e. perceptions of its leadership and vision, financial performance, quality of product and services, workplace environment, emotional appeal, and social responsibility (Reputation Institute n.d.)) in every country and region where it has operations. A closed-ended, quantitative survey instrument will be created and sent to regional headquarters for adaptation, implementation, and analysis in the assigned country markets. The original Spanish questionnaire will need to be translated into other languages, such as English, Portuguese, German, and Chinese Mandarin. The challenge here is to maintain consistency in meanings. One technique is to allow bilingual professionals to translate and back-translate the document and to make sure that the original meanings are not lost in translation. Even the use of an original research instrument in two or more countries that speak the same language demonstrates there are nuances in usage of the language that will demand an adaptation of word choices. For example, there are significant differences between the Spanish spoken in Spain and that spoken in Nicaragua, and subtle differences between the Spanish spoken in the various countries of Central America.

Other components of the construction of a research instrument will determine its effectiveness in making it easy for participants or respondents to answer all the questions or to rate statements (and, most likely, to compare and contrast responses across countries). An instrument should have a logical organization, with answering choices or scales easy to navigate by the participant. A scale from one to five, where one is strongly disagree and five is strongly agree, may be understood in one country but not in another, or may not be easily translated from one language into another. Therefore, maintaining the tone and nature of the answer and creating an acceptable scale for use in a given country is critical to achieving a successful data gathering process. In particular, inappropriate language concerning issues of ethnicity, religion, and politics should be carefully avoided to prevent misunderstandings and negative reactions among respondents.

Involving local personnel or **domestic consultancy** (e.g. host agency or corporate personnel, host research consultants, host freelancers or experts, etc.) will increase the "**internal validity**" of the instrument (i.e. the statements or questions are measuring what they were intended to measure). Additionally, the characteristics of the target stakeholder group (e.g. age, level of literacy, experience and knowledge of the subject under investigation) should be considered when determining the complexity of the language. Language should not be a barrier to multinational research, but a comparative advantage that improves the experience of the research respondents and, hence, the quality of the data collected. As a reminder, we need quality data for formative (before a plan), monitoring (during implementation), and summative (during evaluation) research in national and global public relations and communications management.

Protocol for Data Gathering

The gathering of primary data should follow a strict set of steps. The method employed may affect the level of participation and the information facilitated by respondents. Clearly articulated guidelines should be shared with the teams responsible for research in all of the countries involved and used to train those who will have direct interactions with participants.

In the case of virtual data gathering, such as an online survey, a rigid timeline, an iteration of messages to encourage participation, and controls to avoid communication to those who have already responded should be developed and implemented. As in other stages of the applied research process, a close coordination between a central office (global or regional headquarters) and the national public relations teams or agencies will make the accomplishment of timelines and research goals possible. During this process, cultural and social habits and norms may complicate the coordination and implementation of the research project both internally and externally. For example, the way people perceive time can complicate the timelines of multinational research. Planning and execution may be slower in countries where people do not follow strict calendars and lateness is common. This can be seen in the attention and responses of corporate and agency employees in various world locations (despite having a unified corporate culture that embraces the values and ways of thinking of the headquarters) and the behaviors of respondents in various markets where everyday life runs at different speeds (e.g. life in a big city versus a small town, life in a country with a work-versus-leisure orientation). For instance, a public relations professional in a given nation may believe that one more week will not make a difference in the research plan, while a respondent who receives an electronic message with a link to an online survey may not understand the urgency felt by the sponsored organization over recording their views and opinions.

Procedures for Data Analysis

The previously discussed issues can affect the timing of data analysis. Nonetheless, in this stage of the research process, the regional or global headquarters may pressure its national branches or affiliates to process data faster and submit partial reports, in order to expedite aggregation of the results. Aggregated findings can be used to evaluate organizational and public relations performance in a variety of spheres. Clear guidelines for data analysis should be articulated by the research leaders and distributed to national teams in a timely manner. All of the procedures we have discussed in this chapter concerning multinational applied research can be coordinated with the use of online file-hosting services such as Dropbox, Box.net, Windows Life SkyDrive, SugarSynk, and SpiderOak, which allow documents, images, and videos to be uploaded, downloaded, and modified; global agencies and MNCs have their own online platforms for the sharing of information among their worldwide operations.

Challenges in International Research

The main challenge of conducting research internationally lies in the willingness of the organizations to accept research as an important component in public relations plans and agency proposals. Unfortunately, there are still many MNOs today that do not include or approve appropriate research budgets in the public relations function. Organizational and agency public relations professionals should be prepared to fight this battle for financial and other types of resources in order to achieve the much needed formative, monitoring, and evaluation campaign in global and multicultural plans and campaigns. J. Grunig et al. (2006, p. 30) state that, "for at least 25 years, public relations professionals and researchers have struggled to develop measures that would establish that public relations is effective or adds value."

Let's look at the example of Telefónica, a Spanish broadband and telecommunication provider with operations in Asia, Europe, and Latin America. Telefónica, S.A. is a Spanish multinational telecommunications company headquartered in Madrid, Spain. It is one of the largest telephone operators and mobile network providers in the world. It provides fixed and mobile telephony, broadband and subscription television, operating in Europe and America. The telecommunication and technology sectors are the fastest growing practices in global public relations agencies. One of Telefónica's brands is Movistar, which seems to be popular in Nicaragua. The Nicaraguan branch of Movistar follows directions on how to set goals and evaluations for public relations from its regional office in Guatemala through Telefónica's Direction of

Institutional Relations. The main challenge faced by the corporation is in the differing characteristics of each of the countries in Central America where Movistar operates, which make it difficult to set up public relations strategies to compete for a prominent place in the market.

As already explained, public relations research includes primary and secondary data, as well as qualitative and quantitative methods. Therefore, the challenges to conducting research internationally will be introduced as generic themes. We encourage professionals and students to gain access to training programs and specialized publications on public relations research. International research faces multiple challenges to achieving the formats and standardization requested by organizations in formulating and evaluating public relations plans, among them language, easily available parameters and statistics, methods selection, data gathering infrastructure and cultural nuances, and timely analysis and reporting.

Language Obstacles

Language affects all the stages of the research process from the gathering of secondary data to the translation of verbatim quotes in order to illustrate findings. Expert bilingual and multilingual professionals are needed to achieve efficient data gathering in languages other than the spoken or official language of the organization's headquarters. Language also affects the coordination process in managing a multinational research project, which may slow the agreement of research protocols. Normally, questionnaires or interview guides are written by professionals from the main office of the organization or global agency and then translated into other languages by regional or host professional or outsourcing services. The accuracy of the translation and back-translation of questions and statements is of primary importance in ensuring that participants understand what is being asked of them. The quality of the questions will affect the quality of the results.

Many MNOs and global agencies use existing data for secondary research. Returning to the South East Asian campaign of the hypothetical consumer-goods corporation, organizational and agency professionals are very likely to use census data (parameters) and statistics from various studies conducted by official national or international sources. Ideally, the sources, parameters, and statistics will be reliable. Access to national data may have various degrees of difficulty among targeted countries; the same goes with the quality of the data. These two aspects will determine the possibility of comparing and contrasting the sets of data; that is, the challenge will be to make sure the agency, organization, or outsourcing service is comparing apples to apples. Patterns and trends among participating countries should be easily identified and tracked in the data, and similar indicators gathered.

Method selection, data-gathering infrastructure, and cultural nuances all affect one another. Would a closed-ended, online survey be the method of choice among the targeted populations of South East Asia? Are members of middle-class households in Indonesia accustomed to answering online surveys? How many of them have access to a high-speed Internet connection? Would they prefer a face-to-face survey method? Would they trust more a domestic research firm than an MNO or global agency?

Case Study   Announcement of an Acquisition and Visual Identity Change by a Multinational Financial Group

The Peruvian branch of Burson-Marsteller (now Burson, Cohn & Wolfe, BCW) – part of the communication services conglomerate, WPP (introduced in Chapter 1) – planned, executed, and evaluated a campaign to support the acquisition announcement of ING Latin America – a regional operation of the financial service group based in the Netherlands – by Grupo de Inversiones Suramericana (South American Investment Group, SURA), a holding group based in Colombia. *Revista G*, a Peruvian business publication, called this the most important financial transaction in South America of 2011. The campaign won the 2012 ANDA Excellence Award in Public Relations in Peru, which the global agency considered an evaluation measure of the campaign's effectiveness.

The need to find a new majority shareholder originated with the 2008 financial crisis in Europe, when ING requested a financial bailout from the Dutch government. As part of the government rescue plan, ING needed to give up its retirement funds and insurance businesses in Latin America (i.e. Chile, Colombia, Mexico, Peru, and Uruguay). Rumors spread throughout this market, including speculations about potential international corporations who might buy ING's operations on the subcontinent. In particular, the imminent departure of ING from Peru implied the arrival of a new majority stockholder of the joint venture AFP Integra/ING Fondos/InVita Seguros. These three companies jointly participated in the communication plan to announce their new major shareholder and the exit of ING.

The first step Burson-Marsteller took after winning the account was to conduct formative research on the situation (internal and external factors), its antecedents, and the potential reactions of primary publics. Though Burson-Marsteller Peru had served the AFP Integra/ING Fondos account since 2010, the magnitude of the financial transaction and the aggressive competition demanded a new bidding process, which the agency won with ease. The previous knowledge of the main client's operations and of the global financial sector overall gave Burson-Marsteller a lead during bidding.

The second step of formative research was the identification and description of primary publics, such as employees, current shareholders, affiliated clientele (holders of pension funds and insurance policies), retirees, regulatory agencies, government officials, mass media, and public opinion leaders. The analysis of the situation and the definition of target publics allowed for the articulation of three strategies: to shield the three companies by securing the business continuity with AFP Integra (the most recognized of the three firms) as the focus of the communication effort; to position the financial service company or group that would become the major shareholder of the joint venture; and to be prepared for three possible scenarios related to each of the three potential corporate buyers. Subsequently, three key messages were developed to emphasize the entry of a new major shareholder instead of the departure of ING, to highlight the support of the incoming corporate shareholder for the continuation of the business, and to emphasize the protection of affiliated clientele and the security of their funds, which was identified as a priority.

The campaign was structured in four stages: pre-announcement, day of announcement, maintenance, and closing of the sale. Monitoring research was used to gauge the reactions of primary publics during each of these stages and to make necessary adjustments of strategies and tactics. The actions performed at each stage were as follows:

Pre-announcement: Map of scenarios and critical issues, platform of messages, production of communication materials (e.g. news releases, Q&A, letters to employees, affiliated clientele, shareholders, government officials, public opinion leaders, etc.), communication protocol with the responsibilities of spokespeople and logistics, articulation of statements as counter arguments to deflate rumors, preliminary meetings with media representatives, and permanent coordination with top management and the Boards of Directors of the client companies.

Announcement day: Stakeholder communications, media relations, and media interviews with general managers of AFP Integra, ING Fondos, and SURA. Additional key messages were crafted and communicated about the new major shareholder (the SURA Group).

Maintenance (100 days): Media interviews with the new joint venture AFP Integra and Grupo SURA; familiarization tour/press trip of Peruvian journalists to the headquarters of SURA in Colombia; news releases with corporate, financial, and other relevant information of Grupo SURA; news releases about the growth perspective of the soon-to-be-formalized business partnership.

Closing day of the acquisition: News release and availability of the general manager of AFP Integra for face-to-face interviews with news media, which are considered strategic in the host country.

Soon after the closing day, the new visual identity of AFP Integra as a company of the SURA Group was unveiled internally and externally. Burson-Marsteller continued the work of positioning the new visual and corporate identity of the joint venture. The agency used financial results and media coverage to evaluate the success of the campaign:

- AFP Integra was the retirement fund company that captured the largest number of clients during the second half of 2011.
- There was minimal rotation of clients during the change process.
- There were more than 100 relevant publications in the news media covering the economy, business, and general interest. Qualitative content analysis was used to evaluate the accurate inclusion of key and supporting messages in the news coverage.

Burson-Marsteller further analyzed the news media impacted by the campaign and calculated the total monetary value for the entire news coverage achieved.

Acknowledgments
Burson-Marsteller Peru facilitated the information in this case study.

The Challenges of Doing Research in Developing Countries

By Julius Che Tita, PhD
Department of Journalism and Mass Communication
University of Buea, Cameroon

The purpose of my research was to examine how **transnational corporations** (TNCs) in Cameroon coordinate their **corporate social responsibility** (CSR) efforts between their headquarters and their subsidiaries in sub-Saharan Africa. Though a relatively new field, CSR has garnered considerable attention in terms of research and practice in developed countries and across Asia. This is not the case in sub-Saharan Africa, a region that has enormous social, economic, and political needs. My study focused on the coordination of CSR by TNCs, because the novelty of the concept of CSR in sub-Saharan Africa meant that it was more likely that this phenomenon was present in TNCs from developed countries than in local corporations.

I originally planned to conduct case studies for the qualitative section of this study, but it took over six months to get the corporations to agree to participate. None was receptive to calls, appointments, emails, or short text telephone messages. Due to this lack of cooperation, the research design was changed to in-depth interviews in order to not rely on specific companies. Securing respondents and interviews was particularly laborious and time consuming. In one particular instance, three face-to-face meetings were required to secure an eventual interview with one corporation. When the interview did take place, the participant objected to its being recorded despite earlier assurances. The first face-to-face meeting involved explaining orally what the research was about, an issue that had been covered in one of our previous correspondences. The next meeting involved setting a date for the interview. The third meeting was supposed to be the interview, but on arrival, the respondent announced that because of other issues, the scheduled interview could not take place. I was asked to hold half the interview on that day and the rest on another – a suggestion I turned down. At the fourth face-to-face meeting, though the respondent had previously agreed to be recorded, they said that the recording was unnecessary and refused to be recorded. During the fieldwork, it was common for participants to object to being recorded, and only after very lengthy explanations did they change their minds. However, in this case, the abrupt cancellation of the recording affected my demeanor. It took some time for me to recover, which affected the earlier part of the interview.

Even when participants agreed to take part, they were very restless during the sessions, often becoming impatient after only 15 minutes. Before one of the scheduled interviews, the participant told me he had just come from a meeting and he had another booked in 30 minutes, despite knowing full well that the interview had been programmed for an hour at least. Another participant, after 15 minutes, asked for my interview protocol and demanded to know why I still had so many questions. In another interview, a more senior colleague insisted on accompanying the respondent throughout the session. Some of the participants were very reluctant to divulge information. During one interview, the participant, even when he provided documents that proved that over 92% of the company was foreign-owned, objected to his corporation being labeled a transnational company. The company workers' email addresses bore the email extension of a well-known Fortune 500 company. However, as the interview progressed, it became evident that constant references were made to the parent company and that there were directives from the head office.

Access to international corporations was difficult, and even when sample questions were sent to prospective participants, this did not facilitate cooperation. It was easier to gain access to corporations where I personally knew someone who worked there. In such cases, the inside contact person made all the explanations before the day of the interview and the respondent was more cooperative. Insiders included past students, former classmates, relatives, and friends. Despite previous setbacks, I encountered a lot of cooperation from respondents who had a social relationship with me. I also encountered less difficulty with corporations that had European and North American respondents. This was not the case with corporations with Asian or African managers.

The second data-collection method involved sending out questionnaires. Everything was done to improve participation. First, an email prenotice letter was sent to each prospective corporation. Pre-notice letters have been known to increase response rates of mail surveys by 3–6 percentage points. A survey invitation letter, the survey, an informed-consent form, and the incentive followed two days after the pre-notice letter. This second contact was mail delivery asking potential respondents to pick up the filled questionnaire. Researchers found that that special delivery and telephone follow-up calls increased response rates by 10 and 20 percentage points, respectively. Between the delivery and pick up of the questionnaire, frequent contacts were kept with the administrative assistants of the various corporations to facilitate completion. In Cameroon, because mail can only be picked up at the post office, it is not a common or efficient means of communication, and it is risky sending important and time-sensitive documents by post. I decided to personally deliver all the questionnaires, along with a College of Journalism and Communications pen as an incentive, as a means of increasing the response rate. I requested that all corporations that received the questionnaire acknowledge receipt in a reception ledger that I had provided. The 120 questionnaires were all distributed within a period of three weeks, and the collection began two weeks after the end of distribution.

After six weeks of going out to collect filled questionnaires, only 12 useful ones had been completed. There was a complete reluctance on the part of the corporations to cooperate with the study. Realizing that the response was slow, the research team made calls to the various corporations to solicit their participation – a futile attempt, because the calls only got as far the reception desk, and little effort was made to direct them to the right quarters. Because the questionnaires were also delivered at the reception, there was no specific information as to who to contact. When we informally got some direct contact numbers for those responsible for filling out the questionnaires and managed to contact them, they made all sorts of excuses as to why the questionnaires had not been filled.

After the fieldwork period of three months, a new drive was organized to redistribute 86 replacement questionnaires. This time, we decided to personally hand them to the people in charge of filling them out. This met with limited success, because in many cases the heavy bureaucracy could not allow the distributor to go beyond reception. After four weeks of going round to pick up questionnaires, we only had six back, two of which had been filled out by TNCs that did not carry out any CSR activities.

Over a period of six weeks, we sent out electronic copies of the questionnaire, exchanged emails, and followed up with phone calls. At the end of the exercise, 10 questionnaires had been filled out online. We further contacted a professional research service to assist in the data collection. After two weeks, the research service could only provide eight filled and useful questionnaires. In one instance, after four weeks of constant emails, the Director of Communication at one corporation finally advised me that the coordinator of CSR was best placed to respond to the survey, since the CSR program of the company had just been revised. It took two days of reminders for him to give me the coordinator's contact details. When I got in touch with the coordinator, she claimed she would be out of the office for over two weeks, and gave me the name and phone number of the personal assistant to the General Manager in charge of Human Resources. I kept contacting the Communication Manager, the CSR Coordinator, and the personal assistant of the Human Resources Manager by email and telephone, to no avail. There was a conscious effort by many companies not to participate in the survey.

Five months after the start of the administration of the survey, and having had numerous contacts with the corporations, we decided to work with the 45 responses that had been received.

Research Lessons
Generally, there was a reluctance among top officials to participate in CSR research. CSR is still a new concept in sub-Saharan Africa, and not much has been happening in these corporations. Participation is seen as threatening, making recruitment of participants difficult. Inappropriate CSR performance can lead to reputation damage. There is a sense of mistrust between the researcher and the researched, causing a high possibility of concealment and dissimulation. Moreover, when corporations do participate, they try to paint their corporations in a good light. With one corporation, there was a difference between its interview responses and those on its questionnaire. Administration of research has to take local realities into consideration. Current academic guidelines on procedures to improve participation in survey research deal exclusively with a Western environment. Evidence from this fieldwork shows that personal connections, rather than presentable and well-designed questionnaires, a reputable sponsor, pre-notice letters, and incentives, improve questionnaire administration, unlike in developed countries. Response times in developing countries are long, which must be accounted for when a planning research schedule.

As a result of the long time required and the uncertainty of responses, research in developing countries costs much more than in developed countries. Despite the popularity of interviews and surveys as research methods, other unobtrusive methods such as observation and content analysis should be seriously considered.

Systematic and coordinated research is important in the planning, programming, and evaluation phases of a public relations campaign or plan. The quality of the planning phase depends on the amount and reliability of the information gathered. Public relations professionals should maintain records of everything they do and should complement those records with current data that allows practical and on-point decision-making processes. The organizational function relates to stakeholders whose ways of thinking, attitudes, and behaviors change over time. This is especially true when engaging stakeholders in countries in transition and emergent economies.

Programming is the translation of strategic plans and marks into actions and tactics. When approaching the implementation of public relations across a variety of countries and cultures, comparative research that allows for the assessment of similarities and differences among target stakeholders in selected countries and cultures is essential. As already noted, research allows public relations professionals to set measurable goals and objectives. Assessing whether they are making progress toward the achievement of goals and objectives during the programming stage would increase the likelihood of success. Of course, what is to count as success should previously be clearly articulated by management and public relations teams, as in the case of the large consumer-goods corporation used as an example throughout this chapter. If advances toward achieving goals and objectives among target stakeholders in one or multiple target countries are not shown in monitoring research, adjustments to the plan or campaign should be quickly put in place and additional assessment should be conducted. Finally, evaluation research will allow organizational and agency professionals to gather evidence that hopefully confirms the achievement of set goals and objectives. Comparative data for all the countries involved will show degrees of effectiveness, translating results into the refinement of future plans. Optimistically, evaluation research would result in rewards for the organization and all organizational and agency teams involved.

Discussion Questions

1 What can public relations professionals do to progress public relations measurement and research?

2 Why does public relations research need to move toward an established and standardized approach in measurement and evaluation?

Class Activity

Yahoo! is a global organization that has recently seen a lot of leadership changes. Students should form groups to conduct research on Yahoo!'s reputation at the university. Each group should focus on different colleges, class standings (freshman, sophomore, junior, and senior), and domestic and international students to analyze how different groups perceive Yahoo! as an organization. Primary and secondary research can help formulate the research questions and understand the organizational objectives. Students should choose from various quantitative and qualitative research methods to answer the research questions. The instructor can use Fombrun's six dimensions of corporate reputation to structure the exercise.

References

Broom, G. and Dozier, D. (1990). *Using Research in Public Relations*. Upper Saddle River, NJ: Prentice Hall.

Broom, G.M. (2000). *Cutlip and Center's Effective Public Relations*. London: Pearson.

Daniels, M. and Jeffrey, A. (2012). "International media analysis made simple." Retrieved January 10, 2019 from https://instituteforpr.org// wp-content/uploads/International-media-measurement-6-20-12-aj.pdf.

Dow Jones. (n.d.). "A comprehensive collection of business news and data from Dow Jones." Retrieved January 10, 2019 from http://online.wsj.com/ public/page/ProductX-SignUp-Main.html.

Global Alliance. (n.d.). "The Melbourne Mandate: A new conversation on changing organizations – and changing communication." Retrieved January 10, 2019 from http://www.globalalliancepr.usi.ch/website/page/ melbourne-mandate.

Grunig, J.E., Grunig, L.A., and Dozier, D.M. (2006). The excellence theory. In: *Public Relations Theory II* (ed. C.H. Botan and V. Hazleton), 21–55. Mahwah, NJ: Lawrence Erlbaum Associates.

IPR. (2010). "The Barcelona Declaration of Measurement Principles." Retrieved January 10, 2019 from https://instituteforpr.org/ barcelona-declaration-of-measurement-principles/.

Michaelson, D. and Macleod, S. (2007). The application of 'best practices' in public relations measurement and evaluation systems. *Public Relations Journal* 1 (1).

Michaelson, D. and Stacks, D.W. (2011). Standardization in public relations measurement and evaluation. *Public Relations Journal* 5 (2): 1–22.

OPR. (n.d.). "Peripheral vision: PR communication in 2021." Retrieved January 10, 2019 from https://www.opremployeex.com.au/news/ peripheral-vision-pr-communication-in-2021/.

Paine, K.D. (2011). *Measure What Matters. Online Tools for Understanding Customers, Social Media, Engagement, and Key Relationships.* Hoboken, NJ: Wiley.

Reputation Institute. (n.d.). "Enhance your business through Reputation Intelligence." Retrieved January 10, 2019 from https://www.reputationinstitute.com/.

Singh, D. and Luis, S. (1995). Ethnic and gender consensus for the effect of waist-to-hip ratio on judgment of women's attractiveness. *Human Nature* 6 (1): 51–65.

Stacks, D. (2002). *Primer of Public Relations Research.* New York: The Guilford Press.

Stacks, D. and Michaelson, D. (2010). *A Practitioner's Guide to Public Relations Research, Measurement and Evaluation.* New York: Business Expert Press.

Wilcox, D.L. and Reber, B.H. (2013). *Public Relations Writing and Media Techniques.* London: Pearson.

3

Role of National Culture and Subcultures

Central Themes

- The environment for organizations can differ across countries in a variety of dimensions, including regulations, institutions, labor force characteristics, and culture.
- Dimensions such as power distance, individualism/collectivism, masculinity/femininity, uncertainty avoidance, short/long-term orientation, indulgence/restraint, polychromic and monochromic define a culture.
- A multiplicity of subcultures and languages may coexist in the same nation.
- Colors and graphic design vary across nations and regions.
- Global public relations professionals must consider the nuances of a culture to develop strategies and tactics, including messages that capture the attention of and resonate with target host publics.

Keywords *cosmopolitan publics/society; traditions/holidays; organizational culture; power distance; individualism/collectivism; masculinity/ femininity; uncertainty avoidance; short/long-term orientation; indulgence/ restraint; polychronic/monochronic*

Introduction

Culture is a complex and multidimensional concept, which makes it hard for organizations to comprehend and control. With national, regional, local, and societal cultures so unique to each place, it becomes challenging for organizations to navigate and communicate with such diverse audiences. Let's look at Grupo Bimbo, a Mexican bakery-product manufacturing giant (8000 plus products under some 100 umbrella brands) that has actively engaged home stakeholders in Mexico since 1960. The

Global and Multicultural Public Relations, First Edition. Juan-Carlos Molleda and Sarab Kochhar.
© 2019 John Wiley & Sons, Inc. Published 2019 by John Wiley & Sons, Inc.

company has more than 125000, employees who work in 156 plants (75 in the United States, 72 in Latin America, 7 in Spain and Portugal, and 2 in China). In 2009, it bought Weston Foods, making it the biggest baker in the United States. Therefore, US stakeholders are top of the list for this group of companies. Moreover, Grupo Bimbo and its various brands also have a significant presence in Central and South America, Asia, and Europe, which makes it important for them to understand the roles of the cultures and subcultures of their consumers. Many other global organizations like Grupo Bimbo have to compete in global markets and strategically manage stakeholders and the varied cultures across the globe. These organizations need to develop strategies to relate to a dynamic set of stakeholders; navigating cross-national and cross-cultural relationships is its own challenge.

The opening case of Zara looks at how the organization faced just such a challenge arising from cultural differences. The rest of the chapter focuses on culture as an important aspect of global public relations practice. It first explains national cultures and how they vary across the globe. It then explains the role of culture in global public relations and its impact on the management function. It also talks about organizational culture and how it is shaped by the national culture. Some key theories and concepts are discussed, in order to better understand the complexities of culture for global public relations practice.

Case Study   Opening Case: Zara and Anti-Semitism

In late August 2014, Spanish clothing company Zara and its parent company Inditex were thrown into a transnational crisis just hours after Zara offered a children's pajama shirt for sale in its Albanian, French, Israeli, and Swedish online stores. The shirt, which was produced in Turkey, had navy blue and white stripes with a six-point star in the left corner. Shortly after the shirt was offered for sale, critics around the world accused Zara of promoting anti-Semitism due to the shirt's resemblance to a Nazi concentration camp uniform.

This was not the first time that Zara was accused of selling anti-Semitic apparel. In September of 2007, the Spanish company was involved in a transnational crisis when a woman discovered that a handbag she had purchased in one of Zara's UK retail locations had four green swastika symbols on it. After customers, the media, and activist groups around the world expressed disapproval, a Zara spokesperson released a statement apologizing for the offense and explaining that the bag was produced at one of its factories in India, where the symbol is a traditional Hindu image representing strength. While the swastika was embedded with one meaning in the country where it was produced, it took on an entirely differently meaning elsewhere.

The initial backlash over the shirt began online when the Israeli/ Palestinian independent blog-based magazine *+972* published a story titled "ZARA Presents: A Striped Pyjama with a Yellow Star for Your Child" (Reider 2014). Not long afterward, the shirt sparked massive debate on social media website Reddit when a post was submitted to the group "WTF," which discusses a myriad of controversial social topics. One Reddit commenter based in Thailand wrote, "It's the fact that its a fabric yellow star on top of the fact that the t-shirt is striped with similar colours to the auschwitz uniform," while another user said, "It was close enough that I recognized what the issue was pretty much immediately." Almost simultaneously, users on the social media website Twitter started attacking the company by directly voicing their criticisms and tagging the Zara Twitter handle in their tweets. One tweeter based in New York expressed her anger: "you are obviously a dullard, anti-Semitism, racism & cultural insensitive." Others online expressed their disbelief, with responses ranging from "You had one job, and you came up with a concentration camp blouse?" to "Hey @ZARA, this isn't real right?" Where one might assume affected publics would primarily be regular Zara shoppers or human-rights groups, evidence shows that the global audience was extended to online users who simply had an opinion about the topic.

Zara's Response and the News that Ensued
Within hours after the firestorm of online news coverage about the shirt, Zara's parent company Inditex released a statement on its website explaining that inspiration for the shirt came from "classic American Westerns" and that all shirts would be removed from online stores "due to the potential similarity with the Star of David that has been used as a yellow star patch" (Cengage Learning 2014). The last paragraph of the Inditex news release states:

> Inditex would like to reiterate its utmost respect for all cultures and religions. The Group is a Company where people from 180 nationalities work together representing all the cultures, races and religions of the modern world. Inditex is proud of its cultural diversity. In addition, respect and dignity feature among the principles which guide and define its corporate values. The Group condemns and rejects any form of discrimination. (Cengage Learning 2014)

In the news release, Inditex admitted fault and positioned the company as one that appreciates different cultures and takes a hybrid approach to public relations and business practices. While the apology was published on the Inditex website, the original site that broke news of the shirt, *+972*, also reported that the company's Israeli branch directly reached out and "apologized more profusely" (Reider 2014).

Continuation of the company's strategy to position itself as culturally sensitive was documented on Zara's Twitter page when it tweeted several responses in different languages to the users who initially criticized the company. According to the Zara Twitter page, the company sent out 78 identical replies in English, German, French, and Spanish that said, "We honestly apologize, it was inspired by the sheriff's stars from the Classic Western films and is no longer in our stores." Zara's use of direct multilingual communication with its critics on Twitter is in line with the theory presented by Wang about positioning (as cited in James 2011), which implies that communications themselves must be properly framed in order to facilitate favorable attitudes.

The situation was handled by Zara, but some questions and lessons arise from this example. How can organizations be more sensitive to cultures globally? Would Zara have handled the situation differently if it had had more cultural sensitivity? This is the discussion that the chapter leads into, looking at how organizations can better prepare and train their executives for cross-cultural assignments. The closing case of Disneyland Paris, where they break cultural barriers and make dreams come true, further elaborates the role of culture in practical global public relations.

National Culture and Its Implications for Public Relations Practice

Global and multicultural public relations professionals are advised to learn and understand the cultural values and norms of the host publics they aim to engage or are engaging, and to closely monitor rapid or gradual contextual and societal changes that may influence or are influencing the ways people relate to organizations, causes, influencers, and brands. An example from Chinese culture helps to understand the stable and dynamic nature of societal culture. The citizens of the People's Republic of China enthusiastically celebrate Chinese New Year, also known as the Spring Festival, which each year has a different start date, following the lunar month of the Chinese calendar, and lasts for about 23 days. Transnational organizations in this host country develop public relations and marketing communications activities and efforts that resonate with Chinese publics and consumers. The celebration signals the greatest travel season in the country, because it is the time to reunite with family. This is a predictable facet of Chinese culture that is easily observed by foreign organizations, agencies, and professionals.

A national culture rapidly evolves when dramatic contextual changes occur in its society. Between 1986 and 1990, the Chinese established an "open-door policy" that opened the country to foreign direct investment and launched a market economy and the development of a private sector (BBC 2014). Since then, publics and consumers in China have experienced significant transformations in the way they relate to transnational organizations, emergent media, and brands; they have become cosmopolitan consumers (*Economist* 2014). Chinese cosmopolitans "know at any given moment what movies are playing in New York and what fashions are on the Paris runways" (*Economist* 2014, p. 18). As a consequence of economic liberalization, the Chinese middle class has grown dramatically and become global in its taste for luxury brands and outlook. However, critics say that this state of affairs is unlikely to last.

Among the characteristics of the evolving consumer culture in China are a drive to urbanize; an inclination toward expensive goods; a passion for fashion; the holding of foreign brands in high esteem; an interest in the history and cultural background of foreign products (though brand switching is common); an aspirational and conspicuous nature; a heavy reliance on peer reviews, especially recommendations by friends and family (likes and dislikes make and break brands); and a vivid desire for the new, with no taboos ("Doing it their way" 2014). China is also the world's largest e-commerce market. Here we have an evolving facet of Chinese culture, which shows remarkable similarities with a global consumer class, with more in common across geographical borders than within the nation.

Global public relations are considering cosmopolitanism and its variations as a way of standardizing campaigns without losing sight of unique host differences. Hence, it is not all about brands and products; it is also about causes and issues. **Cosmopolitan publics** hold similar values on major global concerns, such as health, the environment, education, and freedom.

Another thing unique about each country is its **traditions and holidays**, which are dear to its core values and identity. The celebration of independence or founding dates, new year festivities, activities around the arrival of a season, and commemorations of the birth or death of a prominent figure dominate national calendars and signal the patriotic character of a nation. Unique traditions and holidays may be found within subcultures, because of the existence of a variety of religious, ethnic, political, and economic realities in a society; this is especially true in larger nations, such as India and Russia. The colors of a national flag may unite a country, but the flavors in foods cooked by an urban or rural group can resonate loudly with its own members. For example, Venezuelans celebrate the country's independence from Spain on July 5.

This national celebration involves religious fairs showing devotion to Roman Catholic saints in states and cities across the country. The business, government, and religious sectors coordinate events with unique local undertones. Domestic and transnational businesses with national operations follow the calendar of state fairs to plan actions and activities and to get closer to local publics and consumers through special events and targeted public relations campaigns.

However, the world is also highly interconnected. People and ideas are increasingly crossing national borders. The idea of a **cosmopolitan society** implies that global ideas are easier to spread, including traditionally national festivities (e.g. Oktoberfest, Halloween, Christmas, Valentine's Day, Mother's Day, etc.), which are now being celebrated across the world, far from their country or region of origin.[1] Agencies and corporations use these cosmopolitan celebrations to communicate and engage in global and local conversations. But what happens inside an organization and how does an organization define its own culture?

Cultural Belief Systems and Their Influence on Organizational Culture

Does culture exist within an organization? What role does culture play in shaping behavior in organizations? These questions have long been important for scholars and professionals in defining what **organizational culture** is and how or whether it may be influenced.

Organizational culture refers to the beliefs, ideologies, principles, and values shared by the individuals at an organization. Every organization has its own culture, rooted in its practices. Schein (2010, p. 18) defines organizational culture as "a pattern of shared basic assumptions learned by a group as it solved its problems of external adaptation and internal integration, which has worked well enough to be considered valid and, therefore, to be taught to new members as the correct way you perceive, think, and feel in relation to those problems." Organizational culture has an effect on how associates think, behave, and succeed. Culture within an organization shapes what employees consider appropriate behavior and how they interact with one another within the organization. Organizations recognize that it is critical to tap into the skills and insights of a diverse workforce in the new global economy and that a good organizational culture has an important role to play in attracting and retaining talent. Culture is a key factor not only in achieving organizational goals, but also in attracting and keeping desirable employees, creating a positive public reputation, and building respectful relationships with stakeholders.

Organizational culture also provides a sense of direction for employees and keeps them motivated and loyal to the organization. It impacts how individuals and teams deal with the work assigned to them, as well as – most importantly – how outside stakeholders perceive the organization. As public relations professionals, you must understand the impact organizational culture can have not only on an organization's employees but also on its reputation among its external stakeholders. An organization's culture defines its identity. The values and beliefs of an organization contribute to its brand personality. Forbes provides a list of the companies that are most enjoyable to work for (Forbes 2014). Twitter, Apple, and Google are some of the consistent top companies that employees recognize for their culture. In 2014, Edelman, one of the biggest global public relations agencies, was also near the top of the list.

Think about some of the biggest transnational corporations (TNCs) and imagine the kinds of organizational culture that might exist in them. What might it be like inside a consumer product company or a technology company, with its diverse employees? Think about a technology company like Apple or Amazon, and then about a consumer product company like Unilever. How do you think the organizational cultures differ among these organizations?

It is interesting to note that organizational culture is not just patterns of behavior, but also jointly held beliefs. Such beliefs represent what the organization is and why it is the way it is. Organizational culture is shaped by and overlaps with other cultures, especially the broader cultures of the societies in which the organization operates. National culture is a major component of the broader "contextual imperative" that constrains organizational culture (Johns 2006). National culture has a powerful influence and is the essence of organizational culture, and of consequent employee behavior. Other factors like leadership style, language, symbols, procedures and routines, hierarchical levels, functional teams, and how various business functions operate can also define an organizational culture (Cameron and Quinn 2006).

TNCs face a unique challenge in establishing and maintaining a unified culture when operating in multiple host cultures. How should leaders strike the right balance between promoting a single organizational culture, while still allowing for the influence of local cultures? The opening case of Zara and the impact of national culture and traditions on the organization is one of many examples of how organizational and national cultures can overlap and interact.

The local and global forces are unique in each region where a transnational organization operates. The organization has to blend in with the local social cultural influences and match them with the shared goals of the organization, while still functioning smoothly as a part of a single, global entity. Transnational organizations must decide how much to localize their organizational culture and related management practices to fit within the host country context and how much instead to strive to maintain consistency or standardization (Bartlett and Ghoshal 2002).

Just like language, words and images can also imply different things and have different cultural impacts. Global and multicultural professionals use words and images to convey key messages to a variety of host publics. This, in cultural studies, is a process of representation, which focuses on the way language, images, and signs represent objects, people, and situations. Hall (1997) explains that representation is a dynamic process in which meanings are created and recreated. Concerning the role of public relations professionals engaged in global practices, Curtin and Gaither (2007, p. 78) state, "Representation is intrinsic in any material they prepare, any document they write, and any activity they undertake; each of these tasks is encoded with cultural meanings and informs a particular discourse." In other words, professionals use language, associations, and images that will resonate with the host publics and their realities and interests, without losing sight of the intentionality of the stories they tell about their organizations.

Color and graphic design vary across national and regional cultures. Minimalism and simplicity are common themes in Scandinavian graphic design, in which a palette of white and neutral colors in combination with a splash of bright colors dominates. In contrast, warm colors and a combination between primitive and modern imagery are present in African graphic design. The multiplicity of languages and ethnic groups with a complex colonial past impregnate African art expressions with, at times, conflicting views of nature, politics, and society; that is, a visual fusion that is unique, fun, and soulful. For visual communications to capture the attention of and resonate with target publics in host locations, global public relations professionals should consider the unique esthetics in the use of colors and graphic elements when they produce layouts and designs in a given national or regional environment.

Cultural Theories and Concepts

How do you define culture? What are some of the ways you can differentiate one culture from another? Scholars have been trying to answer these questions for years, and have come up with models and theories to contrast cultures along various dimensions. Many of the global public relations and communications management studies on the influence of culture are based on the pioneering cultural work of Geert Hofstede (1984). Hofstede, a Dutch social sociologist, collected data from a large multinational corporation (MNC), IBM, from 40 different countries. Through his empirical data analysis, he concluded, "organizations are cultural-bounded" (p. 252).

Hofstede's six cultural dimensions have furthered the understanding of individuals, society, and communication. These six dimensions are **power distance, individualism/collectivism, masculinity/femininity, uncertainty avoidance, short/long-term orientation**, and **indulgence/ restraint** (Hofstede 2001). These dimensions have been found to relate significantly to public relations practices across the globe. They can be used to better understand cultures and learned norms based on attitudes, values, and beliefs, all of which exist in every nation. A note of caution is necessary here, before we define these cultural dimensions. Cultural dimensions and characteristics can vary within a country where the urban meets the rural, and where the dominant culture meets a variety of subcultures. Here, the need to know your target publics acquires an additional relevance. Further, language is an important force that shapes the way people think and act. Canada's English and French territories and Spain's Catalan, Castilian, and Basque provinces should be treated as subcultures with unique values and histories within a national context.

Hofstede's Cultural Dimensions

The first dimension, power distance, is defined as the extent to which the less powerful members of an organization and individuals in a society accept that power is distributed unequally. In high power distance cultures, individuals respect their superiors and avoid criticizing them. In low power distance cultures, it is very acceptable to challenge one's superiors (Hofstede 1984). Power and inequality are fundamental facts in any society and may vary among different cultures. In organizations, power distance refers to the power inequality between superiors and subordinates. In high power distance organizations, there is a line between managers and subordinates and a clear organizational hierarchy. Low power distance organizations tend to have a flat organizational structure. The Power Distance Index scores given by Hofstede (2010) for 76 countries are higher for East European, Latin, Asian, and African countries and lower for Germanic and English-speaking Western countries. Malaysia, Guatemala, Panama, and the Philippines are countries with high power distance. Austria, Israel, Denmark, and New Zealand are countries with low power distance, where people prefer to have a consultative style.

The second dimension of individualism/collectivism reflects the degree to which a society views its members as individuals or as group members (Hofstede 1984). Individualistic societies emphasize an individual's own interests and the interests of their immediate family. Highly collectivistic societies value groups' actions instead of individual actions. Individuals in highly collectivist cultures are integrated from birth onwards into strong, cohesive in-groups, often extended families (with uncles, aunts, and grandparents). In organizations, high individualistic values will focus on tasks over relationships and tend to care more about self-actualization. Low individualistic value individuals will value relationships over tasks and put organizational benefits above their own interests. Global public relations professionals could emphasize individualism or collectivism in messages and visuals to address the predominant orientation of a given culture both inside and outside their organizations.

The third dimension of masculinity/femininity defines the gender roles in a society. Masculinity is described in cultures where the dominant values are expected to be ambitious, assertive, and competitive. Cultures high in femininity have a dominance of feminine values, such as a preference for a "friendly atmosphere, position security, and physical conditions security" (Hofstede 2001, p. 281). In high masculinity organizations, very few women can get higher-level and better-paying jobs. In low masculinity organizations, women can get more equitable organizational status. Gender equality or difference shapes interpersonal relations and could be reflected in the language and themes we use to engage host publics around the world.

The fourth dimension of uncertainty avoidance is the degree to which people in a culture generally prefer structure to risk or ambiguity (Hofstede 1984). Cultures high in uncertainty avoidance are made anxious by situations that are unstructured, unclear, or unpredictable. On the other hand, cultures low in uncertainty avoidance are reflective, less aggressive, relatively tolerant, and unemotional. In high uncertainty avoidance organizations, there are more written rules in order to reduce uncertainty. In low uncertainty avoidance organizations, there are fewer written rules and rituals. Studies show that in countries with the highest score on uncertainty avoidance, employees prefer set rules that are not to be broken even if breaking them is in the company's best interest. Furthermore, these employees plan to work for the company for a long time, preferring the certainty of their present position over the uncertainty of better advancement opportunities elsewhere. In countries characterized by high risk avoidance, few consumers are prepared to take the social risk of trying a new product first. Willingness, openness to change, and innovation impact global public relations techniques and efforts to introduce new ways of thinking or behaviors. Resistance or acceptance of changes should be considered in strategically planning and executing campaigns aiming to move a target public from one attitudinal, perceptual, or behavioral stage to another.

Hofstede (2001) adopted the Eastern cultural dimension, Confucian work dynamic, as his fifth work-related cultural dimension and renamed it short/long-term orientation. The Chinese Culture Connection (1987) identified the Confucian work dynamic based on traditional Chinese cultural values. Long-term orientation focuses on the degree to which a society embraces, or does not embrace, long-term devotion to traditional values. A long-term orientation indicates that a country adheres to the values of long-term commitments and respect for tradition, and that long-term rewards are expected as a result of hard work. A short-term orientation indicates the country does not reinforce the concept of a long-term, traditional orientation and that people expect short-term rewards for their work. In working with local agencies or suppliers, global public relations professionals need to understand how similar or different is their time orientation, for example. If the time orientations are similar, projects can be accomplished more efficiently; if time orientations are contrasting, this may cause delays and clashes because of unmet timelines and poor work productivity.

The sixth dimension of indulgence/restraint was added in 2010 from Minkov's label "indulgence versus restraint," which was based on World Values Survey items. A high indulgence society allows relatively free gratification of basic and natural human desires related to enjoying life and having fun. A high-restraint society controls gratification of needs and regulates it by means of strict social norms. Indulgence tends to prevail in South and North America, in Western Europe, and in parts of sub-Saharan Africa. Restraint prevails in Eastern Europe, in Asia, and in the Muslim world. Mediterranean Europe takes a middle position on this dimension (Hofstede 2011).

Anthropologist Edward T. Hall described culture through the concept of time orientation. **Polychronic** versus monochronic time orientation describes how cultures structure their time. The monochronic time concept follows the notion of one thing happening at a time, while the polychronic concept focuses on multiple tasks being handled at one time, where time is subordinate to interpersonal relations. Cultures such as those in Northern Europe are monochromic, preferring to work sequentially (e.g. finishing with one customer before dealing with another). Southern Europeans are polychronic, being more comfortable working simultaneously on all the tasks they face.

Cross-cultural Management and Training

Public relations professionals are increasingly working for transnational organizations and clients and going global. Cross-cultural competence is a skill that has become essential for managers at transnational organizations and agencies (Hampden-Turner and Trompenaars 2000). Professionals with an opportunity or desire to experience global and multicultural practices are encouraged to delve into the cultural knowledge and skills they will need to be effective. Training in and acquiring cultural understanding helps professionals improve knowledge of self and manage the stress often caused by cultural differences. Expatriates are selected for foreign assignments based on their technical competence, ability to adapt, and leadership. The most important thing is that professionals first adapt to the host country's culture and operating systems; ideally, they should also learn the host country's language and explore its work and non-work environments. Training, cross-cultural briefings, and other pre-departure preparations reduce the chances of expatriate failure (Khan et al. 2011). These preparation activities should include the expatriate's spouse or partner and other family members.

The process of acquiring cross-cultural competence is long and demanding, spanning years. Public relations students can learn how to be culturally competent by taking courses with an international perspective, going on study-abroad programs or taking internships abroad, attending lectures or speaking events with a global focus, and developing friendships with international students or joining international student-run organizations. Professionals also need continuous preparation in this area, especially those accepting assignments in other countries. They will go through the stages of cultural sensitivity, as elucidated by Shapiro et al. (2008): romantic sojourner, foreign worker, skilled worker, and partner. The final stage is where the professional is so immersed within the culture that he or she is balanced and respectful, yet as enchanted as when he or she was a recent arrival.

Freitag and Stokes (2009) argue (and we would agree) that professionals do not need to leave their hometown to experience an international environment. There are many foreign interests trading and operating in your country for which you might end up working. Professionals may participate in virtual teams working on regional or global campaigns, such as Bacardi International's corporate social responsibility campaign, "Champions Drink Responsibly." However, seeking and taking advantage of overseas assignments should be a priority if one is to become a total global professional. According to Freitag and Stokes (2009, p. 13), "Practitioners with appropriate cultural preparation will be more likely to seek and accept international assignment opportunities, to perceive their experiences to have been successful and satisfying, to gain additional cultural competence with each assignment, and to reinforce their international assignment seeking behavior."

Fleisher (2003) also makes recommendations for how professionals can develop cross-cultural competencies, such as encouraging regular interaction between domestic and foreign employees, allowing domestic employees opportunities to attend meetings and conferences in foreign locales, providing intercultural communication and sensitivity skills training, supporting the acquisition of foreign language skills, streaming news from foreign countries, supporting the taking of "Doing Business In..." courses at nearby universities, and taking part in managerial exchanges with managers from other countries. Once in a foreign assignment, professionals will be benefited by mentoring opportunities across national boundaries. "Having a host-country mentor had a significant positive effect on the expatriate's organizational knowledge, organizational knowledge sharing, job performance, promotability, and perceptions of teamwork," explains Carraher et al. (2008). Having a home-country mentor also has positive effects on organizational knowledge, job performance, and promotability.

Cross-cultural training (CCT), in all forms (i.e. general and specific – cognitive, affective, behavioral), facilitates all facets of an expatriate's adjustment (Okpara and Kabongo 2011). The objective of CCT is to educate members of one culture to interact and communicate effectively with members of another. It also helps expatriates experience a smooth and quick adjustment to their new responsibilities. The most effective types of training appear to be the experimental ones, especially those focused on the host-country culture (specific). Not every agency or transnational organization offers CCT; therefore, students and professionals may need to seek out resources and training opportunities. For instance, the Indian city Chennai has a bustling Korean population; over 200 Korean companies and as many as 4000 Koreans operate and live there (BusinessLine 2014). Global Adjustments, a CCT company focusing on integrating foreigners with the Indian community, launched a Korean-language website to help expatriates and their families engage with the city and connect with the local communities.

The case study on Disneyland Paris is a great example of how national cultures and subcultures impact the practice of public relations.

Conclusion

In the Internet era, perhaps the most salient question to ask is how one can achieve the objectives of global public relations? And how can the international use of social networks facilitate clear connections at the cultural level? It is important to not forget that public relations communications – through technology – is an opportunity, not a threat. Global public relations techniques will continue to expand and develop new methods, multicultural stakeholders will change over time, new stakeholder groups will emerge, and social networks will provide direct communication with audiences around a shared experience. Religion, as an important element of culture, will become more focused and better integrated into society and global public relations activities. As practical services reduce in cost, the demand for public relations services will increase – contributing to an increase in professional specializations, market authority, and valued advisory roles. Most importantly, global public relations will continue to benefit multiculturalism and religion within the global scope of operation.

Case Study   Disneyland Paris – From a Symbol of American Imperialism to One of France's Most Popular Attractions

The Walt Disney Company was started in 1923 and has been entertaining international audiences ever since. The company spans from media networks to The Walt Disney Studios, Disney Consumer Products, Disney Interactive, and its world-famous parks and resorts. Disneyland Park, the first theme park, was opened in 1955 in Anaheim, California and was soon followed by the 1971 opening of Walt Disney World Florida. Tokyo Disneyland opened in 1983, the first international Disney park, and proved to be a success (Tuleja and O'Rourke 2008).

Continuing its expansion plan, Disney turned to Europe and chose Paris as its next destination for its geographical, historical, political, and economic proximity with the majority of Western European countries. The new Disney theme park, however, was not welcomed in the City of Love. The park, initially called EuroDisney, was accused of corrupting French culture with its "disneylandization" (Kuisel 1993). EuroDisney was seen as a threat to the French self-identity, and Mickey Mouse as a representation of American cultural imperialism. French director Ariane Mnouchkine described the park as "a cultural Chernobyl" in 1992 during a private conversation with Robert Fitzpatrick, the park's first chairman, who made Mnouchkine's words public (Mnouchkine 2003).

EuroDisney opened on April 12, 1992. In June of that year, a group of protesting French farmers blocked the entrance to the park with their tractors, preventing hundreds of families and several buses of schoolchildren from entering. The farmers were protesting against US agricultural trade policies and were seeking to attract attention to their cause. They had successfully blocked a motorway, causing a 15-mile traffic jam, days earlier, but that protest had received minimal media attention. The blockade of EuroDisney, however, received coverage from major French and international TV stations. Disney officials tried not to get involved with the dispute because, as Disney spokesman Nicholas De Schonen explained, it was "a matter between the farmers and the French government" (Tempest 1992).

The park suffered from negative public opinion and low attendance until Frenchman Philippe Bourguignon took over as its new chief executive officer (CEO) in 1993 and began to turn things around. The initial color palette was not well received by visitors, as it included several tones of purple, which is often a sad color associated with death and crucifixion in a predominantly Catholic Europe (Blonsky 1992). Market research revealed this difference in color perception between Europe and the United States, and the use of purple has been drastically reduced ever since. The name "EuroDisney" also proved to be unpopular with the European community. Michael Eisner, former Disney CEO, explained that Americans saw the word "Euro" in front of "Disney" as glamorous and exciting, but the word "Euro" for Europeans was associated with business, currency, and commerce (Eisner 1999). In 1994, the park was renamed "Disneyland Paris," and the original logo and company colors were abandoned.

Breaking Cultural Barriers

Continuing its rebranding efforts, Disneyland Paris began to address its negative news coverage and criticisms by embracing its European audiences and repositioning itself as a source of inspiration, fashion, and art within France and the rest of Europe.[2]

European Inspirations
The Once Upon A Time Walt Disney Exhibition was held in the Le Grande Palais, home of great impressionist artists such as Delacroix, Renoir, and Manet, as a collaboration between the French culture minister and Disney's CEO. It paid tribute to Walt Disney and exposed the European influences on his life and work. It displayed Disney not as a businessman, but as an artist and one of the greatest storytellers of the twentieth century. It highlighted the integration of cultural references into this work and the inspirations he took from various European artists, writers, illustrators, and painters, such as Perrault, the Brothers Grimm, F.D. Bedford, and J.M. Barrie.[3]

Tackling France's Growing Love for Rugby
The park decided to take advantage of the 2007 Men's Rugby World Cup, hosted by France, to bring the world to Disneyland Paris. In recognition of their contribution to one of the world's largest sporting events, Disneyland Paris invited all tournament volunteers to spend a day in the park alongside the French national rugby team. Players from the England rugby team visited Disneyland Paris with their families during the tournament and enthusiastically posed for pictures with Belle and the Beast in front of Le Chateau de la Belle Dormant (Sleeping

Beauty's Castle). These visits generated positive publicity for the park, as they were covered by major news outlets in both France and the United Kingdom.

Showing a New Side

Disneyland Paris was originally seen as a foreign intrusion into French culture and was criticized for being "too American." In order to change the way the park was perceived by Europeans, particularly the French, Disneyland Paris decided to show itself through its visitors. As a hub for artistic expression, the park partnered with photographer Martin Parr to take on this new project. Through a series of snapshots at the park, Parr was able to capture candid moments of children having fun during their visit and showed the park as a place to let your imagination run wild. His collection was exhibited during summer 2008 at the Parisian boutique Colette. Lou Doillon also joined the efforts and captured the emotions and amazement of people from various generations, nationalities, and cultures as they experienced the destination. Her collection explored the relationships and reactions between family, friends, and strangers during their Disneyland Paris experience.

Making Dreams Come True

Mickey Star was a French televised contest launched in 2009 and designed to help promote Mickey's Magical Party.[4] In celebration of Mickey Mouse's 80th birthday, four lucky winners were selected to dance live alongside Mickey and his friends during the launch event.[5] Children aged 5–10 were encouraged to participate in the casting by uploading videos of themselves dancing to a song of their choice. The celebration was broadcasted to millions of viewers on TF1, a private national French TV station. In addition to the contest, Disneyland also released a new theme song for Disney's Magical Party 2009 called "It's Party Time."

Mouse Celebrity Makeover

During Mickey's Magical Party, 15 celebrities from several European countries partnered with Disneyland Paris to recreate Mickey's famous ears for the benefit of Rêves (Dreams), a charity association that works to realize the dreams of children with life-threatening illnesses. The participating celebrities had the opportunity to personalize their own pair of Mickey ears to reflect their personality and style. The list included names from the world of music, sports, design, and cinema, such as Isabella Rossellini, Phil Collins, Estelle, Luella Bartley, Giles Deacon, Henry Holland, and Daisy Lowe. From Sébastien Chabal's rugby ears to former Spice Girl Geri Halliwell's polka-dotted pair, the iconic ears received extensive media attention and attracted large crowds. The entire collection of "My Mickey Ears" was displayed at the official premiere of Mickey's Magical Party in Paris. Following the display, the ears were auctioned for the benefit of Rêves.

Blending Cultural Interests

Reinventing Fashion
Paris is the fashion capital of the world and home of many high-end fashion designers. In order to combine the city's love for fashion and Disney's vast collection of character costumes, Disneyland Paris has organized several catwalk fashion shows revealing new and high-fashion character garments. In celebration of Disneyland Paris' 15th anniversary, 25 top designers, including Dame Vivienne Westwood, Chantal Thomas, Ágatha Ruiz de la Prada, Luella Bartley, and Azzedine Alaïa, joined forces to create a more contemporary style for some of Disney's leading ladies, such as Belle, Ariel, Tinker Bell, the Queen of Hearts, Maleficent, and, of course, Minnie Mouse. The high-fashion gowns and accessories created for the "Designer Princesses" event were showcased to the general public before being auctioned to benefit the United Nations International Children's Emergency Fund (UNICEF). Five years later, in 2012, Disneyland Paris celebrated its 20th anniversary with the "Designer of Dreams Fashion Show," which showcased brand new Disney character costumers made by some of Europe's most prestigious fashion houses. The catwalk featured creations by international designers from Belgium, the United Kingdom, Germany, Russia, Ireland, Spain, Italy, and the Netherlands.

Culinary Inspirations
When it comes to cuisine, Paris is enduringly French and also undeniably cosmopolitan (Parkhurst-Ferguson 2006). Over the years, Disneyland Paris has partnered with top chefs to strategically combine the artistic influences and gastronomy of French cuisine with Disney delicacies and themes. One of its culinary innovations was a limited-edition Mickey Mouse macaroon cake created by top chef Philippe Andrieu and the Ladurée patisserie. Chef Thierry Marx also created animated delicacies out of street food such as popcorn, toffee apples, and cookies. Another favorite was Christophe Michalak's Buzz l'éclair, a delicacy inspired by Buzz Lightyear. These culinary creations and delicacies both appealed to the palate and generated media coverage for the park (Champs-Elysees n.d.).

The Art Beyond the Gates

In order to really connect with the French, Disneyland Paris made sure to engage audiences far beyond the park's gates. In 2008, it partnered with Troy Henriksen to create the first contemporary gallery in Paris' Metro. In 2009, alongside Collective 1980 and Régis-R, it literally took the arts to the streets by painting the Champs-Élysées. The artists combined Disney and Halloween features on frescos that changed the street's appearance at night through black-light technology. In 2010, Disneyland Paris took over the heart of Paris once more with a giant fresco along the Champs-Élysées. The fresco's theme, "It's Delicious to be Mean," was a creation of David Bersanetti, who used more than 17 000 pieces of candy to complete it.

Influence of Religion in Global Public Relations Practices: The Case of Islam

By Hamid Shokri

Today, public relations professionals must have a good knowledge of international affairs and be adaptable to continually changing geopolitical scenarios. Because information technology is developing rapidly, it is essential for public relations professionals to be able to act effectively on a global level.

As people of all backgrounds and cultures come into contact with one another, global public relations can make significant contributions to foster cooperation and understanding among nations. The recent surge of widespread social studies has encouraged a move from concerns about comparing and classifying cultures to an examination of the actual interaction between people and the outcome of communications between different cultures.

The **religious community**, due to the inherent characteristics of religion (inflexibility), has been wary of change in the context of culture in Iran throughout the nation's history. The largest changes in national policy came within the context of war and were led by religious leaders. An example of such an instance was the conquest of Persia by the Arabs, which resulted in almost the entire population converting to Islam.

There are three significant perspectives related to the religion's influence on global public relations. Each perspective builds off the previous one to create an intercultural review process for global public relations. The first perspective is **cultural background**. Discussions on the role of religion in communications and intercultural relations often refer to cultural background for guidance. From this perspective, certain cultural aspects of a nation may necessitate the inclusion of religion because it is so important to the culture.

The second aspect of the review process is the **manufacturing perspective**. After the role of religion in a culture is researched, this perspective is used as a process for building cross-cultural communications.

The third perspective is the **perspective of combination**. For many people, facilitating cross-cultural communications – in the form of mergers or acquisitions – requires an active dialogue between religious sentiments and communications. Consideration for and integration of these two entities has determined the path of cross-cultural communications in the past.

Islam's Role in the Integration of Global Public Relations

The religion of Islam, as a cultural element, plays a decisive role not only in global public relations operations, but also in social behavior and interpersonal processes. Religion influences the behaviors and reactions of people from different cultures as they interact with one another. Global public relations require an accurate idea of the role that religion plays in campaigns, for instance.

In the *Qur'an*, in Sura Al-Imran verse 200, people are invited to establish social relationships, have patience, and adopt piety in order to achieve salvation. Interestingly, as a matter of ethics in the public relations community, this verse refers to the beauty of dynamic expression. The transfer of information and knowledge, in a study of the Qur'an, suggests the importance of relationship building and communications.

Clergymen, as religious advocates, have consistently emphasized the science and art of public relations. Public relations creates many opportunities for transferring knowledge and information, including: informing and facilitating two-way communications platforms with target stakeholders (such as feedback or consultation); amplifying an awareness of others' opinions; and allowing for knowledge diffusion in our hearts. In the eyes of some Muslim advocates, public relations is not only important, but healthy and honorable.

Models: Ideal and Practical

The behaviors and norms that people practice are, typically, inconsistent with their values and beliefs. People tend to act practically in ideal patterns that reduce decisions down to whether the person likes or dislikes a particular stimulus. This holds true for most religious practices and social relations; the moral models by which people identify are affected by ideal patterns that lead them off course.

Effective functioning of public relations from the perspective of religion means that the audience must be addressed in its own language in order for it to take action. Therefore, public relations professionals must make use of three important criteria to encourage action: religious leaders as spokespersons/advocates, God-centered messaging, and the use of love and justice in campaigns (as commanded in theological doctrine, i.e. the *Qur'an*). These criteria can open the hearts of others by appealing to the power of spiritual influence. Because of the nature of such an influential appeal, public relations professionals should follow guidelines for the use of religious symbols in public relations functions and activities. There are four guidelines for ideal and practical models when using religious symbols for global public relations purposes:

1) **Exchange (ways to communicate with the public and authorities).** Within the religious perspective on public relations, one of the great themes calls for the development of social relations, the strengthening of the bonds of friendship, and the preservation of consideration for others.

2) **Community (people-oriented communications).** While discussing public relations functions for Muslims, Imam Ali (AS) said, "be kind and compassionate people with eye and chest full of love, behold." The development of relationships with people and organizations needs "direct contact"; meeting face-to-face, having conversations, and meetings with social groups are important methods of communications for public relations professionals.

3) **Accountability (critical functions).** It is essential not to be indifferent to public opinion, listening and responding to questions or ambiguities. This is among the most important jobs in public relations. One should be critical of the organization's performance, analyzing public opinion and the views of experts and scholars.

4) **Dignity.** Imam Ali (AS) says, "people have two classes or categories, or you are Muslim or non-Muslim religious brothers, but you are fellow humans." Despite this distinction, dignity in public relations practice is important to harmony. Global public relations, on the basis of international Islamic moral value, should include elements of virtue, forbidding evil, and mutual respect.

Discussion Questions

1 How could corporate identity impact the global public relations efforts of a multinational?

2 How could strategic planning anticipate cultural challenges in intercultural communications?

3 How did the French cultural belief system and Disney's corporate identity affect the success of Disneyland Paris?

4 How did Disneyland Paris' public relations efforts outside of France reinforce its several park initiatives?

5 What was Disney's strategy in addressing its lack of cultural sensitivity toward the French?

Class Activity

Ikea was found in 2008 to have consistently chosen Swedish and Norwegian place names to associate with its best furnishings and Danish place names for doormats, rugs, and carpets (O'Mahony 2008). Doormats and rugs such as Köge, Sindal, Roskilde, Bellinge, Strib, Helsingör, and Nivå are all "seventh-class" citizens in the hierarchical world of Ikea furnishings. Students should consider what they would have done to manage this cultural crisis. They should use Geert Hofstede's cultural dimensions scores to plan their strategy.

Notes

1 Cosmopolitanism "presents a political-moral philosophy that posits people as citizens of the world rather than of a particular nation-state. In this regard, cosmopolitanism represents a spirited challenge to more traditional views that focus on age-old attachments of people to a place, customs, and culture." *Encyclopedia Britannica*, retrieved January 10, 2019 from http://www.britannica.com/EBchecked/topic/1921047/cosmopolitanism.

2 This case uses selective events to highlight the effects of culture in public relations.

3 The Art Ludique Museum opened in Paris in 2013 with an exhibition of Disney's "Pixar, 25 Years of Animation."

4 Following the 15th anniversary celebration, Disneyland Paris' public relations and advertising teams, with the support of consultancies, designed a plan of special annual events to renew interest and improve the experience for visitors to the park.

5 The group of selected winners displayed characteristics of diverse ethnic backgrounds and racial groups.

References

Bartlett, C.A. and Ghoshal, S. (2002). *Managing across Borders: The Transnational Solution.* 2nd ed., Harvard, MA: Harvard Business School Press, 2002.

BBC. (2014). "China profile – Timeline." Retrieved January 10, 2019 from http://www.bbc.co.uk/news/world-asia-pacific-13017882.

Blonsky, M. (1992). *American Mythologies.* Oxford: Oxford University Press.

BusinessLine. (2014). "Chennai engages with Korean community." Retrieved January 10, 2019 from http://www.thehindubusinessline.com/economy/chennai-engages-with-korean-community/article5753955.ece?ref=wl_industry-and-economy.

Cameron, K.S. and Quinn, R.E. (2006). *Diagnosing and Changing Organizational Culture: Based on the Competing Values Framework.* Chichester: Wiley.

Carraher, S.M., Sullivan, S.E., and Crocitto, M.M. (2008). Mentoring across global boundaries: An empirical examination of home- and host-country mentors on expatriate career outcomes. *Journal of International Business Studies* 39: 1310–1326.

Cengage Learning. (2014). "Zara removes striped kids' shirt that resembles Holocaust prison wear." Retrieved January 10, 2019 from https://community.cengage.com/GECResource2/info/b/bus_comm/archive/2014/09/02/zara-apologizes-for-concentration-camp-shirt.

Champs-Elysees. (n.d.). "Ladurée creates a Mickey macaroon." Retrieved January 10, 2019 from http://www.champs-elysees-paris.org/?p=1856.

Chinese Culture Connection (1987). Chinese values and the search for the culture-free dimensions of culture. *Journal of Cross-Cultural Psychology* 18: 143–164.

Curtin, P. and Gaither, K. (2007). *International Public Relations: Negotiating Culture, Identity, and Power.* Thousand Oaks, CA: Sage Publications.

Economist. (2014). "Chinese consumers: Doing it their way." Retrieved January 10, 2019 from https://www.economist.com/briefing/2014/01/23/doing-it-their-way.

Eisner, M. (1999). *Work in Progress: Risking Failure, Surviving Success.* Westport, CT: Hyperion.

Fleischer, C. (2003). The development of competencies in international public affairs. *Journal of Public Affairs* 3: 76–82.

Forbes. (2014). "The top companies for culture and values." Retrieved January 10, 2019 from http://www.forbes.com/sites/kathryndill/2014/08/22/the-top-companies-for-culture-and-values.

Freitag, A.R. and Stokes, A.Q. (2009). *Global Public Relations: Spanning Borders, Spanning Cultures.* London: Routledge.

Hall, S. (1997). "The work of representation." In *Representation: Cultural Representations and Signifying Practices* (ed. by S. Hall), pp. 13–74. London: Sage Publications.

Hampden-Turner, C. and Trompenaars, A. (2000). *Building Cross-Cultural Competence: How to Create Wealth from Conflicting Values*. New Haven, CT: Yale University Press.

Hofstede, G. (1984). *Culture's Consequences: International Differences in Work-Related Values*. Newbury Park, CA: Sage.

Hofstede, G. (2001). *Culture's Consequences: Comparing Values, Behaviors, Institutions, and Organizations across Nations*. Thousand Oaks, CA: Sage.

Hofstede, G. (2010). *Cultures and Organizations: Software for the Mind*. New York: McGraw-Hill.

Hofstede, G. (2011). Dimensionalizing cultures: The Hofstede model in context. *Online Readings in Psychology and Culture* 2 (1): 8.

James, M. (2011). A provisional conceptual framework for intentional positioning in public relations. *Journal of Public Relations Research* 23 (1): 93–118.

Johns, G. (2006). The essential impact of context on organizational behavior. *Academy of Management Review* 31 (2): 386–408.

Khan, A., Khan, R., and Raman, M. (2011). Developing international executives: the capacity-building approach. *Development and Learning in Organizations* 25 (2): 10–14.

Kuisel, R.F. (1993). *Seducing the French: The Dilemma of Americanization*. Berkeley, CA: University of California Press.

Mnouchkine, A. (2003). "Disneyland Resort Paris, France: 1992." Retrieved January 10, 2019 from http://content.time.com/time/specials/packages/article/0,28804,2024035_2024499_2024904,00.html.

Okpara, J. and Kabongo, J. (2011). Cross-cultural training and expatriate adjustment: A study of Western expatriates in Nigeria. *Journal of World Business* 46: 22–30.

O'Mahony, P. (2008). "Ikea guilty of 'cultural imperialism': Danes." Retrieved January 10, 2019 from https://www.thelocal.se/20080220/10054.

Parkhurst-Ferguson, P. (2006). *Accounting for Taste: The Triumph of French Cuisine*. Chicago, IL: University of Chicago Press.

Reider, D. (2014). "ZARA presents: A striped pyjama with a yellow star for your child." *+972*. Retrieved January 10, 2019 from http://972mag.com/zara-presents-a-striped-pyjama-with-a-yellow-star-for-your-child/96058.

Schein, E.H. (2010). *Organizational Culture and Leadership*, vol. 2. Chichester: Wiley.

Shapiro, J.M., Ozanne, J.L., and Saatcioglu, B. (2008). An interpretive examination of the development of cultural sensitivity in international business. *Journal of International Business Studies* 39.

Tempest, R. (1992). "Protesters block Euro Disneyland : France: Irked by US trade policies, farmers use tractors to keep cars and buses out of the park." Retrieved January 10, 2019 from http://articles.latimes.com/1992-06-27/news/mn-837_1_euro-disneyland.

Tuleja, E.A. and O'Rourke, J.S. (2008). *International Communication for Business*. Boston, MA: Cengage Learning.

4

Professionalism and Ethical Reasoning

Central Themes

- The practice of public relations can present unique and challenging ethical issues that should be considered when making decisions and acting on behalf of organizations and stakeholders.
- Protecting integrity and the public trust is fundamental to the profession's role and reputation.
- Organizations are responsible for their actions; so too are public relations and communications management professionals.
- Practicing across borders may place the values of home and host societies on a collision course, which calls for the articulation of professional, corporate, and industry codes of ethics and the clear setting of aspirational values.

   Keywords *integrity; ethical decision-making; professional responsibilities; codes of ethics; values*

Introduction

The recruitment, hiring, and training of public relations professionals in various world locations are complex but important tasks. There are locations where talent is abundant. There are places where public relations is taught in higher-education institutions. Other would-be professionals study journalism and gain additional training in seminars and conferences. It is not uncommon to find lawyers, business administrators, and engineers managing the public relations function in all types of organizations worldwide.

Global and Multicultural Public Relations, First Edition. Juan-Carlos Molleda and Sarab Kochhar.
© 2019 John Wiley & Sons, Inc. Published 2019 by John Wiley & Sons, Inc.

Most multinational corporations (MNCs), multilateral organizations, agencies, and consultancies normally staff the public relations function with a combination of local professionals and expatriates. It is expected that once a professional becomes a member of the public relations and communications team, he or she will be embedded in a corporate culture and management philosophy that somewhat standardizes ethics, norms, and professional practices. It is customary that organizations and agencies will employ local talents whose values, experience, and preparation are close rather than distant from those of employers. There are regions in Africa, Asia, Eastern Europe, and Latin America where recruitment and hiring do not happen in the target country for a new or expanding operation, but in neighboring countries. South Africa, South Korea, Slovenia, and Argentina, to name just a few, are countries that supply educated and skillful public relations and communications professionals to multinational organizations (MNOs) and agencies expanding to neighboring countries. They have demonstrated high levels of professionalism because of a constant evolution of the practice and field of study in their home countries. These countries also exert leadership in the development of public relations and communications management in their regions.

The educational and professional levels of local talent may be closely related to the level of professionalization of public relations in a given country. The level of sophistication and advancement of public relations in a location may be bound to local socioeconomic and political conditions, among other factors. The modern practice and area of study originated in the West, but has spread worldwide. This expansion or emergence does not seem to be equally institutionalized in every market. Thus, this chapter explains what it takes for an occupation to become or be called a profession, what are the indicators of professionalization, and how these indicators vary in different national and regional contexts and change over time, with implications for the status and practice of public relations. Moreover, the chapter also addresses ethical standards and issues that shape the practice locally and globally.

What Defines a Profession?

From a market perspective, a profession is a set of distinctive specialized practices that have achieved legitimacy in the labor market. Sociology of the professions informs this brief definition. These are the most cited indicators that characterize a profession:

- Recognition as a specialized function within organizations of all kinds.
- Foundations in a formal academic and scientific body of knowledge; that is, an area of study that is the focus of a critical mass of devoted scholars.

- Possession of unique applied knowledge and techniques that confer those who practice the craft a special status in the labor market.
- Differentiated practices from other related fields; in the case of public relations, a practice different from advertising, journalism, and marketing. This indicator may be challenged by integrated practices that emergent communications technologies allow. However, integration also means coordination of the commercial and institutional messaging systems of organizations.
- A requirement that practitioners earn a license or accreditation to practice; permission to practice that may be regulated or enforced by trade or governmental entities. In public relations, most countries with professional associations have opted for the accreditation requirement, but in a voluntary fashion.
- Formal studies in higher-education institutions that confer degrees, certificates, and diplomas. Formal public relations education is growing worldwide, though most programs are in the United States and Western Europe.
- Underpinnings in an ideology and ethical principles that explicitly imply a commitment to the wellbeing of society. This important indicator will be discussed later in the chapter.
- Trade or membership associations that unite professionals for the achievement of mutual benefits and career advancement.
- Acknowledgment by the state in laws and legal codes as a particular occupation or professional practice in the labor market. The state, through legislation, establishes the requirements of who could be hired or who could practice a profession in public and perhaps private and other types of organizations or agencies. Very few countries and territories have enacted such specific legislation to regulate the practice of public relations and communications management, including Brazil, Panama, Peru, Puerto Rico, and Nigeria. There are not systematic data and reports on how public relations legislation is enforced, how many practicing professionals are licensed and how many professionals are practicing without being licensed.
- Operations in a labor market where professionals have a certain level of control over supply and demand of services, as well as over the cost of services, other fees, and salaries.
- Power of organized professional groups before governmental agencies to influence decisions that may affect professionals and their practices. Similarly, capacity to influence the education system regarding the development of the body of knowledge and programs needed to learn and obtain degrees with an emphasis in public relations and communications management. The close relationship between the professional and academic communities has in many countries become essential to shaping education and training in the practice and field of study. In fact, many professionals have opted to practice and teach simultaneously or to transition to a teaching job after years of professional experience.

The model of professional in residence at higher education and training institutions has become popular and necessary to withstand the growth of the practice. Research teams that include academics and professionals have become common, in order to delve into conceptualizations and theories that inform major aspects of concern and challenges for the practice and education of future professionals.

- A system of labor access and promotion in which nepotism and personal influence or favoritism are discouraged and skills, abilities, and knowledge are encouraged, being the main criteria for recruitment, selection, and advancement.
- Dispute-resolution, arbitration, or sanction mechanisms in the case of conflicts between professionals and employers or clients.

Professionalization in Global Public Relations

As a modern profession, public relations has escalated hierarchies in organizations to occupy the seat of the chief communications officer (CCO). Again, this is not happening uniformly worldwide. Therefore, the higher the levels of professionalization, the higher the esteem, legitimacy, and influence of the public relations function in organizations in a given society. With higher levels of professionalization, an occupation or profession can attract better quality talent and resources, and have a greater impact on business and society. The better organizations act and communicate their interests, the better they can engage their stakeholders and the more likely they are to achieve their goals. Indicators of professionalization imply a certain order of the field of practice and study in the labor market. When the rules of the game are clearer, service and consulting transactions tend to flourish in a positive and productive environment.

A professionalized and institutionalized occupation should be associated with more employment opportunities, a greater number of educational offerings, and a healthier pool of talent. The authors of this publication have noticed that global agencies open branches in countries that reach stable levels of growth and governance, such as Poland in the 1990s and Peru in the 2000s. Professional and academic events seem also to follow the emergence of public relations as a modern profession on the global stage.

The State of the Profession Across the Globe

Assessing the professional status of public relations and communications management worldwide is a daunting task. It is challenging because, as explained before, professionalization has a variety of market-driven dimensions. Nonetheless, we will highlight the regions of countries that appear to excel in the professionalization indicators for which information is available.

In two content analyses of peer-reviewed academic publications, North America, Western Europe, and East Asia ranked as the regions with the most scholarship on the profession, the professional, and the practice (Rajul et al. 2014; Molleda and Laskin 2005). The United States and United Kingdom are best represented in the scholarship, followed by South Korea, Germany, India, China, and New Zealand. Africa, Latin America, and the Caribbean are the least represented regions.

Licensing or Accreditation?

In 2014, the first author of this textbook participated in the Brazilian Special Commission of Professional Flexibility, which was coordinated by the Federal Council of Public Relations Professionals (CONFERP). The commission's aim was to modify the law that regulates the practice in Brazil to allow people with higher-education degrees other than public relations and work experience to register as public relations professionals within certain limits and meeting some requirements. CONFERP was created in 1969 to enforce the public relations license enacted in 1967 (CONFERP 2014). Brazil became the first country in the world to enact such legislation to regulate who practices public relations. Since the council's creation, the enforcement of the law has been challenging.

As already noted, license and accreditation is one of the requirements for an occupation to evolve into a profession. The debate of whether to adopt one or another has been lost-lasting. Only a very few countries have adopted the licensing requirement. Three of them – Brazil, Panama, and Nigeria – did so under military governments. The need for a licensing requirement has been given low ratings in US-based studies (Cameron et al. 1996; Sallot et al. 1997, 1998). The need for a license or accreditation was rated low in Latin America (Molleda et al. 2010). However, Gupta (2007) found that licensing was rated very high by Indian professionals. Most countries have embraced the option of accreditation, which is based on professional knowledge, skills, and experience. The pattern is mixed, but the debate is on.

Established in 1957, the Public Relations Institute of Southern Africa (PRISA) has developed a layered system of professional accreditation. The PRISA Registration System is based on expertise and academic qualifications, which is consistent with international accreditation standards such as the Accredited Public Relations (APR) in Australia, Canada, New Zealand, and the United States (PRISA 2013). The APR program includes four steps: application by a potential candidate; an orientation session; a verification process and portfolio of evidence; and a final assessment (written and oral) by an accreditation committee.

Accreditation is voluntary. It needs to be supported by an infrastructure that may include other requirements of established professions, such as higher education programs, practical training, representative professional associations or institutes, and a body of knowledge. Accreditation sets experience and education standards and demonstrates commitments from trade groups (which promote it) and professionals (who go through the assessment process to earn accreditation).

For example, in 2014, the Global Alliance for Public Relations and Communication Management (GA) hosted its Second Research Colloquium and Eighth World Public Relations Forum (WPRF) in Madrid, Spain. For these academic and professional events, GA partnered with the Spanish Association of Communication Directors (DIRCOM). In the same year, the organization also sponsored the GA COMM PRIX Awards, recognizing outstanding performance in public relations and communications management around the world. The GA also furthered its leadership workshops, speakers' bureau, and scholarship program for a Master of Science in Communications Management in partnership with the USI Università della Svizzera Italiana and a Reputation Management Learning Program in partnership with the US Reputation Institute.

The GA aims to represent and assist in the development of national, regional, and international public relations associations. The GA's mission includes unifying the profession, raising professional standards across the world, sharing knowledge for the benefit of its association and institutional members, and becoming the global voice for the profession in the public interest. In particular:

> The Global Alliance's vision is to enhance the role and value of public relations and communication management to organizations, and to global society. We pursue this vision through leadership and service to the profession, defining universal principles that unite our professional associations and their members, while embracing a diversity that enables different applications in different parts of our global community. (GA n.d.)

The GA started its operation in 2002, after a series of conversations and a foundation period beginning in 1996 (GA n.d.). The leading organizations that achieved the creation of the GA were the Canadian Public Relations Society (CPRS), UK Chartered Institute of Public Relations (CIPR), International Association of Business Communicators (IABC), International Public Relations Association (IPRA), Public Relations Institute of Ireland (PRII), PRISA, and Public Relations Society of America (PRSA). Many local, national, regional, and international public relations and communications associations are yet to become members of the GA network, which represents an opportunity for growth.

Why Are Ethics in the Profession Important?

The public relations profession and professionals have dual responsibilities and divided loyalties with organizations and stakeholders. A true relationship and honest dialogue can only be achieved with a trusted broker or boundary spanner. Public relations and communications management professionals, moreover, have the duty of interpreting their organizations and clients to target publics and of interpreting the publics to the organizations and clients.

Most importantly, the profession's and professionals' best weapon is credibility. This credibility is internal to their employers and clients and external to their partners and stakeholders, such as communities, businesses, governments, and media. For instance, a credible professional is likely to maintain and achieve mutually beneficial relations with media representatives. Similarly, credible professionals should be able to gain access to the decision-making table of their organizations and clients.

The prestige of a professional follows him or her wherever the job opportunities are. Integrity and reputation can be achieved by embracing personal, corporate, and professional values and following ethical principles in making decisions and taking actions.

Code of Ethics for the Practice

The practice of public relations can present unique and challenging ethical issues. At the same time, protecting integrity and the public trust is fundamental to the profession's role and reputation. Bottom line, successful public relations hinges on the ethics of its professionals. The current state of ethics in public relations practice depends heavily on the codes of ethics held by the major professional associations. Membership in these groups is voluntary, meaning that one is not required to belong to such an association in order to practice public relations. Members agree to abide by a code of ethics that is written for the entire group. Some codes of ethics are written in terms that forbid a list of certain activities; others espouse a set of ethical principles that should be followed. Whether written in positive or negative terms, most of the professional associations in public relations have a code of ethics.

The organization PRSA has a code of ethics that is widely regarded as the industry standard. The code created and maintained by the

PRSA Board of Ethics and Professional Standards sets out principles and guidelines built on core values. Fundamental values like advocacy, honesty, loyalty, professional development, and objectivity structure ethical practice and interactions with clients and the public. Translating values into principles of ethical practice, the Code advises professionals to:

- Protect and advance the free flow of accurate and truthful information.
- Foster informed decision-making through open communications.
- Protect confidential and private information.
- Promote healthy and fair competition among professionals.
- Avoid conflicts of interest.
- Work to strengthen the public's trust in the profession.

Code guidelines stress the use of values and principles when facing everyday tasks and challenges. Professionals should:

- Be honest and accurate in all communications.
- Reveal sponsors for represented causes and interests.
- Act in the best interest of clients or employers.
- Disclose financial interests in a client's organization.
- Safeguard the confidences and privacy rights of clients and employees.
- Follow ethical hiring practices to respect free and open competition.
- Avoid conflicts between personal and professional interests.
- Decline representation of clients requiring actions contrary to the Code.
- Accurately define what public relations activities can accomplish.
- Report all ethical violations to the appropriate authority.

While the Code covers members, PRSA maintains that all public relations professionals should look to it as a model of professional behavior. Additionally, PRSA regards the Code as a model for other professions, organizations, and professionals. The GA bases its professional principles on the fundamental value and dignity of the individual. It believes in and supports the free exercise of human rights, especially freedom of speech, freedom of assembly, and freedom of the media, which are essential to the practice of good public relations. Following this, the GA pledges:

- To conduct ourselves professionally, with integrity, truth, accuracy, fairness, and responsibility to our clients, our client publics, and to an informed society
- To improve our individual competence and advance the knowledge and proficiency of the profession through continuing education and research and, where available, through the pursuit of professional accreditation
- To adhere to the principles of the Code of Professional Standards for the Practice of Public Relations.

Corporate Transparency

Corporate transparency has taken on a new meaning in today's world. Not long ago, the only public statements a company ever made were professionally written press releases and the rare, stage-managed speech by the chief executive officer (CEO). Now organizations share information and post internal memos and even strategy goals online. McDonald's VP of corporate social responsibility believes that credibility is a form or currency that is achieved through transparency. Transparency is not only about *what* companies communicate but also about *how* they communicate.

MNCs are being forced to open up in a host of reporting areas, from tax and government contracts to anti-corruption and sustainability programs. Governments are demanding greater corporate accountability, and nongovernmental organizations (NGOs) are pushing for increased corporate transparency. Transparency International (TI) has published a study on corporate reporting, evaluating 124 big publicly listed companies based on the clarity of their anti-corruption programs, their corporate holdings, and their financial reporting (see Table 4.1). The list on the left presents the most and least transparent firms globally. One measure on which the firms are judged is country-by-country reporting of profits, taxes paid, and the like. According to TI's research, most companies aggregate their accounts in a way that makes it hard to see what assets and revenues they have in any given country. The biggest push for greater

Table 4.1 Shades of opacity. The most and least transparent firms, 2013.

Company	Country	Industry	Index[a]
Eni	Italy	Oil & gas	7.3
Vodafone	Britain	Telecoms	6.7
Statoil	Norway	Oil & gas	6.6
BHP Billiton	Australia	Mining	6.1
Banco Santander	Spain	Financials	6.0
Sberbank	Russia	Financials	1.5
Agricultural Bank of China	China	Financials	1.4
Bank of Communications	China	Financials	1.3
Honda	Japan	Consumer goods	1.3
Bank of China	China	Financials	1.0

[a] On a scale of zero (highly corrupt) to 100 (very clean).
Source: Transparency International.

openness has been among the extractive industries. Progress has come at the regional level: EU states have begun to pass into law a new directive requiring country-by-country, and in some cases project-by-project, reporting of extractive groups' payments to governments. Oil producers, meanwhile, are starting to publish more details of production-sharing contracts with governments.

Mounting evidence suggests that the market gives a higher value to firms that are upfront with investors and analysts. Organizations that share the key metrics and performance indicators that investors consider important are more valuable than those that keep information to themselves.

Beginning in the late 1990s, a private movement emerged that pressured apparel corporations to disclose the identity of their global supplier factories. The brands targeted, such as Nike and Levi Strauss, were reluctant to release information on their contracts, citing the relationships as proprietary. Nike's business model was built on outsourcing to factories for which it took no responsibility in terms of monitoring, compliance, and reporting. A student movement (United Students Against Sweatshops) was launched with the intention of using the market power of students to force the companies to examine workplace conditions at factories they owned or with which they worked. The mounting pressure led to companies like Nike and Levi Strauss publishing their supplier lists in 2005.

A lesson learned from this example and many others is that the organizations that do best in today's co-creation environment are those that have integrated transparency as part of their organizational culture and not just their communications strategy. The case study on Foxconn discusses some of the ethical issues and challenges faced by modern MNCs.

Case Study   Foxconn

Foxconn Technology Group was founded by Terry Gou in 1974 under Hon Hai Precision Company, Ltd. (Foxconn 2014). Headquartered in Taipei, Taiwan, Foxconn is the world's largest contracted electronics manufacturer, offering clients services in joint design and development and contracted manufacturing for electronic parts (Foxconn 2011). At its core, Foxconn engages in six types of technology, ranging from manufacturing computers to consumer electronics. The manufacturer labels itself as an "innovative technology developer" more than an electronics manufacturer (Foxconn 2011).

In 2010, Foxconn faced global scrutiny after 18 of its employees, 17–25 years of age, attempted suicide (Chan 2013). News media coverage reflected poorly on Foxconn's management and the working conditions employees faced. Foxconn, which works closely with companies like Apple, Sony, and Dell (Balfour and Culpan 2010), faced further global scrutiny for the way it handled the situation.

This case study will recount the steps Foxconn's management took before, during, and after the suicides. First, the case will examine the steps it took during the crisis-management stage of the fallout. Second, it will compare Foxconn's corporate, social, and environmental responsibility reports from the year before the suicides and the year of the suicides to show what services were offered to employees under stress. This comparison may show what steps Foxconn took after the fallout to provide additional support for its workers. Finally, it will provide a summary of the remediation attempts made in the years following the suicides. The three pillars of the case allow the reader to derive their own understanding of how effective, or ineffective, Foxconn was in communicating and remedying the fallout of this globally recognized crisis.

Suicides

In 2010, 18 attempted suicides by Foxconn employees resulted in 14 deaths and left four people severely injured (Chan 2013). Most of the employees who attempted suicide were between the ages of 17 and 25 (AsiaOne 2010). The majority of the suicides took place at one of two Foxconn factories in Shenzhen, China. The manufacturer faced scrutiny from the media for not addressing the suicides in a timely and appropriate fashion. *Bloomberg Businessweek* described Foxconn's handling of the situation as a "slow and initially clumsy response" (Balfour and Culpan 2010). The media already had a negative opinion of Foxconn because of a major defamation lawsuit in 2006. Foxconn came across as a bully to the media, and many media analysts were shocked over the extent of the suits (Li 2010).

A statement made by CEO Terry Gou alluded to the "emotional problems" of Chinese employees. Gou, however, stated that because the workers lived in the facilities, the blame should come back to the company (Chan 2013). "The first one, second one, and third one, I did not see this as a serious problem," Gou said (Balfour and Culpan 2010).

As the suicides progressed and the public began to pay more attention, Foxconn tried to reduce the reputational impact of the deaths by stating that the number was well below the national average. Corporate Public Communications Director Liu Kun emphasized the size of the company and stated that the reasons for the suicides were varied (Chan 2013). Kun also said as recently as 2014 that the generational gap and the high turnover rate for Foxconn employees had made communications between management and employees more difficult (Muyuan 2014).

After the ninth suicide, in May, Foxconn management began to realize the extent of the crisis it was dealing with. Foxconn provided a psychological questionnaire for new hires and implemented a no-suicide pledge policy for its current employees, which received backlash and was later dropped (Chan 2013). The manufacturer strung nets along its buildings to catch any future jumpers (China News 2010). In the same month, Foxconn set up a counseling center, open 24 hours a day, and increased wages by about 30%, with the promise of an additional increase in October (Balfour and Culpan 2010).

Another point of contention for the media was Foxconn's labor union's silence during the crisis (Yu 2010). Union Chairwoman Chen Peng reportedly made "insensitive public comments that 'suicide is foolish, irresponsible and meaningless and should be avoided'" (Heffernan 2013). Peng was formerly a personal assistant to Gou before he appointed her to the new position (Heffernan 2013).

Eventually, Foxconn hired public relations firm Burson-Marsteller to develop a strategy for the company, which included giving guided tours to media (Johnson 2011). The Chinese government also told media outlets to scale back coverage for fear that "copycat" suicides would take place (Li 2010).

2009 CSER Report

Foxconn had about 700 000 employees at the end of 2009, according to its 2009 Corporate Social and Environmental Responsibility (CSER) Annual Report (2010). The report emphasized the importance of employees' wellbeing and reiterated the steps management took to make employees' experiences positive. All employees lived in dormitories on site, where sponsored activities were offered outside of the workday, in which they were encouraged to participate. The company also offered benefits, including "regulatory social security funds, employer-sponsored trust funds, employee accident funds, employee voluntary donation funds, and employee assistance funds" for both workers and immediate dependents (Foxconn 2010, p. 22).

Foxconn also considered employee communications. Employees' concerns were heard via complaint boxes placed in "conspicuous" locations so that employees could easily file complaints to management. The complaints were reviewed in secrecy on a daily basis by the most relevant departments, according to the report. The larger goal of the complaint boxes was to help study "shifts in employee perception over time" (Foxconn 2010, p. 23). An employee relations department also facilitated conversations between employees and management.

In March 2007, a labor union was established. The union had more than 210 000 members from Shenzhen alone. According to the report, the four primary duties of the labor union were to aid in the fair representation, construction, involvement, and education of Foxconn's employees. Another communication tactic used by Foxconn was to provide a newsletter to all employees entitled the *Bridgewater Monthly Gazette*. The gazette published news stories on the latest technological advances and quality control to enhance internal communications. The *Gazette* also published uplifting comics to boost morale.

Foxconn offered many other services to its employees. Physical and mental health counseling was offered, including seminars on managing stress. To further the education of its employees, the manufacturer offered diploma, undergraduate, postgraduate, and PhD programs, along with professional skills training.

2010 CSER Report

In contrast to the previous year, Foxconn employed about 935 000 people by the end of 2010, according to the 2010 CSER Annual Report (2011). That year, Foxconn added on to the many services offered to its employees in 2009. A new health monitoring system was established with a healthcare website, which allowed employees to check their medical records at their convenience. Focusing on employees' health and wellbeing seemed to be a priority for Foxconn in 2010. The corporation added an additional 300 square meters to its existing medical offices and established a counseling clinic, which housed private rooms for counseling, group counseling, and telephone counseling. The clinic was open 24 hours a day, 7 days a week, and employees could visit in person or receive counseling over the phone.

While Foxconn continued to use the complaint boxes for different departments, as it had in 2009, a hotline was also created to take complaint calls. By the end of 2010, over 40 000 cases had been reported to Foxconn. The manufacturer's labor union had a more active role in 2010, according to the report. It hosted a variety of contests and competitions to "improve the quality of life at work" for employees.

Conclusion

Despite Foxconn's annual reports listing services for its employees, there seems to have been a disconnect between what was said and what was done by the manufacturer. Foxconn did not respond to the crisis in a timely fashion, and some of its officials failed to exhibit professionalism when they spoke of the crisis.

Given the sensitivity of the situation and its delayed approach, Foxconn was represented unfavorably in the media as a result of the deaths and injuries, which were recognized globally. A standing negative reputation from an earlier defamation lawsuit against journalists probably elevated the issue.

As evidenced by this case, details such as timeliness and sensitivity are crucial aspects of professionalism and ethical reasoning. Open communications between management and employees may have limited the extent of the negative press coverage for the manufacturer, but ultimately, operating ethically and considering serious ethical issues such as the treatment of employees should be at the forefront of all companies' agendas.

The Global Alliance: A Perspective on a Global Industry's Professional Journey

By Daniel Tisch, APR, FCPRS

The Impetus for Global Professionalism

The GA, formed in 2002, is the confederation of the world's major public relations professional associations and institutions. Its mission is to unify public relations associations and professionals – in the academic and professional worlds – with the goal of collaborating on standards, knowledge-sharing, advocacy, and other common priorities in the public relations profession.

Prior to 2002, although there had been many large public relations professional associations – each with their own definitions of public relations, codes of ethics, and professional standards – true global initiatives had been limited, for a number of reasons. Around the turn of the century, changes in professional aspirations, technological advancements, and globalization advanced collaborations between public relations associations. This led to the creation of an international confederation of associations: the GA.

Prioritizing a Code of Ethics

In 2001, the first international collaboration between the associations – taking place a year before the founding general meeting of the GA in July 2002 – resulted in the development of a Global Code of Ethics.

To reinforce the Alliance's top priority even further, ethics was the theme of the inaugural edition of the GA's signature conference, the WPRF, first held in Rome in June 2003.

Instead of seeking to replicate or supplant the multitude of ethical codes among the various member organizations, the drafters of the GA Code of Ethics focused on identifying universal principles. The compact three-page document included a declaration of principles, a code of professional standards, and a code of practice. The Code of Ethics identified key characteristics of good public relations practice (including a commitment to the free exercise of human rights, principles of professionalism, and provisions of ethical behavior). Additionally, the GA leaders made the choice to develop an educational guide to help members apply the Code of Ethics through a six-step process of defining and resolving ethical conflicts.

Advancing Global Knowledge and Standards

Over the years, the GA has undertaken a series of projects aimed at sharing knowledge and elevating standards in various dimensions of public relations, including education, credentials, and practice. One of the earliest (and still ongoing) examples of knowledge sharing is its Landscapes project, which profiles the state of public relations in countries around the world. Its well-researched pieces, usually compiled by graduate students at the University of Florida, have been a popular resource for public relations professionals seeking opportunities in new markets.

The GA has worked with other professional bodies to advance common principles and standards in public relations measurement and evaluation. The most notable of these projects is the Barcelona Principles (2015), compiled in collaboration with the International Association for Measurement and Evaluation of Communication (AMEC). Included among the many significant features of the Barcelona Principles are provisions positing that: goal-setting and measurement are important (including organization, quantity and quality, and frequency); advertising value equivalents (AVE) are not the value of public relations; social media can and should be measured; and measuring outcomes is preferred to measuring media results (outputs).

In the years following publication of the Barcelona Principles, the GA continued to work with industry partners to achieve a broad consensus for standards in measurement and evaluation of public relations programs and activities.

In 2013, the GA launched the COMM PRIX Awards, a "best-of-the-best" competition in which members of participating associations are judged against one another based on the program's success in strengthening the organization's key stakeholder relationships. Entrants who have earned local, national, or international awards – regardless of the public relations discipline – compete against one another for the top prize.

Also in 2013, the GA and the University of Southern California's (USC) Annenberg School for Communication and Journalism embarked upon the world's first ongoing study of public relations and communications management practice, the Global GAP Survey. Modeled after the long-standing Generally Accepted Practices (GAP) study – which, since 2002, has conducted studies every two years in the United States – the Global GAP Survey aims to analyze current practices, trends, and new developments in the profession. The Survey provides comparative data to be used for analysis between countries and continents. Most importantly, it charts the development of multinational perspectives on how the public relations and communications management professions are evolving in different settings.

The results of the inaugural Global GAP Survey were announced at the 2014 WPRF in Madrid, Spain. This first edition saw the participation of six country partners – Australia, Brazil, Canada, New Zealand, South Africa, and the United States – each featuring both an association and an academic partner. The GA and USC plan to expand the study, with additional national partners, for subsequent editions.

A Global Voice of Advocacy: A New Mandate for Public Relations

In recent years, the GA has shifted its exclusive focus on achieving internal consensus within the profession to using its consensus-building capabilities to equip member associations, academics, and professionals with the tools to influence external audiences. It has undertaken this task by using its diverse network of public relations associations and academic leaders to co-create global resources that help raise standards, share knowledge, strengthen associations and professional communities, and make the business case for the profession. The two most prominent examples of this approach are the Stockholm Accords of 2010 and the Melbourne Mandate of 2012 (the WPRF's eponymous convening site and year).

The Stockholm Accords provide public relations professionals with a framework that can be presented to their organizations, highlighting the scope of what public relations professionals do (or what they should do) in their profession. They resulted from an initial attempt to generate a more universal articulation of the role and value of the public relations profession for the global public relations community. Later, they aimed to enable external audiences – regardless of region, culture, or continent – to understand the work of public relations professionals and the value they bring to organizations and society. The Accords are unique in their simultaneous focus on the societal, organizational, and operational values of public relations in six spheres: sustainability, governance, management, internal communications, external communications, and the alignment of internal and external communications. The process of drafting them involved the collaboration of leading practitioners and academics, in some 30 countries, through a series of web-based working groups. After months of work, the group compiled the consensus document, which was endorsed unanimously by delegates at the 2010 WPRF.

If the Stockholm Accords' purpose was to provide a present reflection of public relations and communications management practice, the Melbourne Mandate of 2012 was an attempt to identify the emerging roles of public relations heading into the future. The GA's working assumption was that the characteristics of communicative organizations – as well as the roles, responsibilities, and values of public relations professionals – were rapidly evolving, in a world where audiences and stakeholders had unprecedented communications access and power. GA leaders believed that addressing these concerns could produce a powerful advocacy platform for professionals around the globe. The Melbourne Mandate held that there are three key emerging roles for contemporary public relations:

1) leading the definition of an organization's character and values;
2) building a culture of listening and engagement; and
3) instilling responsible behaviors in professionals and organizations.

In addition to the Mandate, the GA developed a companion "toolkit" to assist public relations professionals in finding applications for it in their organization. The toolkit includes a model to help measure whether an organization is living up to its organizational values in the minds of its internal and external stakeholders, examples of MNCs that have embedded elements of the Mandate in their communications vision and strategy, case studies of ethical and responsible behavior, and a framework that can help professionals align their own professional knowledge and skills development with the principles of the Mandate.

Momentum into the Future

The 2014 WPRF in Madrid marked a shift to a different track for the GA – rather than using the annual event as the culmination of a conversation, it was used as the starting point for one. As more than 800 professionals from 66 nations gathered to consider the theme of "Communication with Conscience," the GA started a discussion on leadership. The conversation focused on exploring some of the ways in which public relations and communications professionals can take on a leadership role that not only builds up their communicative organizations, but also contributes to their society. The dialogue in Madrid identified the following key universal principles:

1) Public relations and communications management must aspire to a social purpose, serve social cohesion, and aim to bring communities together.
2) Public relations and communications management can enable social integration by listening, identifying agendas, and creating shared narratives and safe places for dialogue around the social challenges of each society.
3) Public relations and communications professionals must take responsibility for identifying how they can serve their own societies.
4) By realizing the power of communications, each public relations and communications professional can be a leader. True leadership achieves personal, organizational, and societal transformation.
5) By reflecting on transformational leadership moments, the profession can learn to serve organizations better, and by doing that, serve society better.

These themes are meant to guide future conversations among public relations professions around the globe. One common thread central to all of the GA's work – especially in the dialogues in Stockholm, Melbourne, and Madrid – is a desire to foster enhanced professionalism in public relations.

The GA's work reflects a vision: there is enhanced legitimacy in global collaboration, consensus, and co-creation; universal principles must coexist with flexible applications in different cultures and contexts; and the best strategies and practices for the profession of public relations must originate from within the profession itself.

Discussion Questions

1 Which do you think had a greater impact on Foxconn's public perception: the delay in the response or the way it communicated the crisis publicly?

2 What steps could Foxconn have taken early on to prevent such a fallout as a result of the crisis?

3 What was the most unethical or unprofessional aspect of this case? How could it have been changed or prevented?

Class Activity

In 2006, a blog appeared called "Wal-Marting Across America." It featured the adventures of Jim and Laura as they traveled from Las Vegas to Georgia by RV, staying in park-for-free Walmart store parking lots. While at these different Walmart locations, the couple would interview employees about their jobs. They decided to get approval from Working Families for Walmart, an organization that Laura had signed up to in order to show support. Working Families made the decision to pay for Jim and Laura's entire trip.

So, where was the problem? The fact that these were paid bloggers and hired by the public relations firm Edelman was not disclosed. Readers were led to believe that the tour had no relation to Walmart and that it was just two people who had decided to start to make a blog about their experiences. Once the secret was out, the story blew up in the public relations world. Students should discuss in groups the ethical implications of this case for Edelman and for Walmart. This happened in 2006. Considering how the social media space has changed, what could Edelman or Walmart have done differently today?

References

AsiaOne. (2010). "11th Foxconn employee commits suicide at work." Retrieved January 10, 2019 from http://news.asiaone.com/News/Latest%2BNews/Asia/Story/A1Story20100526-218580.html.

Balfour, F. and Culpan, T. (2010). "The man who makes your iPhone." *Bloomberg Business Week*. Retrieved January 10, 2019 from http://www.businessweek.com/magazine/content/10_38/b4195058423479.htm#p1.

Barcelona Principles 2.0. (2015). Institute for Public Relations Website. Retrieved March 11, 2019, from https://instituteforpr.org/barcelonaprinciples-2-0-updated-2015/.

Cameron, G.T., Sallot, L.M., and Weaver-Lariscy, R.A. (1996). Developing standards of professional performance in public relations. *Public Relations Review* 22 (1): 43–61.

Chan, J. (2013). "A suicide survivor: The life of a Chinese migrant worker at Foxconn." *Japan Focus*. Retrieved January 10, 2019 from http://japanfocus.org/-Jenny-Chan/3977.

China News. (2010). "Another Foxconn employee falls to death despite company, government appeals." Retrieved January 10, 2019 from http://english.sina.com/china/2010/0526/321604.html.

CONFERP. (2014). "Legislação." Retrieved January 10, 2019 from http://conferp.org.br/?s=Legisla%C3%A7%C3%A3o.

Foxconn. (2010). "2009 corporate social and environmental responsibility annual report." Retrieved January 10, 2019 from https://www.yumpu.com/en/document/read/4550491/foxconn-2009-csr-report.

Foxconn. (2011). "2010 corporate social and environmental responsibility annual report." Retrieved January 10, 2019 from http://www.facing-finance.org/wp-content/blogs.dir/16/files/2012/04/Foxconn_CSR-Report_2010.pdf.

Foxconn. (2014). "Group profile." Retrieved January 10, 2019 from http://www.foxconn.com/GroupProfile_En/GroupProfile.html.

GA. (n.d.). "Who we are." Retrieved January 10, 2019 from https://www.globalalliancepr.org/who-we-are/.

Gupta, S. (2007). Professionalism in Indian public relations and corporate communications: An empirical analysis. *Public Relations Review* 33 (3): 306–312.

Heffernan, M. (2013). "What happened after the Foxconn suicides." *CBSNews*. Retrieved January 10, 2019 from http://www.cbsnews.com/news/what-happened-after-the-foxconn-suicides.

Jain, R., De Moya, M., and Molleda, J.C. (2014). State of international public relations research: Narrowing the knowledge gap about the practice across borders. *Public Relations Review* 40 (3): 595–597.

Johnson, J. (2011). "1 million workers. 90 million iPhones. 17 suicides. Who's to blame?" *Wired*. Retrieved January 10, 2019 from http://www.wired.com/2011/02/ff_joelinchina/all/1.

Li, R. (2010). "Foxconn seen as bullying the media." *South China Morning Post*. Retrieved January 10, 2019 from http://www.scmp.com/article/715795/foxconn-seen-bullying-media.

Molleda, J.C. and Laskin, A.V. (2005). "Global, international, comparative and regional public relations knowledge from 1990 to 2005: A quantitative content analysis of academic and trade publications." Retrieved January 10, 2019 from https://instituteforpr.org/pr-knowledge-2005/.

Molleda, J.C., Moreno, A., Athaydes, A., and Suárez, A.M. (2010). Macroencuesta latinoamericana de comunicación y relaciones públicas" [Latin American macro-survey of communication and public relations]. *Organicom* 7 (13): 118–141.

Muyuan, C. (2014). "Foxconn soldiers on in Shenzhen." *China Daily*. Retrieved January 10, 2019 from http://www.chinadaily.com.cn/business/2014-04/23/content_17457219.htm.

PRISA. (2013). "Accreditation." Retrieved January 10, 2019 from https://www.prisa.co.za/accreditation/.

Sallot, L.M., Cameron, G.T., and Weaver-Lariscy, R.A. (1997). Professional standards in public relations: A survey of educators. *Public Relations Review* 23 (3): 197–216.

Sallot, L.M., Cameron, G.T., and Weaver-Lariscy, R.A. (1998). PR educators and practitioners identify professional standards. *Journalism & Mass Communication Educator* 53 (2): 19–30.

Yu, X. (2010). "Better relations to curb frustrations." *China Daily*. Retrieved January 10, 2019 from http://www.chinadaily.com.cn/cndy/2010-05/31/content_9909192.htm.

5

Transnational Corporations and Global Public Relations Agencies

Central Themes

- International trade has increased rapidly through the development of transportation and communications technologies and a multiplicity of free-trade agreements among nations and regions.
- Transnational corporations (TNCs) and global public relations agencies are important players in international business and world affairs.
- TNCs need to consider the demands and expectations of a complex set of home and host publics.
- Corporations with a combination of internal departments and professionals and external agencies and outsourcing services manage public relations and communication practices.
- Large TNCs handle their internal communications and corporate affairs with their own public relations professionals, especially programs of employee and shareholder relations.
- Social media and owned, earned, and paid media are essential components of internal and external global and local programs and campaigns.

Keywords *transnational corporations; international business; trade; global agencies; global campaigns; home and host publics*

Introduction

International businesses dominate trade and commerce globally. The World Trade Organization provides databases and publications on the evolution of international trade over the years and its projected growth and impact in this century (WTO n.d.). International trade has sped up through the development of transportation and communications

Global and Multicultural Public Relations, First Edition. Juan-Carlos Molleda and Sarab Kochhar.
© 2019 John Wiley & Sons, Inc. Published 2019 by John Wiley & Sons, Inc.

technologies, as well as a multiplicity of free-trade agreements among a combination of nations and regions. Corporations that operate in many countries simultaneously have spearheaded the growth in the exchange of goods, raw materials, and services. In this chapter, they are addressed as transnational corporations (TNCs), where in many other textbooks they are called global, international, or multinational corporations (MNCs). The first section explains the decision to adopt the term "transnational" in this text.

Corporations operating in several countries manage their overall public relations function from their headquarters with various degrees of centralization and decentralization. Netherlands-based Unilever Group, for instance, is a food and personal care products firm. The transnational conglomerate has a chief marketing and communication officer who also leads the firm's sustainability work, its drinking water business (i.e. Pureit), and the Unilever brand itself from offices in Rotterdam and London (Hoovers 2014). Unilever is a world leader in manufacturing dressings, savory products, and spreads, with brands such as Hellmann's, Knorr, Wish-Bone, and Ragú. The corporation's other products include Breyers and Ben & Jerry's ice creams, Lipton tea, Dove and Lux soaps, and Sunsilk hair care. Unilever holds a leading position in laundry detergents and operates tea and oil plantations in India, Kenya, and Tanzania, among other countries. Asia, Africa, and Central and Eastern Europe account for 40% of the group's sales, followed by 33% in the Americas, and 27% in Western Europe (Hoovers 2014). Emergent markets thus account for 57% of total sales (Unilever n.d.-a).

The conglomerate includes the following tabs on its online global media center: "Press Releases," "News and Features," "Speeches and Interviews," "Footage," "Executive Biographies," "Images and Logos," "Media Contacts," and "Sign Up for Press Releases" (Unilever n.d.-b). The firm's website also includes an investor center and media contacts for its global teams in London and Rotterdam, as well as locally in the United Kingdom/Ireland, the United States, and many other countries worldwide.

In addition to having its own marketing and communications unit, Unilever has worked closely with several global public relations agencies, including Burson-Marsteller, Edelman, Golin (Lipton account), and Ogilvy (see Table 5.1). Global agencies are also introduced in this chapter because they function as TNCs and offer their services to TNCs. Global agencies also offer their service to nongovernmental organizations (NGOs), governments, and multilateral organizations, among other world players.

The firm's community outreach is particularly supported by the Unilever Foundation, which has developed partnerships with global organizations such as Oxfam, Population Service International, Save the Children, United

Table 5.1 Unilever brands' media contacts in the United States.

Brand	Agency
AXE	Edelman
Ben & Jerry's	Ben & Jerry's Corporate
Breyers	Golin Harris
Caress	Weber Shandwick
Clear	Weber Shandwick
Degree Men	Weber Shandwick
Degree Women	Weber Shandwick
Dove	Edelman
Fruttare	Golin Harris
Good Humor	Golin Harris
Hellmann's	Weber Shandwick
I Can't Believe It's Not Butter	Golin Harris
Klondike	Golin Harris
Knorr	Unilever US Corporate
Lever 2000	Mbooth
Lipton Tea	Golin Harris
Magnum	Golin Harris
Motions	SIREN
Nexxus	Kaplow PR
Noxzema	Weber Shandwick
Pond's	Weber Shandwick
Popsicle	Golin Harris
Promise	Pollock and Associates
Q-Tips	Weber Shandwick
Shedd's Spread Country Crock	Golin Harris
Simple	Weber Shandwick
St. Ives	Kaplow PR
Suave	Weber Shandwick
Suave Men	Weber Shandwick
TIGI	SIREN
TRESemmé	SIREN
Vaseline	mbooth

Source: https://www.unilever.com/news/media-contacts/.

Nations International Children's Emergency Fund (UNICEF), and the World Food Programme (Unilever n.d.-a). Thus, Unilever's global public relations and communications management is complex and extensive. That is why the corporation announced in 2013 the streamlining of its marketing program to six core elements: communications; marketing insight; category and brand strategy; brand marketing plans; innovation and renovation; and in-market brand management, execution, tracking, and optimization (Stein 2013). Also in 2013, on Universal Children's Day, Unilever launched Project Sunlight, a global long-term campaign to encourage people to adopt more sustainable lifestyles (including by using its products, of course, among other alternatives) (Campaign India 2013). Launching a global campaign presents significant management challenges for the public relations teams and their agencies, implying processes of coordination and control, as well as a balance between global and local strategies and tactics. This is explained in Chapter 7.

What Are Transnational Corporations?

The power of TNCs has increased over the decades, as have expectations about their constituencies or stakeholders. In a publicly traded corporation, shareholders emphasize sales performance and productivity because higher profits will result in higher returns. Employees at headquarters and in subsidiaries in host countries want a safe workplace environment and fair, if not high, compensation. Customers in many countries want high quality products and services, which justifies pricing policies. Society – through community groups, activists, and influencers – advocates for corporate taxes, corporate support for social or environmental causes, and trustworthy behavior. The strengths of these competing stakeholder groups vary among countries where the corporation operates (Steiner and Steiner 2012).

The acceptance of local or host publics is essential for TNCs to achieve legitimacy and sustainability of their operations. Locals may fear takeover by foreign-owned TNCs because this can lead to job loss and unemployment. TNCs may also be blamed for the replacement of local businesses (affecting domestic entrepreneurship), monopolizing the best human and natural resources, and decreasing domestic research and development capabilities.

Moreover, they may also be accused of being foreign-policy instruments or agents of their home-country government, of disrupting local elections and politics, and of controlling sensitive or critical sectors in the host economy. TNCs, therefore, should strategically and trustfully communicate and show through their decisions and actions their positive impact on the host countries where they operate. Specifically, they are advised to acknowledge, for instance, how they generate quality employment and market growth, as well as the transfer of best practices and even technological advances. To this end, they could explicitly emphasize their technological capabilities, their marketing communications and public affairs expertise, their ability to export, their contribution to domestic diversity of products and services, their contribution to increasing foreign direct investment in the host country, and their corporate social performance and practices of corporate social responsibility (CSR).

Most large TNCs, such as Unilever, manage their internal communications and corporate affairs with their own public relations professionals, especially via programs of employee relations and shareholder communications. However, many of their external communications and programs are handled through coordination between in-company departments, global agencies, and a variety of outsourcing services. Having a mix between in-house departments and global agencies is advantageous because they complement one another's capabilities, resources, and expertise. This is why we include a section on global agencies in this chapter.

Global Public Relations Agencies

In Chapter 1, we discussed the strategic communications hubs around the world and how the use of an agency by a TNC is determined by its in-house capabilities, the scope of the work, and the complexity of the markets it is trying to reach.

The global PR industry grew by 5% in 2017, based on the Holmes Report's annual ranking of the world's top 250 PR firms. The report reveals that the Top 250 PR firms reported fee income of around $11.7bn in 2017, compared to $11bn in 2016.The Holmes Report defines public relations as including all of the activities in which an organization engages in order to strengthen its relationship with any public or stakeholder group. Thus, public relations fee income includes not only fees derived from traditional public relations activities (media relations, community relations, employee communications, investor relations, public affairs) but also fees (but only fees) related to activities such as research, design, advertising, and social media relations – as long as those activities are carried out by a firm whose primary activity is public relations.

According to Morris and Goldsworthy (2008), public relations consultancy started in the United States about 100 years ago, with most of the early consultancies built around individual personalities like Ivy Lee, Edward

Bernays, and John W. Hill. The growth of multinationals and the emergence of the IT industry made it possible for public relations consultancy to develop into an international business. By the late 1990s, large marketing groups like WPP, Omnicom, Publicis, Havas, and IPG owned public relations consultancy firms, which helped large conglomerates reach out to their international audience (Morris and Goldsworthy 2008). Chapter 1 details all of these large groups and the network of agencies each has.

The Unilever example explained how TNCs work with global public relations agencies across their networks. The revenues and networks of global public relations agencies are as large as those of any TNC. Edelman has a staff of around 5500 across its global network in Asia Pacific, Middle East & Africa (APACMEA), Canada, Europe, Latin America, and the United States. In APACMEA, Edelman has 1500 staff members in 24 offices across 13 countries and serves clients like Tata, HP, and Starbucks. In Europe, Edelman was established in London in 1967 and today has 1000 professionals in 18 offices across 13 markets. Edelman also works with more than 13 affiliates and partners across the Europe region. In 1994, when Brazil emerged as a global economic force, Edelman entered Latin America as a region. Edelman ranks among the top six agencies in Latin America, with offices in São Paulo, Rio de Janeiro, Buenos Aires, Miami, Mexico City, and Bogotá.

Edelman specializes in corporate communications, consumer marketing, CSR, crisis communications, public affairs, stakeholder engagement, sustainability, B-to-B and B-to-C brand marketing, strategic planning and creative execution, content marketing, research, and social media, digital, and traditional media relations. Recently in 2019, Edelman announced and appointed its New York chief creative officer, Jimmie Stone as Chief Creative Officer of Latin America. In his new role, Stone will develop and lead a team of creatives around Latin America, building on the efforts of the agency's creative leaders in Mexico, Eduardo Cisneros, and Brazil, Rogerio Gonçalves. Edelman works across industries and sectors like:

- Aerospace and defense
- Consumer packages goods
- Education
- Energy
- Financial services
- Food and beverage
- Health
- Life sciences
- Metals and industrial equipment
- Nonprofit
- Retail
- Specialty chemicals

- Sports and entertainment
- Technology
- Telecommunications
- Transportation
- Travel and hospitality.

Edelman is an independent agency and not part of any network. Imagine the reach and network of a global conglomerate like WPP (Table 5.2). WPP describes itself as the world leader in marketing communications services and is made up of leading companies in:

- Advertising
- Media investment management
- Data investment management (formerly known as consumer insight)
- Public relations and public affairs
- Branding and identity
- Healthcare communications
- Direct, digital, promotion and relationship marketing
- Specialist communications.

Public relations agencies are in many ways similar to management consultants and accounting and law firms. They charge fees related to time spent on client work. Staff salaries are the largest single cost of an agency (around 50% of their income). The second largest single cost is rent, followed by other administrative costs. Public relations agencies typically charge annual "fixed fees" to their clients based on their knowledge of the amount of time and work involved or estimated based on agency experience with similar programs. Another model that agencies frequently use is a "retainer fee" model. Here, the client pays a modest retainer fee and can draw on the agency's services when required. When a service is needed, the client pays according to the hourly rate of the client team involved. For example, a senior consultant will have a different hourly fee than a junior staff member; the client is charged according to how many hours each team member puts in. The client decides whether to hire a public relations executive internally or retain an external public relations agency.

Table 5.2 Facts and figures about.

Number of employees	>179 000 (including associates)
Number of offices	3000
Number of countries	111
Reported revenues	£11.5bn (as at December 2014)
Reported billings	£46.2bn (as at December 2014)
Market capitalization	£20.5bn (as at April 2015)

Globalization has resulted in many businesses with operations in several countries, and they need the expertise and counsel of large communications conglomerates and agency networks to synergize their communication efforts. The case study explains one such example where Genesis Burson-Marsteller used its network to create a global event.

Case Study   Genesis Burson-Marsteller – Beyond the "Hour"

Founded over 20 years ago, Genesis has become a leading public relations and public affairs firm in India (Genesis Burson-Marsteller n.d.). Prema Sagar, Founder and Principal of Genesis, has grown the "big small firm" into a network of seven offices spanning key South Asian metropolitan markets across India (Genesis Burson-Marsteller n.d., para. 3). Genesis now has a strong affiliate footprint in over 200 cities across India and neighboring countries (Genesis Burson-Marsteller n.d.). Genesis challenges itself to be "committed to Being More" for clients (para. 3); it emphasizes an "integrated approach [that] helps [it] provide the best council to build, nurture and protect [client] reputation" (Genesis Burson-Marsteller n.d., para. 4).

Genesis, continuing on its journey to provide integrated communications services to global markets (in addition to Indian ones), has used strategic mergers to expand the reach of its "evidence-based, ideas-driven and result oriented campaigns" (Genesis Burson-Marsteller n.d., para. 2). "In 2005, [Genesis] joined Burson-Marsteller, a leading global public relations and communication firm" to form Genesis Burson-Marsteller (Genesis Burson-Marsteller n.d., para. 5). Burson-Marsteller is an affiliate firm of the Young & Rubicam Group – a collective global marketing communications network (Genesis Burson-Marsteller n.d.; WPP n.d.-b), and Young & Rubicam Group is an associate company of the international communications services conglomerate, WPP (Genesis Burson-Marsteller n.d.; WPP n.d.-a). Genesis Burson-Marsteller's strategic merger has allowed it to expand its client-service capabilities into new markets; as a result, the firm has acquired clients in neighboring nations, such as Pakistan, Bangladesh, and Nepal (Genesis Burson-Marsteller n.d.).

World Wide Fund for Nature

The World Wide Fund for Nature (WWF) is "the world's largest conservation organization" (WWF n.d.-a,b). Founded in 1961, WWF is a charitable trust whose mission is to "conserve nature and reduce the most pressing threats to the diversity of life on Earth" (WWF n.d.-b, para. 1). The organization's vision is to stop the degradation of the planet's natural environment and "build a future in which people live in harmony with nature" (WWF n.d.-b, para. 1). WWF's people-centered focus is organized around six key areas in the global community: "forests, marine, freshwater, wildlife, food and climate" (WWF n.d.-c, para. 1).

WWF uses partnerships with corporate, humanitarian, and marketing entities, leveraging the strengths of its partners to collaborate on local and global conservation projects (WWF n.d.-c). Over the years, companies such as Coca-Cola, the United States Agency for International Development (USAID), and Avon Products have helped WWF experts deliver conservation solutions affecting the environment (WWF n.d.-a). Since its inception over 50 years ago, WWF has funded over 13 000 projects with support from over 1 million stakeholders (WWF n.d.-e).

Earth Hour

In 2007, the WWF launched its environment awareness campaign: Earth Hour (Zeenews 2012). The annual campaign's goal is to increase awareness of issues relating to climate change and its effects on the Earth (Zeenews 2012). To support global efforts to combat the effects of climate change, on the last Saturday in March, participants are asked to turn off all their lights and electrical appliances for 1 hour (Beyond the Hour n.d.; Zeenews 2012). This global environmental movement was created by WWF to challenge individuals, businesses, schools, and communities to take a stand against frivolous energy usage by reducing their carbon footprint (WWF n.d.-d; Zeenews 2012). The Earth Hour initiative seeks to inspire people to make energy-conscious decisions that reduce problems related to climate change; people can positively contribute to the goal of the campaign through small daily changes in their energy-consumption habits (Beyond the Hour n.d.).

The first Earth Hour event took place in Sydney, Australia (WWF n.d.-d). The campaign resulted in over 2 million people and 2000 businesses reducing energy consumption in the city by more than 10% (Beyond the Hour n.d.; WWF n.d.-d; Zeenews 2012). The success of the inaugural event led to the campaign's expansion the following year (WWF n.d.-d). In 2008, Earth Hour went global, with "more than 50 million people" (representing 35 countries) participating in the movement worldwide (WWF n.d.-d, para. 2). In the years following its launch, audience engagement in the Earth Hour campaign has increased exponentially, demonstrating the value and relevance of the initiative's goal (WWF n.d.-d).

Beyond the Hour

In 2009, India joined the Earth Hour campaign (Zeenews 2012), but after three years the campaign began to lose momentum there (Burson-Marsteller n.d.). In 2012, WWF enlisted the help of Genesis Burson-Marsteller to build a public awareness campaign that would address a new set of challenges facing Earth Hour in India (Burson-Marsteller n.d.). To promote the growth of the Earth Hour campaign, Genesis Burson-Marsteller created a strategy that would use diverse, culturally representative messaging designed to address "regional variances, different languages and cultural nuances" (Burson-Marsteller n.d., para. 2). The goal was to engage target publics in underrepresented cities throughout India, through localized events, partnerships, and endorsements from celebrity ambassadors (Burson-Marsteller n.d.). Genesis Burson-Marsteller created an integrated communications message focusing on "Earth Hour as a movement that goes beyond the 'hour' and actually demonstrates the power of each individual's action" (Burson-Marsteller n.d., para. 3).

Tactics

Genesis Burson-Marsteller used an integrated communications approach, utilizing offline and online tactics, to engage target publics (Burson-Marsteller n.d.; WWF 2012). The strategy was to engage target audiences offline, and then nurture and grow the relationship online (Burson-Marsteller n.d.). Earth Hour organized local events with specialized messages for participants in the region; also, Genesis Burson-Marsteller partnered with local media to introduce the "Beyond the Hour" message of the campaign (Burson-Marsteller n.d.). Genesis Burson-Marsteller strategically used celebrity ambassadors, with personal ties to targeted regions, to engage publics and media (Burson-Marsteller n.d.). An example of such a tactic was a cricket match during Earth Hour in Mumbai, which featured Indian cricket legend, Sachin Tendulkar. Other representative celebrity ambassadors included Chinese actress Li Bingbing and Brazilian supermodel Gisele Bundchen. Genesis Burson-Marsteller used special-event tactics to generate enthusiasm, garner support, and increase participation among local audiences.

Genesis Burson-Marsteller's online tactics used social media to spread the campaign's message across India (Burson-Marsteller n.d.). Social networking platforms such as YouTube, Facebook, and Twitter were used to encourage participants to share their Earth Hour experience across the country and around the world (WWF 2012). Globally, people were encouraged to make pledge videos proclaiming their commitment to participate in Earth Hour and, further, challenging others to make the same pledge of taking "environmentally-responsible actions" (WWF 2012, para. 4). The videos uploaded to YouTube were shared across many other social media platforms, spreading the reach of the campaign even further (WWF 2012). Through social media outlets, Earth Hour generated global support.

Outcomes

Genesis Burson-Marsteller's Earth Hour 2012 campaign in India was a well-earned success. Though Genesis Burson-Marsteller had only 45 days to plan and execute the Earth Hour campaign, it was able to exceed all of its goals (Burson-Marsteller n.d.). Overall, the campaign provided an opportunity for the Earth Hour movement to reach more Indian citizens than ever before. In total, over 9 million people in more than 150 cities in India participated in the Earth Hour campaign in 2012 (Burson-Marsteller n.d.). The success of the campaign rested on Genesis Burson-Marsteller's ability to authentically engage new publics and to leverage advocacy and support from the media and celebrity ambassadors (Burson-Marsteller n.d.). In 2013, Genesis Burson-Marsteller was awarded the Certificate of Excellence from SABRE India in the Special Event category (Holmes Report 2013; Burson-Marsteller n.d.).

Discussion Questions

1 What are some other tactics Genesis Burson-Marsteller could have used to navigate India's diverse landscape?

2 How did Genesis Burson-Marsteller work to make the Earth Hour 2012 campaign different than in previous years?

3 What research could have been conducted on the cultural landscape prior to implementing tactics?

4 What are some criteria that should be met before selecting a celebrity ambassador?

5 What are some suggested methods for reaching audiences in rural areas?

6 How did the national identity of Earth Hour impact Genesis Burson-Marsteller's work in the local Indian market?

Class Activity

TNCs and global public relations agencies have to work effectively in teams. In groups of four or five, students should perform a detailed country analysis of a TNC operating in one of the following countries: China,

India, the Philippines, Japan, Brazil, Mexico, Argentina, Germany, France, or Italy. They should analyze the country's political, economic, legal, and cultural environment, outline the challenges and opportunities of conducting business there, and provide relevant guidelines and recommendations for public relations agencies managing the TNC operations.

References

Beyond the Hour. (n.d.). "The countdown to Earth Hour 2019." Retrieved January 10, 2019 from http://www.beyondthehour.org.

Burson-Marsteller. (n.d.). "Case study: Beyond the Hour 2012." Retrieved January 10, 2019 from http://www.burson-marsteller.fr/case-studies/beyond-the-hour-2012/.

Campaign India. (2013). "Unilever looks to spread sunshine in phase one of Project Sunlight." Retrieved January 10, 2019 from http://www.campaignindia.in/Video/367268,unilever-looks-to-spread-sunshine-in-phase-one-of-project-sunlight.aspx.

Genesis Burson-Marsteller. (n.d.). "About us." Retrieved January 10, 2019 from http://www.genesisbm.in/who-we-are/about-us.

Holmes Report. (2013). "Coca-Cola and perfect relations win platinum at SABRE Awards India." *The Holmes Report*, July 26. Retrieved January 10, 2019 from http://www.holmesreport.com/latest/article/coca-cola-and-perfect-relations-win-platinum-at-sabre-awards-india.

Hoovers. (2014). "2010 sales." Retrieved January 10, 2019 from http://subscriber.hoovers.com/H/company360/productsOperations.html?companyId=93845000000000.

Morris, T. and Goldsworthy, S. (2008). *PR: A Persuasive Industry?* London: Palgrave Macmillan.

Stein, L. (2013). "Unilever to streamline comms, marketing." *PRWeek*, December 5. Retrieved January 10, 2019 from http://www.prweek.com/article/1273932/unilever-streamline-comms-marketing.

Steiner, G.A. and Steiner, J.F. (2012). *Business, Government, and Society: A Managerial Perspective*, 13e. New York: McGraw-Hill Companies, Inc.

Unilever. (n.d.-a). "About Unilever." Retrieved January 10, 2019 from http://www.unilever.com/about/who-we-are/about-Unilever.

Unilever. (n.d.-b). "News & features." Retrieved January 10, 2019 from http://www.unilever.com/news.

WPP. (n.d.-a). "At a glance." Retrieved January 10, 2019 from https://www.wpp.com/about/at-a-glance.

WPP. (n.d.-b). "Young & Rubicam Group." Retrieved January 10, 2019 from https://www.wpp.com/companies/young--rubicam-group.

WTO. (n.d.). "Trade and tariff data." Retrieved January 10, 2019 from http://www.wto.org/english/res_e/statis_e/statis_e.htm.

WWF. (n.d.-a). "Partnerships play a key role in WWF's efforts to influence the course of conservation." Retrieved January 10, 2019 from http://www.worldwildlife.org/pages/partnerships.

WWF. (n.d.-b). "Who we are." Retrieved January 10, 2019 from http://www.worldwildlife.org/about.

WWF. (n.d.-c). "Our work." Retrieved January 10, 2019 from http://www.worldwildlife.org/initiatives.

WWF. (n.d.-d). "What is Earth Hour?." Retrieved January 10, 2019 from https://www.wwf.org.uk/earthhour/what-is-earth-hour.

WWF. (n.d.-e). "About us." Retrieved January 10, 2019 from http://www.wwf.org.la/about/.

WWF. (2012). "WWF announces Earth Hour 2012." Retrieved January 10, 2019 from http://www.worldwildlife.org/press-releases/wwf-announces-earth-hour-2012.

Zeenews. (2012). "Earth Hour 2012: World goes dark for an hour." Retrieved January 10, 2019 from http://zeenews.india.com/news/eco-news/earth-hour-2012-world-goes-dark-for-an-hour_767414.html.

6

Nongovernmental Organizations (NGOs), Multilateral Organizations (MOs), and Activist Networks

Central Themes

- The world is polarized by the participation of a variety of interest groups and all types of organizations with social, environmental, human rights, and political agendas.
- Nongovernmental organizations (NGOs) often seek to cultivate public awareness, support, and involvement in their activities.
- NGO public relations tend to engage heavily in relationship-building activities.
- NGOs are helping reshape global politics by putting pressure on decision-makers through various communications campaigns.

Keywords *nongovernmental organizations; multilateral organizations; activist networks; United Nations; transnational advocacy; digital advocacy; grassroots; public interest communications; activism*

Introduction

Strong, influential voices are competing for attention with big global players, such as multinational corporations (MNCs), in the international public marketplace. The organizations and groups that promote social or environmental causes, or economic development and media freedoms, are involved in the major issues, initiatives, and controversies of the day. Global public relations professionals offer their services and talents to nongovernmental organizations (NGOs), multilateral organizations (MOs), and activist networks. If they work for MNCs, they monitor their activities and, ideally, cultivate relationships that benefit their organizations, industry sectors, or clients.

Global and Multicultural Public Relations, First Edition. Juan-Carlos Molleda and Sarab Kochhar.

The UN Rule of Law defines NGOs or civil-society organizations as "a not-for-profit group, principally independent from government, which is organized on a local, national, or international level to address issues in support of the public good" (United Nations 2015, para. 1). The United Nations offers five categories of NGO: advocacy, assistance, and pro-bono services such as Amnesty International and Human Rights Watch; associations and commissions such as the International Bar Association and World Justice Project; centers of excellence and institutions such as the African Institute of Capacity Development and Swisspeace; foundations such as the Ford Foundation and Open Society Institute; and the International Committee of the Red Cross.

International gatherings and discussions are trendy in the nongovernmental sector. The Aspen Institute, for instance, provides nonpartisan opportunities to address critical challenges and solutions the world faces though seminars, young-leader fellowships around the globe, policy programs, public conferences, and other events (Aspen Institute 2015).

MOs are "formed between three or more nations to work on issues that relate to all of the countries in the organization" (Abola 2014, para. 1). Examples of MOs are the European Union (EU), the International Monetary Fund (IMF), the World Bank (WB), the Asian Infrastructure Investment Bank (AIIB), and the Organization of American States (OAS).

Merriam-Webster (2015) defines activism as "a doctrine that emphasizes direct vigorous action especially in support of or opposition to one side of a controversial issue." Activist networks and groups such as Sierra Club and Greenpeace are guided by their convictions. These networks have many followers, but also detractors. For instance, the Center for Organizational Research and Education (CORE) aims to uncover the truth about anti-consumer activism. CORE (2015, para. 2) states, "[t]hese groups promote false science, scare campaigns, and sometimes even violent 'direct actions' to threaten our right to choose certain products." Richard Berman seems to be behind CORE. Citizens for Responsibility and Ethics in Washington (CREW) explains, "Richard 'Rick' Berman is a longtime Washington, DC public relations specialist whose lobbying and consulting firm, Berman and Company, Inc., advocates for special interests and powerful industries … [and] wages deceptive campaigns against industry foes, including labor unions; public-health advocates; and consumer, safety, animal welfare, and environmental groups" (CREW 2014, para. 1). The authors of this textbook do not want to take sides in this controversy, but it is important that students and professionals understand the activities and impacts of these outspoken and dedicated groups.

Strategies and Tactics of NGOs, MOs, and Activist Networks

The world is polarized by the participation of a variety of interest groups and all types of organizations with social, environmental, human rights, and political agendas. This section explains some of the structures, campaigns, and communication plans used by these groups and entities.

NGOs

Founded in 1971 in Paris, Médecins Sans Frontières (MSF, also known as Doctors Without Borders) is an international humanitarian aid NGO and Nobel Peace Prize laureate that operates in 68 countries with close to 32 000 staff (Doctors Without Borders n.d.-a). MSF produces its own public relations content and promotes multiple books, films, and television shows produced by others about its operation and humanitarian missions, especially in war-stricken areas of the world (Doctors Without Borders n.d.-b).

The organization's website not only communicates what MSF is and what it does, but also includes a section for the recruitment of doctors, office staff, and volunteers, as well as a section for donations. The Press Room section includes news releases and other media materials, as well a stream of media coverage. The media page also facilitates media contacts at MSF's international headquarters in Geneva, Switzerland, and provides contacts in 28 country offices (1 Africa, 4 Asia, 16 Europe, 1 Middle East, 3 North America, 2 South America, and 1 Oceania) (Doctors Without Borders n.d.-c).

Launched in 2011, one of MSF's unique global campaigns is Positive Generation: Voices for an AIDS-Free Future, which includes CDs, books, documentaries, and a website. The purpose of the project is to raise awareness through music and indigenous storytelling about the reality of HIV/AIDS in sub-Saharan Africa and, specifically, how people can live highly positive lives with HIV/AIDS treatment, which can also prevent further transmission of the virus; however, it also highlights how shortfalls in funding for HIV programs in developing countries threaten the recent progress made in the fight against the virus, putting the lives of thousands of people at risk (Doctors Without Borders 2011, para. 2).

Multilateral Organizations

Since 1999, the UN Foundation has planned and implemented the Better World Campaign. According to the UN Foundation (2012), the purpose of the Better World Fund, which was created with a US$1 billion donation from entrepreneur and philanthropist Ted Turner, aims "to foster a strong relationship between the United States and the United Nations that promotes core American interests and builds a more secure, prosperous, and healthy world" (UN Foundation 2012, para. 1).

Activist Networks

In the summer of 2015, impactful images of 13 protesters dangling from a bridge in Portland, OR invaded news and social media worldwide. For almost 40 hours, activists from the Netherlands-headquartered Greenpeace stopped the way for an icebreaker owned by Royal Dutch Shell aiming to navigate to the Pacific Ocean and up the Alaskan coast. Dozens of other protesters in kayaks and canoes also tried to block the vessel's path. Activists were concerned about the multinational oil corporation's drilling operations in the Arctic. This was a high-risk, high-reward, and visible campaign tactic, which Greenpeace protesters claimed to be a symbolic victory. The 40-country-office activist organization uses these kinds of high-impact tactics to call the attention of the media and policy-makers to pressing environmental problems.

Several authors have developed detailed explanations of how to develop corporate campaigns and strategic attacks against corporate and governmental interests (e.g. Klein 1999; Manheim 2001, 2011). Greenpeace's protests against Shell would be considered a sabotage or disruption (Manheim 2001). The environmental activists may have known they could not stop the icebreaker forever, but strategized a visible way to call attention to the gravity of oil drilling in an environmentally sensitive area like the Arctic. Framing the issue and setting the agenda for media and policy-makers are strategies used by activists with this show of force (Manheim 2011). For instance, the home page of the Greenpeace USA website contained a straightforward call to action with a background photograph of the activists hanging on the Oregon bridge and a "Take Action" button: "Make your voice heard. Tell President Obama to reject Arctic drilling!" (Greenpeace USA 2015).

Some coalitions that advocate for causes and issues employ less confrontational campaigns. They develop communication plans and actions as agencies and corporations do, with the aim of achieving social change. For example, EDC Free Europe is a coalition of public-interest groups representing more than 50 organizations (trade unions, consumers, public health and health professionals, advocates for cancer prevention, environmentalists, and women's groups) across Europe concerned about endocrine-disrupting chemicals (EDCs) (EDC Free Europe 2015). This coalition uses media events, fundraising efforts, petitions, education and training, and direct call to action through face-to-face and digital channels and tools. It joins numerous groups that advocate for toxin-free products worldwide, especially in developed countries.

Case Study   UNICEF in Eastern and Southern Africa – The Right to Have Rights Project

Introduction

The United Nations International Children's Emergency Fund (UNICEF), an NGO, was created on December 11, 1946, after World War II left European children hungry and disease-stricken. UNICEF served to give these children the supplies they desperately needed: food, clothing, and healthcare (UNICEF Eastern and Southern Africa n.d.-b). UNICEF broadened its scope in 1950 to encompass developing countries in order to assist the needs of children and women globally. According to UNICEF (n.d.-b, para. 1), its mission statement reinstates its duty to "advocate for the protection of children's rights, to help meet their basic needs and to expand their opportunities to reach their full potential." In 1959, the Declaration of the Rights of the Child, "which defines children's rights to protection, education, health care, shelter, and good nutrition," was accepted by the UN General Assembly (UNICEF Eastern and Southern Africa n.d.-b, para. 4).

UNICEF in Eastern and Southern Africa

UNICEF operates in 190 countries across the world, 21 of which are located in Eastern and Southern Africa: Angola, Botswana, Burundi, Comoros, Eritrea, Ethiopia, Kenya, Lesotho, Madagascar, Malawi, Mozambique, Namibia, Rwanda, Somalia, South Africa, South Sudan, Swaziland, Tanzania, Uganda, Zambia, and Zimbabwe (UNICEF n.d.-b). UNICEF's (n.d.-b) website states that it concerns itself with issues of young child survival and development, basic education, gender equality, HIV/AIDS, child protection, social policy, and emergency preparedness and response.

The Right to Have Rights Project

Civil registration is a major issue in Africa. In September 2012, 46 ministers from countries across the continent met in Durban, South Africa, for a 2-day conference discussing this issue and ways to improve it (UNICEF n.d.-a). "Children without a birth certificate have no legal status," said Elke

Wisch, UNICEF Deputy Regional Director for Eastern and Southern Africa. According to UNICEF (n.d.-a, para. 2):

> Birth registration is essential for children to access health care and education, as well as for orphans to inherit from their parents. Birth registration protects children from child labor, recruitment into armed forces and militias, human trafficking, early marriage as well as other forms of exploitation.

In Mozambique, UNICEF began the campaign The Right to Have Rights to ensure that children were properly documented with a certificate at birth (UNICEF n.d.-b). This campaign is a public–private partnership between the Ministry of Justice, the Ministry of the Interior, and UNICEF, with funding from the Swedish Embassy of Mozambique and Lúrio Green Resources SA, a forestation company that operates in Nampula Province (UNICEF n.d.-b). The project began June 19, 2014 in the Rapale district. It will span across the Nampula Province to more than half a million people in three of its districts (UNICEF n.d.-b).

Challenges of the Campaign

UNICEF in Eastern and Southern Africa is concerned with proper documentation, because it provides African citizens with the ability to attend school and obtain child-support grants (UNICEF Eastern and Southern Africa n.d.-c). Currently, only 38% of children born in Eastern and Southern Africa have a birth certificate. The range of registration spans from 3% in Somalia to 95% in South Africa (UNICEF Eastern and Southern Africa n.d.-c).

Implementation and Success

The campaign began in the Nampula Province in the districts of Rapale, Ribaue, and Mecuburi. With a budget of US$5.2 million, UNICEF hoped to reach 520 000 children and adults in these districts. According to an official UNICEF (n.d.-b) news release, "less than half of children under the age of 5 in Nampula have birth certificates, with the figure dropping down to only 17% for the population aged 0 to 64" (UNICEF Eastern and Southern Africa n.d.-a, para. 9).

Future Implementation and Obstacles

It is hoped the program's successes will fuel a campaign that will span across more districts and provinces in Mozambique (UNICEF Eastern and Southern Africa n.d.-a). In 2013, UNICEF implemented a similar program in

Tanzania's Mbeya region, this time making use of new technology. The government of Tanzania, UNICEF, and Tigo, with support from VSO International, created and used a mobile application to document children under the age of five.

The same development is being pushed across African regions (Bisin 2014). With multiple programs and a common goal, the issue of proper birth registration may be resolved, but this challenge needs time and funding, along with cooperation from African governments.

Evaluation

This campaign received positive reactions from the citizens it influenced and the government that supported it. The program was able to reach thousands, but it still faces challenges (UNICEF Eastern and Southern Africa n.d.-a).

The Right to Have Rights campaign is seen as a positive step toward the protection of girls. After the abduction of 200 schoolgirls in northeast Nigeria in mid-April 2014, birth registration was brought to the forefront of the conversation as a potential solution to protect women globally from human trafficking (Hillebrenner 2014).

In addition to human trafficking, birth registration would also prevent child marriages by accurately tracing African children's ages. According to a gender profile conducted by the Zambian Governance Foundation for Civil Society, birth registration is an intrinsic component of child protection and can implicitly and explicitly be utilized to promote associated rights addressed throughout the Convention on the Rights of the Child (CRC). Nkonkomalimba (n.d.) states that the violation of the right to a name and nationality, and preservation of identity, affects girls more than boys because of issues around defilement and early marriage.

This campaign has also stressed the need for legislation in support of registration. The Council on Foreign Relations lists passing laws mandating birth registration as a strategy to stop child marriages (Lemmon and ElHarake n.d.).

Acquiring a birth certificate in some African regions is no easy feat. Birth registration may be costly for some, and the facilities where they are given out may be too far to reach (Bisin 2014). Although the campaign was able to influence a few districts in one part of the continent, its message and goal are for all of Africa to be granted the right to formal documentation.

Case Study   Amnesty International

The Vision

On May 28, 1961, a worldwide human-rights movement was established after an article by Peter Benenson entitled "The Forgotten Prisoners" was published in the *Observer*, describing how two Portuguese students were imprisoned for "toasting" their freedom. According to Amnesty International (n.d.-f), Benenson, a British lawyer, launched Appeal for Amnesty in 1961 to call the public to action in protest of the injustice of political and religious condemnation against human rights. This seminal moment not only marked Amnesty's birth, but exemplified the principle by which this global, non-profit organization has striven to operate over the past 50 years: "[W]e are at our most powerful when we stand together for human rights" (Amnesty International n.d.-c, para. 6).

Amnesty International is an independent and privately funded non-profit NGO that advocates for human rights in 150 countries. The Amnesty community is made up of over 7 million members, supporters, and activists working from its headquarters in London and from regional sections (offices/operations) in 80 countries around the world. As summarized in the United Nations' Universal Declaration of Human Rights, Amnesty campaigns for "full human rights," which includes, but is not limited to: abolishment of the death penalty, justice for crimes against humanity, freedom of expression, and women's rights (Amnesty International n.d.-c,g). Amnesty serves all global citizens regardless of their nationality or ideological background. This global advocacy group does not identify with any specific government, political ideology, religion, or economic interest (Amnesty International n.d.-c).

As a future-oriented organization, Amnesty deeply identifies with reliance and adaptability to the ever-evolving threats in the world. Salil Shetty, Secretary General (equivalent to CEO) of Amnesty, takes pride in the non-profit's ability to "always [stay] one step ahead" of human injustice with an ongoing commit to the "relentless probing for truth" (Shetty 1997, para. 10). This is accomplished with vigilant adaptation to the evasive tactics of provocateurs and by embracing emergent technological opportunities to address human rights (Shetty 1997).

The Infrastructure

Amnesty's global communications structure is unique in its design and execution. It could, perhaps, be conceptualized as a "hierarchical matrix." Such an extensive operation – which rests on investigating and advocating for human rights around the world – requires some flexibility in the communication infrastructure. The International Secretariat (head-quarters) in London is the operational head of the non-profit, with all business going through it, while the International Council Meeting is the governing body, making the ultimate decisions on transnational strategy, budgets, and all other organizational issues (Amnesty International n.d.-d). Information, research, statements, and campaigns are all vetted through the International Secretariat, which checks for accuracy in factual information and consistency with Amnesty's mission. Organization-wide directives all come from the headquarters and are disseminated through-out the Amnesty network (Amnesty International n.d.-f). These sections are structured and hierarchical.

The various regional sections of Amnesty – comprising the internal stakeholders (i.e. volunteers, interns, employees, members, activists) – require a certain amount of independence in their various day-to-day actions. Members of Amnesty, throughout all global markets, are responsible for their own fact-finding ventures and the organization of social action around a particular issue (hence the matrix). There are a number of investigative procedures at the disposal of Amnesty members, including but not limited to: monitoring domestic and international media reports; disseminating information on humanitarian concerns; and interviewing parties involved in alleged human rights violations. The number of potential social movement-motivating actions members have in their cache is plentiful, as well. Amnesty members must leverage public support to put pressure on companies, governments, or political groups violating human rights; some tactics used include lobbying, petitioning, protesting, and various awareness-raising efforts (e.g. concerts, community activities). In addition to self-mobilization, Amnesty partners with local and global interest groups for a more efficient campaign. Student groups and local community activist groups are the most common resources for support of various human rights injustice campaigns (Amnesty International n.d.-f).

The Strategy

Being a world leader in humanitarian causes requires strategic planning far past the immediate challenges of the day; transnational organizations such as Amnesty must have long-term goals that continue to motivate and inspire stakeholders. In April 2010, after months of external analysis and research, Amnesty adopted a 6-year future-oriented plan designed to set goals, outline an operational plan, and provide a tangible statement of commitment to human rights advocacy moving into the future (Amnesty International n.d.-d). Amnesty International's Integrated Strategic Plan 2010 to 2016 provides a framework of accountability toward stakeholders; the central goal is to "[empower] rights-holders whose rights are challenged and [strengthen] the human rights movement" as a whole (Amnesty International n.d.-d, p. 4). The strategic plan focuses on five key objectives (each with corresponding goals): human rights change, partnerships, excellence, investment and growth, and resources. The first, human rights change, will pursue the empowerment of indigent people, defend unprotected persons from violence and discrimination, and protect people's right to express themselves freely. The second, partners, not only endeavors to build more partnerships, but also seeks to promote and develop the global human rights movement to create solutions to issues as a global community. The third, excellence, refers to effective communications – including responses to challenges and opportunities – as well as promotion of glocalization through active participation from members and other stakeholders. The fourth, investment and growth, seeks opportunities for Amnesty to invest in its own infrastructure – such as technology, new governing practices, and development of leadership and volunteers – all with the goal of staying relevant and sustainable moving forward. Finally, the fifth objective, resources, focuses on tactics that encourage further growth in stakeholder membership; this includes retaining existing members and acquiring more donors (Amnesty International n.d.-d).

The Campaign

The Control Arms Campaign is one of Amnesty's most recent examples of a successful campaign. Initiated in 2003, Amnesty partnered with Oxfam and the International Network on Small Arms (among other NGOs) to organize a global Arms Trade Treaty (ATT) (Amnesty International n.d.-a,b). The goal was to introduce international legislation for firearms sales that would take into consideration the implications resulting from them. Because over half a million people die every year by gun violence – and millions more are otherwise affected – Amnesty sought to create a legally binding control over the gun trade.

A core tenet of this proposal was a simple notion that Amnesty and other campaign participants came to refer to as the "golden rule": governments are responsible for not allowing the transfer of firearms when there are immediate implications that the weapons will be "used to seriously violate human rights or commit war crimes" (Amnesty International n.d.-a,b, p. 15).

As the Control Arms Campaign unfolded over the first several years, Amnesty used a number of different tactics to garner support for its cause. It staged events around the world to raise awareness in the media and among global stakeholders. From London to Cambodia, Amnesty mobilized through protests and promotion of the Control Arms cause.

Both traditional media (e.g. news releases, op-eds) and social media were used as tools to directly appeal to decision-makers and influencers on the international stage (Amnesty International n.d.-a,b). The Control Arms Campaign even pioneered new forms of awareness with the "first-ever global photo petition – the Million Faces – to which anyone could add their picture" (Amnesty International n.d.-a,b, p. 14).

Strategic and focused advocacy was utilized to leverage the support of governments for a new treaty (Amnesty International n.d.-a,b). UN conferences were targeted as key arenas for informational meetings and campaign events and activities; Amnesty also provided research briefings and detailed legal counsel on the dangerous outcomes from irresponsible arms transfers (Amnesty International n.d.-a,b). As the campaign progressed over subsequent years, more and more supporters lobbied their government representatives, diplomats, and ministers for action in regulating the gun trade (Amnesty International n.d.-a,b). Amid the building pressure and support for the treaty, 2012 marked the year in which the United Nations voted to begin negotiating the terms of the treaty (Amnesty International n.d.-a,b).

On April 2, 2013 – with a virtual consensus agreement – the United Nations voted to adopt the ATT; this came after years of deliberation within the organization and months of drafting the treaty's text by internal stakeholders (Amnesty International n.d.-a,b). As of September 24, 2014, the treaty had met the mandated 50 ratifications necessary for acceptance as active international law, effective December 24, 2014 (Amnesty International n.d.-a,b; Control Arms 2014). With the success of the treaty, the Control Arms Campaign met the objective of creating an international standard for the gun trade. Although this was a monumental first step, the accomplishment cannot overshadow the most important aspect of the campaign: impact (Amnesty International n.d.-e). The true goal was to alleviate (and ultimately prevent) human injustices caused by gun violence – the treaty was just one part of this.

The Evaluation

Evaluation is a necessary component in assessing the significance of any communications campaign. Although Amnesty's Control Arms Campaign will require more time to accurately measure its effectiveness, the evaluative entity of the operation is among its most structured and thoroughly monitored. Amnesty takes pride in evaluating its effect on the global community. It commonly uses the term "impact" instead of "evaluation" because, although these terms may seem similar, "evaluation" usually denotes a selective disclosure of outcomes from a campaign. Amnesty prefers to "look at the overall effects of a particular [campaign], including positive and negative, intended and unexpected effects" (Amnesty International n.d.-a,b, p. 2). It feels an obligation to all stakeholders and supporters to provide impact assessments for three reasons (in particular): learning (knowledge accumulation and future improvement), accountability, and transparency (Amnesty International n.d.-a,b).

Amnesty International has specified its impact assessment model in terms of guiding principles and good practice. There are three guiding principles that influence how Amnesty makes an impact assessment. First, it understands the evaluation process is not a one-time assessment that concludes a campaign; rather, it is an ongoing process that assists strategists in decision-making throughout the campaign's life. From the planning stages, to the crafting of objectives, and even to the execution of tactics, impact assessments drive necessary or corrective changes to a campaign's model. The second guiding principle is to understand change in holistic terms. Change is not only about cause and effect, but also about the causation of such outcomes – the how and the why. The third and final guiding principle for Amnesty's impact assessment is to accurately identify which actors are responsible for social change in a human rights campaign. Because Amnesty commonly partners with a number of NGOs, among other allies, measuring its own contribution to a campaign is important to understanding how effective it is as an organization (Amnesty International n.d.-a,b).

Amnesty has outlined seven indicators of good practice: inclusion, participation, rigorous methodology, gender-perspective inclusion, ethics, integrity, and adoption of approaches to learning and accountability. Its goal is to provide stakeholders – both internal (including gender perspectives) and external – with the opportunity for participation in every stage of the campaign design and process. Throughout the methodological assessment, Amnesty emphasizes ethical, multidisciplinary, multivariate, and systematic approaches to data collection and analysis. Lastly, in the interest of educating stakeholders and encouraging organizational, social, and operational growth, it stresses the wide disclosure of all findings (Amnesty International n.d.-a,b).

Discussion Questions

1 What other issues do you think birth registration could solve for African youth?

2 What is UNICEF trying to accomplish with the Right to Have Rights project?

3　Why is birth registration an important issue?

4　For the first several years of the Control Arms Campaign, Amnesty ran what was essentially an awareness campaign. Was this strategy vital to the campaign? How else could the campaign have been executed?

5　After years of lobbying, protesting, and campaigning for a human rights issue, what are some ways for a strategic communication team to keep a campaign alive and relevant?

6　Now that the Control Arms Campaign has concluded, what responsibility does Amnesty have in implementing the treaty, if any?

7　Looking another 20 years ahead, how should Amnesty measure and evaluate the impact of the ATT?

Class Activity

Greenpeace International is an independent global organization that works to change attitudes and behavior to protect and conserve the environment and promote peace. Greenpeace International has initiated an international campaign to help solve the current climate crisis. The organization is using the hashtag #actforclimate to facilitate conversation about this cause. Working in small groups, students should analyze the #actforclimate campaign. They should check the hashtag on social media and look at Greenpeace's website and social media pages. Each group should examine the key messages used in the campaign, its communication channels, and how effective it appears to be.

References

Abola, O.A. (2014). "Development concepts." Retrieved January 10, 2019 from http://www.academia.edu/7993499/EAST_AFRICAN_INSTITUTE_ FOR_MANAGEMENT_SCIENCE_Northern_Uganda_Regional_Office_ P.O_Box_701_Gulu_Plot_1-3_Queen_Avenue_Road_DEVELOPMENT_ CONCEPTS.

Amnesty International. (n.d.-a). "External evaluation of Amnesty International's arms trade treaty." Retrieved January 10, 2019 from https://www.amnesty.org/en/documents/act30/013/2014/en/.

Amnesty International. (n.d.-b). "Amnesty International Impact Report 2012–2013: Making human rights change happen." Retrieved January 10, 2019 from https://www.amnesty.org/en/documents/org30/009/2014/en/.

Amnesty International. (n.d.-c). "Amnesty International is a global movement of more than 7 million people who take injustice personally. We are campaigning for a world where human rights are enjoyed by all." Retrieved January 10, 2019 from http://www.amnesty.org/en/who-we-are/about-amnesty-international.

Amnesty International. (n.d.-d). "Amnesty International's integrated strategic plan 2010 to 2016." Retrieved January 10, 2019 from https://www.amnesty.org/en/documents/POL50/002/2010/en/.

Amnesty International. (n.d.-e). "Assessing Amnesty International's impact: Understanding 'impact'." Retrieved January 10, 2019 from https://www.amnesty.org/download/Documents/ACT1028872014ENGLISH.pdf.

Amnesty International. (n.d.-f). "How we're run." Retrieved January 10, 2019 from http://www.amnesty.org/en/who-we-are/faq.

Amnesty International. (n.d.-g). "Universal Declaration of Human Rights." Retrieved January 10, 2019 from https://www.amnesty.org/en/what-we-do/universal-declaration-of-human-rights/.

Aspen Institute. (2015). "Our people." Retrieved January 10, 2019 from http://www.aspeninstitute.org/about.

Bisin, S. (2014). "A new solution for birth registration." UNICEF Blog, February 25. https://blogs.unicef.org/blog/a-new-solution-for-birth-registration/.

Control Arms. (2014). "The race to 50 is won! Check out our '50 celebrating 50' webpages." Retrieved January 10, 2019 from https://controlarms.org/blog/the-race-to-50-is-won-check-out-our-50-celebrating-50-webpages/.

CORE. (2015). "About us." Retrieved January 10, 2019 from https://www.activistfacts.com/about.

CREW. (2014). "Who is Richard Berman?" Retrieved January 10, 2019 from https://www.citizensforethics.org/who-is-richard-berman/.

Doctors Without Borders. (2011). "Positive generation: Voices for an AIDS-free future." Retrieved January 10, 2019 from https://www.msf.org.za/stories-news/press-releases/positive-generation-voices-aids-free-future.

Doctors Without Borders. (n.d.-a). "Founding." Retrieved January 10, 2019 from http://www.doctorswithoutborders.org/founding-msf.

Doctors Without Borders. (n.d.-b). "Films about MSF." Retrieved January 10, 2019 from https://www.doctorswithoutborders.org/who-we-are/films-about-msf.

Doctors Without Borders. (n.d.-c). "Around the world." Retrieved January 10, 2019 from http://www.doctorswithoutborders.org/about-us/other-msf-offices.

EDC Free Europe. (2015). "About us." Retrieved January 10, 2019 from http://www.edc-free-europe.org/about-us.

Greenpeace USA. (2015). "President Obama: Reject Arctic drilling!" Retrieved January 10, 2019 from https://www.care2.com/news/member/100041282/3874932.

Hillebrenner, M. (2014). "Time to stand with girls demanding change." *Global Public Square*, July 23. Retrieved January 10, 2019 from http://globalpublicsquare.blogs.cnn.com/2014/07/23/time-to-stand-with-girls-demanding-change.

Klein, N. (1999). *No Logo: Money, Marketing, and the Growing Anti-Corporate Movement*. New York: Picador USA Reading Group.

Lemmon, G.T. and ElHarake, L.S. (n.d.). "High stakes for young lives: Examining strategies to stop child marriage." Retrieved January 10, 2019 from https://www.cfr.org/report/high-stakes-young-lives.

Manheim, J.B. (2001). *The Death of a Thousand Cuts: Corporate Campaigns and the Attack on the Corporation*. Mahwah, NJ: Lawrence Erlbaum Associates.

Manheim, J.B. (2011). *Strategy in Information and Influence Campaigns: How Policy Advocates, Insurgent Groups. Corporations, Governments and Others get What They Want*. New York: Routledge.

Merriam-Webster. (2015). "Activism." Retrieved January 10, 2019 from http://www.merriam-webster.com/dictionary/activism.

Nkonkomalimba, M. (n.d.). "Child rights." Retrieved January 10, 2019 from http://zgfoffce.org:8080/jspui/bitstream/123456789/33/2/ZGF_Child%20rights%20gender%20profile_2014.pdf.

Shetty, S. (1997). *Development Project in Assessing Empowerment*. New Delhi: Society for Participatory Research in Asia.

UNICEF. (n.d.-a). "African ministers to agree on steps to strengthen civil registration throughout the continent." Retrieved January 10, 2019 from http://www.unicef.org/media/media_65740.html.

UNICEF. (n.d.-b). "UNICEF's mission statement." Retrieved January 10, 2019 from http://www.unicef.org/about/who/index_mission.html.

UNICEF Eastern and Southern Africa. (n.d.-a). "Major birth and civil registration project to reach thousands in Nampula." Retrieved January 10, 2019 from http://www.unicef.org/esaro/5440_mozambique2014_Nampula-registration.html.

UNICEF Eastern and Southern Africa. (n.d.-b). "What we do in Eastern and Southern Africa." Retrieved January 10, 2019 from https://www.unicef.org/topics/eastern-and-southern-africa.

UNICEF Eastern and Southern Africa. (n.d.-c). "Fast facts on children." Retrieved January 10, 2019 from http://www.unicef.org/esaro/ factsonchildren_5780.html.

UN Foundation. (2012). "About the Better World campaign." Retrieved January 10, 2019 from http://www.betterworldcampaign.org/about.

United Nations. (2015). "Non-governmental organizations." Retrieved January 10, 2019 from https://www.un.org/ruleoflaw/blog/keyword/ non-governmental-organizations/.

7

Coordination and Control, Standardization and Localization

Central Themes

- Strategies such as coordination, control, standardization, and localization are frequently refined by multinational organizations (Mnos) to carry out their public relations functions and practices around the globe.
- The techniques and efforts used to integrate and evaluate global operations follow three principles: efficiency, learning, and flexibility or responsiveness.
- Standardization improves organizational efficiency by integrating public relations operations across various world locations into a more cohesive and collaborative state.
- Localization improves the effectiveness of public relations, or the ability of a program or campaign to achieve a desired effect.
- Environmental factors play a role in an organization's decision to localize.

Keywords *global efficiency; multicultural; polycentric; standardization; localization; coordination control*

Introduction

The advent of globalization has made it imperative to comprehend strategic and tactical public relations choices from a global perspective. Global and multicultural public relations can be best understood as the strategies employed by organizations in any environment in order to engage in effective two-way communication with stakeholders in an effort to build enduring symbiotic relationships. These environments are no longer isolated from one another, meaning the influence an organization has on its stakeholders at home (where it is headquartered)

Global and Multicultural Public Relations, First Edition. Juan-Carlos Molleda and Sarab Kochhar.
© 2019 John Wiley & Sons, Inc. Published 2019 by John Wiley & Sons, Inc.

impacts its influence on publics elsewhere, and vice versa. The impact may occur through communications campaigns, crisis situations, or political or socioeconomic upheavals. Equally important is the transnational environment, where groups' and institutions' activities can have a simultaneous impact in several world locations and, perhaps, globally. As a consequence, organizations planning, executing, and evaluating global programs should understand this multigeographic and virtual dynamic. This chapter will focus on the mechanics of public relations management from a global perspective. Moreover, it will look at how multinational organizations (MNOs) are planning, implementing, and managing their global strategic communications efforts. Strategies such as coordination, control, standardization, and localization are frequently refined by MNOs in carrying out their public relations functions and practices around the globe. In sum, the chapter will delve into the coordination and control mechanisms required to manage the global public relations function while aiming to strike a balance between standardization and localization.

Coordination and Control

Lenovo, the world's second-largest personal computer manufacturer (Shah 2012), has principal operations in China, Singapore, and the United States; seven research centers in China and one each in Japan and the United States; sales headquarters in China, France, Singapore, and the United States; and four manufacturing centers in China and one each in India, Mexico, and the United States (Lenovo 2015). This complex structure is typical of corporations operating globally, and requires coordination and control of functional areas, including public affairs or public relations, among other related communications functions.

Coordination has been defined as "the linking or integrating of activities into a unified system," and control systems as "the measurement of performance so companies can respond appropriately to changing conditions" (Daniels et al. 2013, p. 646). Examples of coordination mechanisms are all the components of the global supply chain, as well as supplier relations, logistics, and the administration between the headquarters and subsidiaries of all communications programs and activities. Examples of control systems include structure and performance assessments. Multinational corporations (MNCs) use coordination and control mechanisms "to synchronize, integrate, and evaluate value activities" (Daniels et al. 2013, p. 574). In particular, the coordination and control of global public relations or public affairs have been conceptualized and documented through cultural and transnational crisis perspectives (e.g. de Mooij 2010; Molleda and Laskin 2010).

The techniques and efforts used to integrate and evaluate global operations follow three principles: efficiency, learning, and flexibility or responsiveness (Bartlett and Ghoshal 2002). These principles, in a global public relations context, take on different connotations. Global efficiency is the coordination and control, with various degrees of centralization or decentralization, of the management of programs, campaigns, plans, and daily activities or tactics. Worldwide learning is the documentation, sharing, analysis, and perhaps awarding or rewarding of the best domestic and multinational practices. Finally, multinational flexibility or national responsiveness is the need to adapt or conform to country-specific legal or social regulations, as well as stakeholders' and consumers' expectations and needs. Two out of the three principles, efficiency and flexibility or responsiveness, imply a continuum between two extremes: standardization and localization. This will be addressed next.

Standardization and Localization

The main assumption of coordination by standardization is operational consistency, which entails the application of "rules and precise procedures" that help an MNO "leverage its core competency as well as minimize inefficiencies" (Daniels et al. 2013, p. 574). In global public relations, standardization means the consistency of programs and strategies across dispersed world markets of the MNO. Coordination by standardization entails "universal rules and procedures that apply to units worldwide" (Daniels et al. 2013, p. 574). This also includes policies, rules, and procedures for global strategic communications and its various areas of specialization. On the other hand, localization is about understanding and accepting unique local challenges.

The decision over standardization versus localization definitely goes beyond product, pricing, and distribution to include the choice of communication strategy adopted by an MNO (Schmid and Kotulla 2011). Pudelko and Harzing (2008) suggest considering both internal and external factors in choosing between them. Molleda et al. (2012) reviewed the literature on standardization and localization from a multidisciplinary perspective to conceptualize and empirically test the extent of localization practiced by MNOs. They conducted a content analysis of the online newsrooms of US-based MNO subsidiaries in China, India, and the United Kingdom, and found a high extent of localization in the form of localized newsrooms on organizational websites, with news releases being the most common localized information subsidy on the corporate portals. The extent of localization was also found to be dependent on the industry type and the level of impact the corporation had on its stakeholders.

A similar study by Halliburton and Ziegfeld (2009) analyzed how major European multinationals communicate using their organizational websites and create corporate identities. The study found evidence that organizations adopt a "glocal" approach, which varies according to the industry type. The discussion on standardization versus localization is significant for the tourism industry due to its uniqueness. Gotham (2005) analyzed how tourism, a truly global industry, integrates with local actions to develop different forms of the industry. Tourism is seen as a process that symbolizes the differences and commonalities between standardization and localization (Gotham 2005).

The Standardization–Localization Paradox

Studies on the management of the public relations function in MNOs underscore the need for a balanced approach to standardization and localization (Newburry and Yakova 2006; Molleda and Laskin 2010). Balance is required because the adoption of one approach to the exclusion of the other can have unintended consequences for MNOs. In an attempt to explain the delicate balance necessary between standardization and localization, Wakefield (2009, p. 10) proposed that MNOs should "think global *and* local *and* act global *and* local" (italics in original).

On the one hand, standardization improves organizational efficiency by integrating public relations operations in various world locations into a cohesive, collaborative unit through formal control and informal coordination. From this ethnocentric perspective, public relations techniques and efforts are the same in home and host countries. Standardization enables MNOs to accomplish organizational goals and objectives through consistent communications at a reduced cost across geographical borders. It also allows MNOs to effectively manage transnational crises. However, a standardized approach to public relations programs can be less effective because it does not consider the social, cultural, and political differences between home and host countries.

On the other hand, localization improves public relations' effectiveness, or the ability of a program or campaign to achieve a desired effect. This polycentric perspective assumes that public relations is practiced differently wherever an MNO has operations (Grunig 2006). Localization allows subsidiaries to adapt corporate messages to address the self-interests, expectations, and cultural sensitivities of local stakeholders (Molleda and Laskin 2010). A localized approach can also prevent issues from developing into crises through environmental scanning conducted at the local level (Molleda and Laskin 2010). However, the increase in autonomy of the public relations departments of a subsidiary caused by localization can also lead to inconsistent communications about the organization (Botan 1992; Wakefield 2011).

The Localization Decision

While much of the research on global public relations has described the factors that influence the standardization–localization decision, little research has been conducted to understand the decision-making process used by professionals in global agencies in deciding whether and how to localize strategies and tactics. Verčič et al. (1996) and Wakefield (1997) conducted the first systematic study of the standardization–localization paradox. This research resulted in the generic/specific theory of global public relations, which proposes a set of eight universal principles derived from the Excellence Theory and five factors that influence the implementation of public relations in different host countries. These five factors are: (i) the level of development of the host country; (ii) its political, legal, and cultural environments; (iii) the language difference between home and host countries; (iv) the degree of activism in the country; and (v) the characteristics of the mass media (Verčič et al. 1996; Wakefield 1997). As suggested by this model, the generic principles are inextricably linked to the application of country-specific public relations programs (Wakefield 2011). Therefore, macro-level organizational variables, such as the complexity of the organization, corporate culture, shared expectations about public relations, and public relations participation in organizational decision-making, should all influence decisions about whether and how to localize (e.g. Dozier and Broom 1995).

Other internal organizational factors play a role in the implementation of local public relations programming. Lim (2010) reports that the autonomy of a subsidiary plays a key role in localization. Subsidiaries in host countries need enough autonomy from corporate headquarters in the home country to tailor public relations efforts to local conditions. After Molleda and Laskin (2010) reviewed the existing literature on the coordination and control of international business and public relations, they proposed that larger or strategically important subsidiaries have more influence and greater autonomy to implement localized strategies. Similarly, they argued that greater localization is likely in host countries when headquarters has a high level of confidence in its subsidiaries. They also posited that different types of public relations activities require different levels of standardization. For example, they observed that investor relations are highly standardized, while community relations are highly localized. Molleda et al. (2012) tested this assertion by comparing the extent of localization of the online newsrooms of MNOs in high-, medium-, and low-contact industries. They observed that high-impact industries (e.g. mining, chemicals, electricity, oil, and gas) had more localized newsrooms than medium- or low-impact ones.

Environmental factors also play a role in an MNO's decision to localize. Lim (2010) identified five environmental factors that should be addressed to achieve local public relations effectiveness: (i) policies and regulations; (ii) culture and language; (iii) local activism; (iv) local hostility and skepticism; and (v) relationships with local media. These categories broadly describe the findings of a number of empirical studies. Similarly, other research has demonstrated that cultural understanding can predict the communications strategies and techniques that are suited to a particular cultural environment (Holtzhausen et al. 2003; Sriramesh and Verčič 2009). Furthermore, Curtin and Gaither (2007) used the circuit-of-culture model to demonstrate how culture, power, and identity affect the practice of public relations in MNCs.

A few scholars have explored the localization decision-making process in more detail. Zaharna (2001) used an intercultural approach to describe three levels of external, country-specific factors that affect localization: country profile, cultural profile, and communication profile. The country profile consists of the "the structural components of a country or national entity that influence international public relations" (p. 137). These country-level components include political, economic, legal, and social structures, as well as mass media and the country's infrastructure. The cultural profile considers cultural differences and indicates the public relations adaptations that may be effective in a particular country. These cultural-level considerations include high and low contexts, monochronic and polychromic, doing and being, future and past tense, and linear and nonlinear.

García (2010) drew from his experience in global public relations to suggest a three-phase process for teaching students about developing global programs or campaigns. The first phase is the preliminary period, which consists in conducting thorough research on the client organization, its standing in the industry, its capabilities to implement a campaign, and how culture will influence all of these factors. The second phase is the preparation period, which is marked by decisions about whether to hire a local agency or to work with subsidiary resources. Finally, the third phase is execution, where the major questions revolve around the relationship between headquarters and the subsidiary.

Localization Strategies and Tactics

Almost no scholarly research documents how localization occurs on a tactical level. Zaharna's (2001) three-level typology comes closest to providing guidance about localizing specific strategies and tactics. Localization of public relations tactics may include adaption of verbal, nonverbal, and visual communications, rhetorical style, and the overall communications matrix. However, research from the international advertising literature can provide some ideas of the ways that global professionals can localize strategies and tactics. A number of content analyses show that the localized advertising strategies of MNOs include the customization of themes, slogans, headlines, subheads, body copy, models, characters, spokespeople, names, layout, background visuals, color, music, commercial length, and advertisement size (e.g. Harris and Attour 2000; Melewar et al. 2000).

Case Study **"Costa Rica: No Artificial Ingredients" – A Global Campaign Created by the Country's Tourism Board**

The Costa Rican government's participation in tourism development began in 1930 with the creation and promotion of the first privately owned luxury hotel, Gran Hotel Costa Rica (Visit Costa Rica n.d.). Foreign tourists entered the country via the Port of Limón (on the Atlantic coast), then commuted to San José (the capital city) by train. In 1931, the first regulation of tourism activity was decreed, by means of Law 91, on June 16, when the National Tourism Board was created. This board operated until 1955, when Law 1917 replaced it with the Instituto Costarricense de Turismo (ICT). The ICT is a governmental organization that promotes and regulates the tourism industry in Costa Rica. It is responsible for promoting tourism attractions and destinations nationally and internationally, for establishing tourism norms, regulations, and incentives, and for certifying Costa Rica's hotels, travel agencies, rental cars, and other tourism service providers under its Certification of Sustainable Tourism program. The ICT coordinates and controls all of Costa Rica's global promotional efforts via internal human and material resources, as well as the outsourcing of specialized public relations agencies with a global reach.

In 1997, the ICT launched the global campaign, No Artificial Ingredients, to promote the natural environment. Costa Rica is 31 600 square miles in area, representing 5% of the earth's biodiversity (Smithsonian Journeys 2010). A quarter of the landmass is protected by law, through national parks or wildlife refuges. In 2009, a research firm evaluated Costa Rica's branding effort and concluded that it was very strong and well positioned. Burson-Marsteller's Latin American hub in Miami has been the country's global public relations agency in North America since 2007.

According to ICT's statistics, Costa Rica's main market is North America (more than 50%). US tourists come from Florida, Texas, New York, Indiana, and California. Canadian tourists mainly come from Toronto, Vancouver, and cities in Quebec. Europe is another important market (close to 20%). The majority of European visitors come from France, Germany, the Netherlands, Italy, Spain, Switzerland, and the United Kingdom. European tourism in Costa Rica is year-round but peaks in the summer (European winter). Since the end of 2012, the ICT has worked with the Central America Tourism Agency (CATA), a promotion agency in Spain. The economic crisis beginning in 2008–09 forced the ICT to increase its visibility and promotion in the European market, especially in areas such as France, Germany, Spain, and the United Kingdom, as well as Belgium, Russia, Sweden, and Switzerland. In 2008, 2 million tourists visited Costa Rica, generating US$2 billion. In 2009, the number of tourists declined by 9% (ICT 2010), but by the end of 2011, they had increased again by more than 10% (Costa Rica Information n.d.). Overall, tourism represents 7.4% of Costa Rica's GDP and 19% of its total exports.

The ICT's main strategy has been to educate and attract all demographics (e.g. families, students, ecotourists, adventure seekers, etc.) that may find Costa Rica interesting. The ICT sponsors and carries out formal and informal research to understand the media use of identified tourists, which helps it develop, execute, and measure effective campaigns. It has successfully developed and implemented social media and interactive online campaigns in its communications efforts to attract potential foreign tourists.

Global Communications Function
The ICT's vision is "to be the leading institution for the country's tourism activity" (Visit Costa Rica n.d.). Its mission is stated in a *National Development Plan*, quoted on the ICT website: "Promote a wholesome tourism development, with the purpose of improving Costa Ricans' quality of life, by maintaining a balance between the economic and social boundaries, environmental protection, culture, and facilities" (Visit Costa Rica n.d.). ICT's main functions are:

> Strengthening of the processes of formulation and implementation of planning for tourism development, attraction and assessment of investors, development of quality and competitiveness systems, development of marketing in an integral way, tourist attention, generation of information for decision-making, reinforcement of processes for improving administration (comptrollership services, income, administrative analysis, among others). (Visit Costa Rica n.d., par. 2)

In particular, the Director of Marketing is in charge of global communications efforts through the departments of Research and Evaluation and Promotion (ICT 2008). The ICT Director of Marketing coordinates its campaigns with the network of embassies and consulates of Costa Rica worldwide, as well as with advertising and public relations firms and travel agency operators. The ICT's institutional policies state: "All of the international and national promotion will be done according to specific plans that have been designed keeping in mind the private sector's and related communities' proposals, responding to a vision and the country's tourism goals at large" (ICT n.d., para. 9).

Public Relations Agencies
Burson-Marsteller handled the ICT's public relations for North America from 2007 to 2013. Other markets are handled either through CATA or in-house. It selected Cheryl Andrews Marketing Communications as its public relations agency of record in August 2013. The ICT is also interested in developing domestic tourism among Costa Ricans, especially during the low season. The ICT targets domestic tourists and encourages travel through local public relations and advertising campaigns. The goal is to use the extensive tourist infrastructure to spread knowledge among citizens about the importance of the tourist industry and the preservation of the natural environment. The ICT's domestic agency is Comunicación Corporativa Ketchum, an affiliated agency of the Omnicom Group with roots in Costa Rica. The ICT works closely with its various outsourcing agencies, both local and global, to develop specialized campaigns and drive efforts to attract domestic and international tourists.

Coordination and Control
The planning of the No Artificial Ingredients campaign was carried out by the ICT's director of marketing and McCann Erickson Worldwide, a marketing communications agency of the Interpublic Group of Companies. Approval for the global strategic communications plan and its objectives, strategies, and tactics was granted by the ICT's board of directors. Execution of the campaign was the responsibility of both McCann Erickson and the ICT's marketing and public relations teams. The main evaluation efforts focused on the assessment of the country brand.

A highly standardized approach was adopted for the campaign, with the ICT (client) exercising control and McCann Erickson (marketing communications agency) coordinating things. A moderate level of centralization was adopted for the content of communications materials, with the language and currency being localized, while the rest of the content was standardized.

No Artificial Ingredients has been one of the hallmark campaigns of the ICT, and its tourism branding efforts, including advertising, sales promotion, marketing, and public relations, are still being used to promote Costa Rica globally today. These efforts have been effective according to the studies the ICT has commissioned. The Foreign Agents Registration Act (FARA) reports the money spent on media relations campaigns carried out by Burson-Marsteller for the Costa Rican Tourism Board since 2009. A total of US $2 966 082 has been spent on monitoring and analyzing news coverage, writing news releases, distributing to key media, organizing events for consumers and agents with travel industry partners, fulfilling media inquiries, and organizing media familiarization trips to Costa Rica (Foreign Agents Registration Act 2011). In the second semi-annual report to Congress, Costa Rica is shown to have paid US$245 930 to Burson-Marsteller for media relations services, where:

> The registrant monitored and analyzed news coverage of the foreign principal in the North American media market; wrote press releases in English and distributed some to media; organized events with travel industry partners for consumers and the travel industry; fulfilled media inquiries; provided background information on Costa Rican tourist attractions and services; and organized media familiarization trips to Costa Rica. (FARA 2012, p. 40)

Familiarization Tours: Teaming Up With Foreign Media Professionals
At the invitation of the ICT, the first author of this textbook participated in a familiarization tour through Costa Rica in the summer of 2010. This was an opportunity to conduct participant observations. Guided by the "no artificiality" theme, the author's itinerary included an eco-lodge, a grand tourism hotel with national and global sustainability certifications, hot springs, zip lining, marine life and wildlife watching, volcanic sights, national parks, pristine beaches, and an indigenous territory. The familiarization tour also included talks on sustainable development and indigenous cultural preservation, given by managers of the lodge and hotel where the author stayed.

Familiarization tours are controlled by the ICT and coordinated by the public relations agency. Foreign journalists and media professionals can request guided tours, or they may be invited strategically by the ICT, targeting various media outlets in specific markets with the potential to reach prospective tourists. Once the list of invitees is finalized, sent out, and confirmed, the marketing team assesses the needs and expectations of the professional guests through emails and telephone conversations. The logistics are planned in detail, and the marketing team sends out regulatory paperwork (including visa documents or formal invitations), itineraries, logistics, timelines, a welcome guide, and information regarding the assigned trained guides and drivers. The ICT is always very careful in explaining and setting expectations for media guests regarding the rules and conditions of travel expenses and sponsorships. Upon arrival, media guests are assigned to their respective guides and drivers, who are responsible for ensuring a successful stay. Each media guest's requests for language translators and assistance in overcoming other cultural barriers and time orientations are specially arranged.

English is an international language that facilitates work with media representatives from various world markets, and it is the preferred language for the ICT familiarization tours, unless otherwise requested by a media guest. The guides and drivers have experienced a variety of behaviors and attitudes from visiting media professionals, and find it easier to interact with and relate to some more than others. Rapport and empathy between guides and guests inform interpersonal relations on the tours, and may affect guests' impressions of their visit. The ICT marketing and promotion team is aware of how preparation, coordination, and personal treatment of visiting media professionals may influence the perceptions they have or develop regarding not only the professionalism and qualities of ICT personnel, but also, more importantly, Costa Rican tourism itself.

The author's guide and driver explained some sensitive issues that should be treated carefully during familiarization tours, such as the exchange of gifts, the safety and comfort of guests, and hotel and tour operators' expertise on environmental and sustainability issues. Close coordination and constant communication between ICT administrative headquarters and the guides and drivers guarantees a smooth running of the tours. Any change or delay in the agenda is immediately reported and adjustments made. Almost all aspects of the familiarization tours are guided by written policies – especially those which refer to guides and drivers' allowed behaviors and interactions with guests. Administrators, guides, and drivers issue standard final reports with evaluations and recommendations. These reports are intended to support stated objectives and register best practices.

By the end of the tour, the slogan "No Artificial Ingredients" had acquired a different meaning for the author. It had become a tangible subject with multiple reinforcements. The campaign's claims and promises were fulfilled greatly in the context of the tour. Media familiarization tours are one example of how the ICT strengthens its global strategic campaign. They support the solid foundations of tourism in Costa Rica by emphasizing the country's long-term programs to preserve and enhance its natural, human, and cultural environments. This is a universal theme that should resonate with today's international tourists, and will continue to do so for generations of tourists to come.

Conclusion

The complexity of global public relations is increased by the existence of a multiplicity of home, host, and transnational stakeholders and consumer groups. These groups are exposed constantly to claims, promises, and calls to action from a variety of organizations with domestic and foreign roots. Organizations operating in multiple markets face the challenge of being consistent with their core messages and yet relevant to local needs and expectations. Coordination, control, and standardization are essential to the success of multinational campaigns. Regarding the standardization–localization continuum, the approach taken by an MNO is not as important as the core foundation and distinctiveness of its offerings and rewards. Here, the authors have presented an international case in which standardization was the strategic preference over localization in certain management functions. Costa Rica is a unique case in that it offers a tourist destination with appealing characteristics for domestic and international tourists in search of natural and safe environments.

This case study was a unique way of applying the fundamentals of strategic communications in a tourism setting. However, in terms of research, studying other economic sectors will help determine the use of specific coordination and control mechanisms, and the extent of standardization or localization of global strategic communications strategies and tactics. Further research is important in order to understand how organizations, operating in a diverse but interconnected world, can accomplish their goals and objectives through the adaptation of coordination control and standardization and localization efforts.

Case Study   Public Relations and the Communications Coordination Strategies in Telefónica Central America – Localization Tactics in Nicaragua

Telefónica is one of the world leaders in integrated operators in the telecommunications sector, providing communications, information, and entertainment solutions with presence in Europe and Latin America. Its corporate headquarters is located in Madrid, Spain. Telefónica operates in 24 countries, with a total customer base amounting to 315.7 million. It has one of the most international profiles in the sector, with more than 77% of its business outside its home market, and a reference point in the Spanish- and Portuguese-speaking market.

In Latin America, Telefónica serviced more than 212.4 million customers as of the end of March 2013, making it the leading operator in Argentina, Brazil, Chile, and Peru. It also has substantial operations in Colombia, Costa Rica, Ecuador, El Salvador, Guatemala, Mexico, Nicaragua, Panama, Puerto Rico, Uruguay, and Venezuela. In Europe, on top of the Spanish operations, the corporation has operating companies in the Czech Republic, Germany, Ireland, Slovakia, and the United Kingdom, providing services to more than 102.7 million customers. In this case study, we will explore how public relations and communications coordination and strategies work in this Spanish multinational, with emphasis on the Central American region, and in particular on Nicaragua.

Multilevel Structure
Telefónica's communications strategy is divided into three major corporate levels. First, we have the corporate, a global structure under the Director of Communications and Corporate Reputation, which structures global communications strategies in regions where Telefónica operates. This level is subdivided into Europe and Latin America, and is based in Spain. Second, we have the regional (in this case, the Central American region), which aligns the strategy in a particular region and promotes joint projects to exploit synergies of scale. There is a Regional Assistant Director of Public Relations and Institutional Communications located in Panama. Finally, we have the country (in this case, Nicaragua), which manages the internal and external communications strategies of the corporation. It has a manager and is under the corporate regional level. Each country monitors its own business and communications results, and reports to its region.

The Sub-direction of Institutional Relations Central America is in charge of two main areas: the Department of Communication and Institutional Relations and the Department of Corporate Social Responsibility, which operate separately by country. In Nicaragua, the head of the Department of Communication and Institutional Relations is responsible for maintaining corporate relationships with different publics of interest in order to facilitate the work of other areas, paving the way for partnerships to facilitate the smooth running of the business. The manager looks after the reputation of the company. This department runs the company's internal and external communications, maintains relationships with the media, is in charge of messages the company transmits to the community (everything that goes out to the community has to be checked by the department first), and ensures the reputation and sustainability of the corporation.

Control and Monitoring at the National (Host) Level
In Telefónica Nicaragua, the Department of Communication and Institutional Relations plans strategic communication and operates a management tool for the control and monitoring of communications, contributing to the corporation's objectives.

At the regional and corporate levels, the department proposes annual and weekly goals. Annual goals are directed to the Executive Committee, consisting of the managers of each area of the corporation, the communications team, and the regional level. Annual goals led by the managers begin with an evaluation of the actions of the previous year, identifying key actions to provide continuity. An example of an annual goal is "stakeholder engagement." As a way of fulfilling this goal, team members set strategies, such as engaging in dialogs with interest groups the department wants to attract or coordinating the participation of external stakeholders in internal corporation dialogs. Another strategy is to reinforce relationships with public entities and interest groups. To fulfill the annual goals, team members set weekly goals every Monday, directed toward members of the participating areas and the regional level; the team members then meet to coordinate the goals and take action. Each member of the communications team shares their tasks for the week, and all tasks are documented in a spreadsheet. The team members meet again the next week and evaluate their success. The annual goal of stakeholder engagement is supported by the weekly strategies and tactics set every Monday. Examples of weekly goals based on the "stakeholder engagement" goal are workshops, Skype conferences, presentations, and social events with stakeholders.

Goals, strategies, and tactics all have desired outcomes. The members of the department prepare a report each week, and these reports are compiled at an annual evaluation. With each weekly report, the department analyzes quantitatively the presence of Telefónica and other multinational operators in print and broadcast news media based on the main topics of interest; the annual report aims to analyze and then present the results of the contribution of communications management in the development of the business.

Corporate Social Responsibility (CSR)
The Sub-direction of Institutional Relations in the region is also in charge of corporate social responsibility (CSR), leading the social function of the corporation and working closely with the community. Telefónica Foundation, in conjunction with local operators, implemented a social responsibility initiative in 13 countries across Latin America, aimed at tackling child labor – the Proniño program. According to the International Labour Organization (ILO), there are currently 211 million children and adolescents aged between 5 and 17 working in the world, almost three-quarters of whom do so in one of the worst forms of child labor. With Proniño, Telefónica Foundation aims to contribute significantly to the eradication of child labor in Latin America through the education of children and adolescents. The Proniño program is aligned with the regional goals of ILO, which seek to eradicate all child labor by 2020.

In Nicaragua, Telefónica works hand in hand with the Ministry of Education. It accomplishes Proniño's mission through reinforcement activities (sports, arts, and crafts) and by giving lectures on how harmful child labor is in the educational sector. Teachers are trained in teaching techniques and computer software in order to support quality education and provide for children to remain in school. Similarly, corporate volunteering is another program where employees invest time and financial resources to support activities like Proniño, environmental activities, and programs for people with disabilities. Various kinds of activity are organized, such as reforestation, supporting the Teletón and Proniño, and school visits to share morning recreation with the children. The Department of Communication, Institutional Relations, and CSR reports to the country director or general manager and works with an annual plan containing goals, objectives, budget, and guidelines.

Corporate Identity and Reputation
Telefónica Nicaragua is one of the leading organizations in terms of sales and customer loyalty in the region. One aspect that should be emphasized in the communications process is that public relations and communications strategies are used not only as a business strategy, but also as a way to create corporate identity and a shared positive philosophy for customers, shareholders, and employees.

Acknowledgments
This case was made possible thanks to the contribution of the Communication and Image Specialist of Telefónica Nicaragua. All data provided in this case study is dated as of March 2013.

Discussion Questions

1 What factors do you think contribute most to deciding which functions of a global public relations campaign will be standardized or localized?

2 What is the interplay between standardization, localization, coordination, and control? How does each concept affect the others?

3 How does an outsourcing public relations agency aid in helping an MNC localize its global campaign?

4 In what situations should an MNC choose to standardize a global campaign, and when should it be localized to different host countries?

Class Activity

Netflix, an online movie and television streaming service, is currently operating in the United States, Latin America, and Europe. It is hoping to expand to more areas in the future. Students should think about which aspects of Netflix's global operations should be standardized and which should be localized. They should also look into how Netflix coordinates and controls its global operations.

References

Bartlett, C. and Ghoshal, S. (2002). *Managing Across Borders: The Transnational Solution*, 2e. Boston, MA: Harvard Business School Press.

Botan, C. (1992). International public relations: Critique and reformulation. *Public Relations Review*, 18 (2): 149–159.

Costa Rica Information. (n.d.). "International tourist arrivals by month and nationality." Retrieved January 10, 2019 from http://costarica-information. com/about-costa-rica/economy/economic-sectors-industries/tourism/ tourism-statistics.

Curtin, P.A. and Gaither, T.K. (2007). *International Public Relations: Negotiating Culture, Identity, and Power*. London: Sage.

Daniels, J.D., Radebaugh, L.H., and Sullivan, D.P. (2013). *International Business Environments and Operations*, 4e. Upper Saddle River, NJ: Prentice Hall.

de Mooij, M. (2010). *Global Marketing and Advertising: Understanding Cultural Paradoxes*, 3e. Thousand Oaks, CA: Sage.

Dozier, D.M. and Broom, G.M. (1995). Evolution of the manager role in public relations practice. *Journal of Public Relations Research* 7: 3–26.

FARA. (2012). "Report of the Attorney General to the Congress of the United States on the administration of the Foreign Agents Registration Act of 1938, as amended, for the six months ending December 31, 2012." Retrieved January 10, 2019 from http://www.fara.gov/reports/SAR_DEC_2012.pdf.

García, C. (2010). Integrating management practices in international public relations courses: A proposal of contents. *Public Relations Review* 36 (3): 272–277.

Gotham, K.V. (2005). Tourism from above and below: globalization, localization and New Orleans's Mardi Gras. *International Journal of Urban and Regional Research* 29 (2): 309–326.

Grunig, J. (2006). "After 50 years: The value and values of public relations." 45th Annual Distinguished Lecture. The Institute for Public Relations, 9 Nov. 2006, New York, The Yale Club.

Halliburton, C. and Ziegfeld, A. (2009). How do major European companies communicate their corporate identity across countries? An empirical investigation of corporate Internet communications. *Journal of Marketing Management* 25 (9): 909–925.

Harris, G. and Attour, S. (2000). Content analysis of advertising 1970-1997: A review and assessment of methodologies. In: *The Handbook of*

International Marketing Communications (ed. S.O. Monye), 237–250. Chichester: Wiley.

Holtzhausen, D.R., Petersen, B.K., and Tindall, N.T.J. (2003). Exploding the myth of the symmetrical/asymmetrical dichotomy: Public relations models in the new South Africa. *Journal of Public Relations Research* 15: 305–341.

ICT. (n.d.) "About us." Retrieved January 10, 2019 from https://www.ict. go.cr/en/ict/about-us.html#pol%C3%ADticas-institucionales.

ICT. (2008). "Organization chart." Retrieved January 10, 2019 from https:// www.ict.go.cr/en/ict/organization-chart/file.html.

ICT. (2010). "Plan nacional de turismo sostenible de Costa Rica 2010–2016: Resumen ejecutivo." Retrieved January 10, 2019 from https://www. slideshare.net/RivieraMayaSostenibl/plan-nacional-de-turismo-sostenible-costa-rica-20102016.

Lenovo. (2015). "Locations." Retrieved January 10, 2019 from https://www. lenovo.com/us/en/lenovo/locations/.

Lim, S.L. (2010). Global integration or local responsiveness? Multinational corporation's public relations strategies and cases. In G.J. Golan, T.J. Johnson, and W. Wanta (eds.), International media communication in a global age. NewYork: Routledge, pp. 299–318.

Melewar, T.C., Turnbull, S., and Balabanis, G. (2000). International advertising strategies of multinational enterprises in the Middle East. *International Journal of Advertising* 19: 529–547.

Molleda, J.C. and Laskin, A. (2010). Coordination and control of global public relations to manage cross-national conflict shifts: a multidisciplinary perspective for research and practice. In: *International Media Communication in a Global Age* (ed. G.J. Golan, T.J. Johnson, and W. Wanta), 319–344. New York: Routledge.

Molleda, J.C., Kochhar, S., and Wilson, C. (2012). "Theorizing the global–local paradox: Comparative research on information subsidies' localization by US-based multinational corporations." Paper Presented at the Association for Education in Journalism and Mass Communication's 100th Annual Convention, Division of Public Relations, Chicago, USA.

Newburry, W. and Yakova, N. (2006). Standardization preferences: A function of national culture, work interdependence and local embeddedness. *Journal of International Business Studies* 37: 44–60.

Pudelko, M. and Harzing, A.W. (2008). The golden triangle for MNCs: standardization towards headquarters practices, standardization towards global best practices and localization. *Organizational Dynamics* 37 (4): 394–404.

Schmid, S. and Kotulla, T. (2011). 50 years of research on international standardization and adaptation: from a systematic literature analysis to a theoretical framework. *International Business Review* 20: 491–507.

Shah, A. (2012). "Lenovo gains over Dell as world's second-largest PC maker". *PCWorld*. Retrieved January 10, 2019 from http://www.pcworld.com/article/253622/lenovo_gains_over_dell_as_worlds_secondlargest_pc_maker.html.

Smithsonian Journeys. (2010). "Costa Rica's natural heritage." Retrieved January 10, 2019 from https://www.smithsonianjourneys.org/blog/costa-ricas-natural-heritage-1-180951287/.

Sriramesh, K. and Verčič, D. (eds.). (2009). *The Global Public Relations Handbook: Theory, Research, and Practice.* (2nd ed.). NewYork: Routledge.

Verčič, D., Grunig, L.A., and Grunig, J.E. (1996). Global and specific principles of public relations: Evidence from Slovenia. In: *International Public Relations: A Comparative Analysis* (ed. H.M. Cuthbertson and N. Chen), 31–66. New York: Routledge.

Visit Costa Rica. (n.d.). "Essential Costa Rica." Retrieved January 10, 2019 from http://www.visitcostarica.com.

Wakefield, R.I. (1997). "International public relations: A theoretical approach to excellence based on a worldwide Delphi study." Dissertation.

Wakefield, R.I. (2009). Public relations contingencies in a globalized world where even 'glocalization' is not sufficient. *Public Relations Journal* 3 (4).

Wakefield, R.I. (2011). World-class public relations one decade later: Does the model still apply? *Public Relations Journal* 5 (3): 1–26.

Zaharna, R.S. (2001). 'In-awareness' approach to international public relations. *Public Relations Review* 27 (2): 135–148.

8

Cross-national Conflict Shifting: How to Manage Transnational Crises

Central Themes

- Multinational corporations (MNCs) that operate across borders in multiple world locations face a variety of environments and issues that challenge their survival and sustainability.
- Having operations in multiple locations indicates that when a significant crisis breaks in one part of the world, it will immediately be known in others.
- MNCs must make decisions, take actions, and communicate about a transnational crisis at home (headquarters) and in host locations. They need to address the concerns, need for information, and demands of accountability from home, transnational (global activists), and host publics.
- Transnational crises (a.k.a. cross-national conflicts) have financial and reputational consequences for the MNCs involved, whose impact may be greater if the crisis or conflict is handled poorly or the corporation is slow and inconsistent in its responses and actions.
- Global public relations professionals at agencies or in-house departments have the responsibility to understand their organization's, or their client's, business and world environments, with the aim of identifying, tracking, and managing issues to prevent transnational crises.
- Reliable information and data are the best tools for global public relations professionals to use in advising MNCs on business and communications decisions and actions.

Keywords *transnational crisis; cross-national conflict shift; issues management; corporate responses; global news flow; home publics; transnational publics; host publics; localized responses; localization of news*

Global and Multicultural Public Relations, First Edition. Juan-Carlos Molleda and Sarab Kochhar.
© 2019 John Wiley & Sons, Inc. Published 2019 by John Wiley & Sons, Inc.

Introduction

The September 2015 Volkswagen (VW) diesel emission scandal broke virtually overnight when the US Environmental Protection Agency (EPA) publicly announced the carmaker's violation by deliberately designing its diesel engines to cheat on emissions tests. The transnational crisis progressed rapidly: from a government agency issuing notice of legislation violation, to a quick corporate acknowledgment of responsibility; from the resignation of the "shocked" chief executive officer (CEO), to the appointment of a new leader; from the cancellation of advertisements and the suspension of middle managers, to the promise that the corporation would do "everything that must be done" to restore trust in VW.

Pressure came from all directions, and there was major scrutiny in VW's home country from shareholders, employees, and the German government. The global reaction to a transnational crisis depends on how coordinated, consistent, and localized responses are in affected and influential world locations (host countries). VW used a multiplicity of platforms to reach primary and secondary stakeholders in its home (Germany) and host (United States) countries, where it conducts manufacturing and does business.

The news and web coverage was intense. The VW communications team operated in 24/7 crisis mode. It tried to manage the tide of news and customer claims, but it was overwhelming. And things only got worse, with new allegations and a slow and inappropriate response to the cross-national recall. The recall affected close to 500 000 vehicles in the United States and more than 11 million worldwide, most of them in Europe.

It is no surprise that the greatest news coverage happened in Germany, the United Kingdom, and the United States, as predicted by theories such as news flow, news values, and cross-national conflict shifting (CNCS).[1] News and digital coverage peaked incrementally, but mirrored a normal curve or crisis cycle following major events, as when VW Chief Martin Winterport apologized for the deception and the 20% decrease of the company's share value – its largest ever one-day fall. Chief Winterport resigned and the news coverage went through the roof.

VW made available a virtual chatroom with customer care representatives who knew the key messages about the diesel recall, and who took additional steps to learn about customers and document their specific cases. Customers were mailed a letter that included the key messages repeated on multiple platforms, such as the corporate website, a new dedicated portal (www.vwdieselinfo.com), social media, and other traditional and digital platforms. These messages included an admission of guilt, an apology, a statement of shared values in contrast to the company's recent actions, a notice of collaboration with authorities, safety and legal assurance, a statement that no further action was needed by owners, a statement of fact-gathering, a notification that the company was searching for the optimal remedy, a plea for patience and a chance to make things right, provision for an open line of communication, and an assertion that the company would survive and recover customers' trust.

To be successful in this situation, VW needed to move fast to address the host-country (US) publics' concerns and need for information. The president and CEO of Volkswagen Group of America, Michael Horn, was the main spokesperson, and his voice and face were carefully orchestrated to deliver apologies to dealers at a meeting in Brooklyn, NY (this was deemed unsuccessful, as its festive tone contrasted with the gravity of the situation), to customers on the crisis website, and in the letter addressed and signed to customers. Furthermore, apologies were issued to employees through in-house meetings, intranet, and public video.

The authors of this textbook wonder why VW did not come clean before the EPA made the legislation violation public. CNCS informs the need to monitor issues and avoid crisis, and helps enunciate the consequences of a poorly managed crisis. According to *The New York Times*, the head of US VW had known about the potential trouble with diesel emissions since May 2014 – much earlier than when top management acknowledged the problem (*New York Times* 2015). Despite the full-force responses to this transnational crisis, the fact is that VW lied and suffered great financial and reputational losses because of it. This chapter explains and provides illustrations of the elements of transnational crisis or CNCS, as well as the responsibility of global public relations professionals to advise business and communications decisions and the actions of multinational organizations (MNOs) involved in them.

Definition of CNCS and Major Components

A newsworthy event originates in one location and instantaneously flows through mainstream and emergent communications, as well as media technologies, in all directions worldwide. In addition to traditional mass-mediated channels:

> When users post news and videos to social media sites, they are not sharing their information and thoughts with a void, without being heard and engaged with. Instead, other users interact (both positively and negatively) to the information being shared, which provides citizen journalists with immediate gratification and feedback for their efforts. (DeMers 2013, para. 9)

A frantic laser matrix over an infinite sky is a good analogy for this communication flow. A breaking news event will be reported and discussed with great interest where it has some or high resonance. Where an event is foreign to a given public, domestic angles become an essential component of the coverage and of controlled public relations techniques, as well as efforts through localization strategies and data. Those producing online content will debate and share views on transnational crises from their own local perspectives. When developing crisis strategies and tactics, global public relations professionals need to consider local concerns, relevance, and impact; communications targeting domestic affected and involved publics must speak the local language and include the local framework.

MNOs, including national governments and multilateral institutions (e.g. the United Nations), are often the subject of transnational crises – that is, of CNCS. The term **transnational** is used in this chapter as a strategic business mentality, where "diverse roles and dispersed operations must be held together by a management mindset that understands the need for multiple strategic capabilities, views problems and opportunities from both local and global perspectives, and is willing to interact with others openly and flexibly" (Bartlett and Ghoshal 2002, p. 299).

Considering factors such as emerging demographics, environmental and natural resources, and global economic interconnectedness is essential. If multinational corporations (MNCs), with their headquarters and subsidiaries, are not on top of the global flow of communications, media, and issues, it may be an enormous disadvantage to have their voices heard clearly and at appropriate volume when conflicting interests collide in the marketplace or in the cyberspace of ideas – that is, in the public sphere. The level of understanding and preparedness for a transnational crisis or CNCS will determine the efficiency and effectiveness of global public relations techniques and efforts in times of difficulties that cross multiple borders (Lim 2010). Thus, "managers in most worldwide companies recognize the need for simultaneously achieving global efficiency, national responsiveness, and the ability to develop and exploit knowledge on a worldwide basis" (Bartlett and Ghoshal 2002, p. 65).

To frame this discussion, we can recall a domestic product-safety incident that became global news as it emerged from Central America in 2007. A Kuna Indian in Panama alerted the country's government and health authorities to the danger of a brand of toothpaste imported from China. His reading of the product's label – specifically, an ingredient listed in the contents known to have detrimental physical impacts – caused concern for his health and the wellbeing of his fellow country people. His actions and those eventually taken by government officials detonated a global hunt for, and eventual multiple recalls of, the tainted toothpastes. The crisis resulted in product recalls and health alerts on six continents, affecting approximately 34 countries. "People around the world had been putting an ingredient of antifreeze in their mouths, and until Panama blew the whistle, no one seemed to know it," reported Bogdanich and Koster (2007, p. A1). A little butterfly in Panama beat her wings and created a storm in China and other nations. This created a transnational crisis for many corporations, governments, and local businesses and retailers.

Transnational crises have profound consequences for many countries, a host of organizations, and associated publics, clients, and consumers in an era of world interdependence and interconnection. For instance, "The toothpaste scare helped galvanize global concerns about the general quality of China's exports, prompting the government [in Panama] ... to promise to reform how food, medicine, and consumer products are regulated ... And other countries are re-examining how well they monitor imported products," as Bogdanich and Koster (2007, p. A1) explain.

Exploring this line of reasoning, this chapter conceptualizes CNCS as a theoretical perspective that explains the main challenges of global public relations education, research, and management. The chapter contributes to scholarship and specialized professional practice by using previous studies and original cases to illustrate the theory.

Conceptualizing CNCS

Organizations operating across borders are increasingly facing transnational crises due to the interconnectedness of the world's economy and media (both traditional and emergent). This phenomenon has been called CNCS (Molleda and Quinn 2004). When a crisis occurs in a host country, the MNO will coordinate local (host), home, and global responses, incorporating varying degrees of communications tactics and actions (Molleda 2010; Molleda et al. 2005; Lim 2010). The organizational structure and corporate culture of the involved multinational may pose challenges to global public relations professionals in planning and executing transnational crisis communications plans. In a study of corporate crisis planning, the authors concluded:

> A less enlightened dominant coalition, a conservative corporate culture, a hesitant approach towards engaging its external constituents, and the lack of access and representation of corporate communications in the dominant coalition, made the job of practitioners [in handling transnational crises] even more strenuous than it already is. (Pang et al. 2006, p. 384)

One of the contributions of this theoretical perspective is the expanded definition of domestic publics to include involved stakeholders in other world locations. A CNCS includes a variety of actors and their voices:

home, host, and transnational publics (Molleda et al. 2005). The greater the number of voices, the more difficult it is for the involved parties to be heard through the collective noise. In transnational crises, government officials, corporate representatives, and international nongovernmental organizations (NGOs) seem to have the strongest voices (Molleda et al. 2005). Significant involvement of home and host governments is more salient when the crux of a crisis involves legal action and directly affects consumers.

The quality of reporting on a transnational crisis has been found to differ according to the news media's country of origin. News coverage in Europe and the United States has been found to be more comprehensive than in other major global markets (Bravo et al. 2013; Molleda et al. 2005). In these two markets, the transnational crisis agenda is more prominently framed and set by the media. The volume of news coverage is significantly larger in home-country locations (where the organizations involved have their main offices). The corporate responses of involved organizations receive a substantial amount of home-country media coverage (Bravo et al. 2013; Molleda 2011).

The international newswire coverage of a transnational crisis will privilege corporate and governmental responses and actions, which could "indicate that newswire services would favor powerful voices or that these sources are habitually available for news reporters during the coverage of a cross-national conflict shift" Molleda (2011, p. 67).

When an MNO faces a conflict or crisis that originates at its home location (headquarters), the challenging situation shifts prominence to host markets, especially where main branches or foreign operations take place. A reversed transnational crisis was documented in which "the conflict involving a transnational corporation … shifts from a home country (USA) to a host country (China) through international media, and results in greater impact in the host country" (Wang 2005, p. 81). A reversed transnational crisis is likely to produce negative appraisals. As a result of this phenomenon, an organization's headquarters (home) may feel pressured to produce further responses in host locations.

Evidence shows that the actors, the issues addressed, the types of corporate and government responses, and, in general, the nature of news coverage have different characteristics in home and host locations. Wang (2005) found that news coverage in China was significantly different from that in the United States. In China, story features – such as event location (Chinese coverage included both home and host locations), focus (Chinese coverage had a more diverse range of topics), and primary problem attribution (Chinese coverage largely ascribed the crisis to product safety concerns) – were distinct from similar instances in the United States (Wang 2005). Bravo et al. (2013) also found differences between home and host news coverage – requiring localized crisis responses – with respect to headlines, leads, key issues addressed, terminology, sources, and quotes. Molleda (2011, p. 67) articulated this proposition based on evidence from another CNCS case: "International newswire agencies will frame conflicts differently and will highlight particular aspects of a CNCS depending on where they are headquartered in relation to the involved transnational corporation's main office." Taylor (2000) documented how culture may determine the involved publics' responses to a transnational crisis that has local impact. Freitag (2001) explained how cultural aspects determine corporate responses to a transnational crisis.

News media outlets and international wire services favor sources from or representing the views of the country where they have their main offices. Wang (2005) supported the assumption that news outlets are more likely to refer to sources from their own country of origin than those from other locations (i.e. Chinese outlets preferred Chinese sources and US outlets preferred US sources), indicating that proximity and prominence are held as news values (see also Freitag 2001). The study also found evidence that news media outlets covering multiple countries as event locations involved more actors and used more sources and direct quotes than news outlets covering one single country (Wang 2005). The traditional and online news coverage of major transnational crises will be concentrated in the main cities of the home and host countries involved (Molleda 2011).

Home, Host, and Transnational Stakeholders

Practicing public relations domestically entails engagement or public-organization relationship building and maintenance with internal and external stakeholders – with various degrees of involvement and impact. Managing public relations across borders increases the number and complexity of involved and affected stakeholders. To be efficient and effective in engaging publics at various national and transnational environments,

> the effective public relations practitioner employed by a transnational will research and respond to a list of strategic constituencies that typically begins with any activist groups pressuring the organization, followed by shareholders and potential investors and, finally, labor unions or employees. The media, as a strategic public, would fall behind the organization's customers or clients; the community where it operates; its competitors or suppliers; and the local, regional or national government of the host country. (Grunig 1992, p. 134)

The sequence of public–organization engagements may depend on where the CNCS originates and the number of countries involved, among other factors. Effective global public relations professionals should consider stakeholders at the home, host, and transnational levels (Molleda et al. 2005; Molleda and Quinn 2004). Despite access to emergent communications technology, such as social media, the publics in each geographical dimension will experience the MNO's actions differently, and may hold unique expectations and anticipate localized communications that place the conflicting situation into their perceived reality.

Home publics are in the country where the MNO has its headquarters. These publics will reside at the local, state, or national levels. Particular attention will be paid to government agencies in the country's capital, which may rapidly become aware of, assess, and demand rapid explanation of any incident involving national business or institutional interests in foreign nations. That is, a Dutch corporation found guilty of paying bribes to government officials in South Africa will also be subjected to the Netherlands' laws. Similarly, conflicting situations happening at home will be shifted to the global stage, affecting the organization abroad, especially in main host locations. The same Dutch corporation found guilty of cooking the books and owing a large amount of taxes may be seen with suspicion and be a subject of investigation in South Africa and other nations where it has additional significant operations.

Host publics inhabit the countries where the MNC operates or intervenes in domestic affairs. National governments and communities involved or affected are of primary importance. The number and level of involvement of host publics may be determined by the location where the incident occurs – that is, in their country, in the region, in another host nation or nations, or in the corporate headquarters – such as in the hypothetical case of the Dutch corporation. It is predicted that the closer the situation to the host country, the greater the impact, the number of publics, and the level of activist involvement of those publics. For instance, a large Brazilian construction corporation building a dam in Bolivia might be blamed by activist groups for design and construction defects that threaten indigenous communities. The accusations might follow extensive media coverage and government investigation, and result in a substantial fine. This incident would be likely to cause public reactions in Brazil, and perhaps in other South American countries where the construction corporation also operated.

Transnational publics navigate cyberspace, newswires, and airways. International NGOs, activist groups, and global media would be listed in this category. The presence of a transnational public is felt everywhere in an interconnected and instantaneous fashion, often connecting and supporting local groups or using television or radio feeds from local broadcasters. Transnational publics often identify and transmit the CNCS to where its influence is most felt or its audiences are more interested in the cause advocated, such as human rights or environmental protection. For example, the transnational activist organization CorpWatch seeks "to expose multinational corporations that profit from war, fraud, environmental, human rights, and other abuses, and to provide critical information to foster a more informed public and an effective democracy" (CorpWatch 2009, para. 2). In September 2007, the organization launched a wiki project named Crocodyl.org in partnership with the Center for Corporate Policy and the Corporate Research Project. The San Francisco-based CorpWatch has developed a global network of researchers and journalists to identify and report corporate wrongdoing wherever it happens. The organization offers reports and other publications aiming to empower governments and citizens in the fight against transnational corporate power.

In many cases, host and home publics are active and paying close attention. In 2004, Walmart opened a subsidiary, "Bodega Aurrera," north of Mexico City at San Juan, Teotihuacán, which is 1.6 miles from the 2000-year-old pyramids of Teotihuacán – a UNESCO World Heritage Site (*Economist* 2004). Local and national politicians, artists, artisans, community groups, activist groups, media, and competitors became actively involved in the fight against this. The opposition alleged the commercial expansion of a US-based corporation was "an insult inflicted on the sacred site by a symbol of American consumerism" (Malkin 2004, p. 6). In general, Mexican consumers and government officials were supportive of the new supermarket, because it brought competitive prices, quality products and services, a convenient location, and sponsorship for social and cultural programs. Many communities in the United States, on the other hand, used the international incident to strengthen their opposition to the expansion of the world's biggest retailer into their own backyards. The argument over Walmart's alleged abuses to Mexican heritage was voiced by local media and city commission sessions (*Gainesville Sun* 2004).

In the end, Walmart succeeded in managing the transnational crisis through public relations techniques and efforts. Walmart responded to home and host publics by proactively communicating the benefits of the supermarket to consumers and local communities, offering timely clarifications to the opponents' allegations, and providing contextual information that addressed domestic concerns both in Mexico and in various communities in the United States that seemed to have a love–hate relationship with the corporation. The retailer also posted updated and timely information on its website. Walmart used global and local spokespeople and third-party supporters. The grand opening of Bodega

Aurrera was a success, and the US opposition stopped using the Mexican controversy as a valid argument to further oppose the corporation's expansion in its own communities (although it continued to focus on its own concerns at home) (*Calgary Sun* 2004).

There are CNCS cases that evolve through variations and diverse degrees of influence in different host locations. In September 2009, Pfizer paid the largest fine ever, US$2.3 billion, to settle a marketing fraud case with the US Department of Justice. The news about the world's largest drug company was in every newswire service and countless media outlets on every continent. Focusing on the contextual information contained in news reports, domestic coverage in many countries pointed to the large penalty involving "the New York-based" (Clark 2009, p. 2) or "US-based" company (Hooi 2009) (reports in London and Singapore, respectively). Clark (2009, p. 2) ended a news report with this contextual information:

> Pfizer employs 90 000 people around the world including 4000 staff in Britain, where the company has a large research and development site at Sandwich, in Kent. Its top-selling products include the anti-cholesterol drug Lipitor, the arthritis drug Celebrex and the erectile dysfunction drug Viagra.

Similarly, Hooi (2009, para. 4), writing for the *Business Times Singapore*, said, "the same year Bextra was withdrawn in the US, the Health Sciences Authority in Singapore had withdrawn Bextra, after reports from Canada and the US linked the drug to an increased risk of heart attacks and skin reactions." Both examples put the US settlement into a domestic context. However, the news story in Singapore included a greater amount of background detail concerning the company, its performance, and its products. Pfizer operates its "first large-scale active pharmaceutical ingredient manufacturing facility in Asia" (Hooi 2009, para. 18) in Singapore. Other aspects contained in the Singaporean version of the news story were: (i) domestic advertising regulations of prescription drugs; (ii) names and uses of various medications produced and commercialized by the pharmaceutical company; (iii) the company's brief history and performance in Asia and Singapore, including research and development and employment statistics and projections; and (iv) quotes from global and local spokespeople, including Pfizer's senior vice president and general counsel.

Surprisingly, in some countries the news story seemed to be downplayed. Although NOTIMEX (a Mexican news agency) reported on the settlement (NOTIMEX 2009), only small notes were found in major Mexican newspapers. Moreover, the news story was also reported in Spanish by the Spaniard Agencia EFE and Reuters. More importantly, Pfizer Mexico did not include any news release or pertinent information on its website (Pfizer Mexico n.d.), although information about the settlement could be found easily on its US site (Pfizer USA 2009). The common Mexican citizen may not have known about Pfizer's settlement through his or her national or domestic media, but the Mexican elite and decision-makers, including shareholders, would have learned about it through international media, including cable television networks such as CNN. Pfizer may have left this online void in Mexico deliberately as a localized strategy to downplay a major legal incident with US authorities.

Evolving Knowledge: Actions and Responses

Stakeholders' reactions and corporate responses to incidents involving public safety vary according to the cultural characteristics of the host environment. Taylor (2000, p. 289) analyzed the Coca-Cola Company's response to an incident where its product allegedly caused Belgian children to become ill: "Given the high levels of uncertainty avoidance and power distance in Belgium, France, and Spain, it makes sense that those nations would respond quickly and severely to any threats to public safety." Home, host, and transnational publics actively engaged the organization. Their actions – specifically, the brand boycott by publics in France and Spain, in addition to where the tampering happened in Belgium – affected the company's stock value and its relationships with host stakeholders. This CNCS also served to identify the deficiencies of a highly centralized management in Coca-Cola's main office in Atlanta, GA, which resulted in a lack of flexibility and understanding of local conditions in the nations involved.

Freitag (2001) studied the cultural and international complexities and cross-national impact of the Ford–Firestone tire crises, as portrayed by media outlets in Canada, Denmark, France, Germany, New Zealand, Poland, the United Kingdom, the United States, and Venezuela. The amount of national news coverage was predicted by the number of affected domestic consumers (in proximity and consequences), the place where the companies were headquartered, and the direct links between the companies and their countries of origin. In France, the large media coverage resulted from a tradition of activism in consumer and labor issues and the prominence of the automobile and automotive manufacturing in the country. In contrast, the news coverage in East Africa focused on assuring consumers that faulty tires would not be dumped on African markets. According to Freitag (2001), cultural aspects determined the corporate responses to the transnational crisis – that is, it was difficult for a Japanese executive to accept the blame and offer an apology for fear of losing face, and Ford's US executives were at fault because of arrogance.

Wang (2005) studied the DuPont Teflon crisis in China, which originated from the EPA's administrative action against DuPont. The crisis shifted to China, where it transformed into a consumer product safety crisis. The study found that DuPont, China was unprepared for the crisis in terms of early signal detection and prompt initial response. DuPont subsequently implemented a series of active-turnaround actions and multiple-response strategies. However, the damage to the company's reputation and the Chinese Teflon market due to its early lapses could be hard to recover from in the short term. The findings also indicated that DuPont employed a strategy mix to offer a competing narrative, given the unfavorable perceptions held by its stakeholders, and redefined the alleged acts as ones of lesser offensiveness. According to Wang (2005), DuPont's combined strategies were found to be internally coherent and partially corroborated by the media coverage. Wang's study documented a case of reversed CNCS, where a conflict involving an MNC shifts from a home to a host country, with greater effect on the host location. The study suggested interpreting such a phenomenon from three perspectives: (i) the **crisis management performance** of the involved MNC (ii) the **level of media interest** in the involved issue; and (iii) the unique and complicated **social and cultural context** of the involved host country.

Kim and Molleda's study (2005) also combined CNCS with crisis management by analyzing Halliburton's bribery probe case in Nigeria. To advance the CNCS theory with a more complex context, including political aspects, the authors offer three propositions dealing with: (i) the prominence of the CEO or top-level management and how much more attention they might attract to the crisis, potentially resulting in greater political repercussions and debates; (ii) the way national conflicts are perceived differently by involved actors in home and host locations and framed differently by host and home media; and (iii) how domestic conflicts of MNCs are sometimes combined with other related crises that negatively affect their reputation in home and host countries and, therefore, require more complex responses and public relations techniques and efforts until the conflicts are resolved.

In 2004, Merck Sharp & Dohme announced a voluntary, worldwide withdrawal of Vioxx, its arthritis and acute pain medication. Oliveira and Molleda (2008) documented the public relations effort of the withdrawal in Brazil. According to the authors, Merck's decision resulted in the development of the most elaborate and critical public relations campaign by the company in contemporary history. In Brazil, as in other world markets, the medication was a top seller. Prompt action was thus required in response to the concerns of the medical community, regulatory agencies, and consumers. The campaign aimed to ease any confusion caused by the product withdrawal and the research disclosure – and additionally to position the company as responsible and as concerned for the wellbeing of patients and the reputation of the physicians who prescribed the medication. The company announced the decision to each subsidiary around the world and offered common guidelines to keep the same institutional discourse. Merck Brazil created a crisis committee. It localized the global strategy by communicating the reasons for the product withdrawal through the use of domestic statistics and the company's compliance to national regulations. The domestic strategy also included the identification of influential and credible personalities to maximize the communications impact on targeted publics, assuring Brazilian consumers of secure reimbursements at drugstores and of the quality of Merck Brazil's product lines.

Molleda et al. (2008) tested the CNCS theory by analyzing international news agencies' coverage of lead-tainted Mattel toys manufactured in China and sold in the United States and other markets worldwide. They concluded Mattel was effective in its crisis communications strategies, providing a transparent and timely response – a critical element of effective public relations, particularly during product recalls. However, from a global perspective, Mattel failed to fully integrate the needs of host, home, and transnational publics in its crisis communications approach. The Chinese government and Chinese manufacturing companies did not take a proactive approach in their crisis communications strategy. Defense of their actions was not communicated until late in the conflict and, once communicated, it likely escalated things instead of assisting in resolving them for the various publics. Had Mattel and the Chinese government jointly approached the problem, acknowledging from the outset their shared roles and responsibility in resolving the global crisis, the intervention of activist groups might have been somewhat negated, and the crisis might not have taken such a grand scope.

Lim and Molleda (2009) analyzed the particular effects of a home crisis on host countries' consumers. The study showed that the type of crisis significantly affected potential customers' attitudes and behaviors in terms of intention to purchase, recommending the company's product to a friend, and requesting more information about the company. A massive product recall produced more negative responses from potential consumers than a bribery scandal affecting a transnational automobile corporation. Prior attitude toward a MNC affected audiences' attitude formation and behavioral intentions.

Molleda and Laskin (2010) combined the original CNCS propositions and body of literature with studies from international business on coordination and control mechanisms. They articulated nine additional presuppositions concerning the intersection of the multidisciplinary theoretical perspectives and concluded that

> the strategies employed by a transnational organization to deal with CNCS depend on and are largely determined by the coordination and control structure of a MNC: centralization versus localization; subsidiary autonomy in marketing decisions; division of responsibilities; and the chain of command. (Molleda and Laskin 2010, p. 337)

Conclusion

The best MNCs avoid CNCS by acting ethically and complying with home and host economic, political, social, and cultural norms. Nevertheless, CNCS is often unavoidable, as the world is a complex place. Thus, it is necessary for MNCs to closely examine the management approach they use to develop global public relations techniques and efforts through functional departments or with the assistance of global agencies or independent indigenous professionals. The communicators should ask whether the availability of culturally appropriate spokespeople and the timely provision of information subsidies according to time zones and indigenous journalism or communications practices would result in a coordinated and consistent global public relations function. Moreover, would the efficient coordination and control of host and home responses and actions, as well as the contextualization of information subsidies provision and controlled online communications use, increase the likelihood of a successful crisis-control program?

Today, those who nurture a transnational mentality (i.e. multinational responsiveness, global efficiency, and worldwide learning) may exert greater control over a crisis and effectively engage home, host, and transnational publics. In that regard, global public relations scholars and students must invest further efforts into research on the evolution, effects, and management of transnational issues and crises. Professionals in MNCs and global and domestic agencies should maintain fluid channels of communications with their headquarters and other influential offices worldwide. The contribution of each part will make greater the whole. Professionals must also be active observers of the reactions of local audiences to global events, particularly in their industries and sectors. The mastery of localization strategies and tactics will allow professionals and their organizations to meet the domestic expectations of host publics, without ignoring the expectations and needs of home and transnational stakeholders.

Case Study   Huawei – The Chinese Telecom Giant

Huawei Technologies is a Chinese transnational corporation (TNC). A former army officer, Ren Zhengfei, founded the company in Shenzhen in 1987. It is a private corporation owned entirely by its employees and one of the largest telecommunication businesses in the world (Prasso 2011). Huawei has expanded from its vast home market to become one of the world's largest global corporations (*Economist* 2012).

Main Challenges

Huawei's highly competitive low-price strategy has been key to its international success (Vance and Eihorn 2011). However, its expansion has faced scrutiny. Multiple countries have claimed national security concerns associating Huawei with the Chinese government and the People's Liberation Army (PLA), which has been detrimental to its continuous growth. The corporation has faced serious suspicions and national security fears in the United Kingdom and Australia, but distrust seems to be highest in the United States (Poling 2012).

The US government has hindered Huawei's expansion in the United States by blocking business deals due to concerns over security threats and exposure to Chinese military hackers (Vincent 2013). The corporation has been accused of having military ties with the Chinese government due to its founder and CEO's service in the PLA. Huawei has also been the target of accusations regarding intellectual property rights violations. Furthermore, Huawei has been accused of allegedly receiving financial support from the Chinese government, and of being a "Trojan horse" used to infiltrate foreign networks (Mishra 2012). In a daring move, Huawei directly addressed these concerns in an open letter to US investigators in 2011, inviting the US government to look closely into its business in order to settle the claims that continued to tarnish its reputation. In the United Kingdom, Huawei addressed the distrust of its products by partnering with Britain's National Security Agency (NSA)-equivalent, Government Communications Headquarters, to set up a Cyber Security Evaluation Centre that comprehensively audits any gear Huawei intends to sell in the country (Greenberg 2012).

Global Communications Strategy

Huawei hired lobbyists, consultants, and public relations agencies and assembled advisory boards in key markets across the world to establish its global operations and distinctive brand (Tiezzi 2013). Over the years, the corporation has continuously adapted and improved its public relations strategy so as to manage its international expansion and build and shape its international identity. In 2003, it turned to Edelman's Silicon Valley office to help establish its brand worldwide. According to its 2006 annual report, it reached US$8.5 billion in revenue in that year, with 65% of its contract sales coming from international markets, and 31 out of the world's top 50 telecom operators acting as its corporate partners, including Vodafone, BT, Telefonica, FT/Orange, and China Mobile. In the same year, Huawei adopted a new visual identity, and new logo, that better reflected its principles of customer focus, innovation, steady and sustainable growth, and harmony.

FleishmanHillard Hong Kong led the global account for three years when the company decided to appoint both it and Manning Selvage & Lee as its agencies of record in 2007. Both agencies were tasked with increasing corporate brand exposure to win greater acceptance from world-class operators. By 2008, FleishmanHillard was leading Huawei in an ambitious going-global program alongside its other Chinese clients, such as Lenovo and TCL (Hong 2009).

In 2009, there was a major turn in Huawei's business strategy. The corporation surprised the technology industry by hiring Matt Bross as its chief technology officer (CTO). This represented a change in strategy for the corporation, which previously ran a secretive operation and selected its top managers from China. It was reportedly proud of its new efforts to become a modern multinational company (Vance and Eihorn 2011).

In 2011, there was another clear change in Huawei's public relations strategy. The corporation employed multiple spokespeople around the world to respond to criticism and dispel false claims against it. This was an instrumental change in the management of Huawei's reputation, because even though the corporation had continued to work with several public relations agencies, it had never empowered them to respond to the majority of inquiries (Dean 2011). In that same year, Huawei turned to FleishmanHillard again to create and develop relationships with the UK consumer market during the launch of its first smartphone in the United Kingdom (Luker 2011).

Also in 2011, Huawei celebrated 10 years of business in the United States while still dealing with some remaining suspicions about its background and business practices. In order to sustain its growing presence in the United States, Huawei launched its first US advertising campaign and hired at least 500 employees in the country. As the company's first formal marketing communications push in the United States, the campaign was meant to raise its national profile and to appeal to the country's consumer base. Jack Morton Worldwide was hired by Huawei to run a brand-awareness campaign and build brand recognition for the launch of its upcoming devices. This strategic partnership was also meant to address concerns about Huawei's Chinese affiliations, and to establish the company as a top manufacturer in the United States.

Identity Against Reputation

Huawei's corporate reputation has been challenged by security concerns and blocked business deals. The varying regional and national attitudes toward the corporation also continue to impact its corporate identity. In one instance, the corporation was featured in two influential magazine cover stories that presented two conflicting corporate identities. *China Entrepreneur* described Huawei as a company proud of its roots and company culture (Qin and Yongqing 2012). The article claimed, "Ren is Huawei," and tied the corporation to its CEO. The *Economist* described Huawei as a corporation trying to address its strategy and cultural problems, while seeking to improve transparency and separate itself from its PLA associations (*Economist* 2011). The conflicting corporate identities presented by these magazines will remain a challenge for Huawei as it continues its international growth.

After a year-long investigation, the US House Intelligence Committee issued a report in 2012 that warned US companies against doing business with Huawei and advised them to stay away from its equipment (Schmidt et al. 2012). Huawei responded by condemning the committee's investigation and report, claiming it ignored its proven track record of network security and the large amount of information the company had provided to the US government. In the report, US intelligence officials called China the world's biggest perpetrator of economic espionage (Engleman and Salant 2012). Huawei's chief spokesman, William Plummer, responded by saying, "Huawei has become a punching bag for Americans wary of China" and arguing that "the outcome was predetermined [as] the political agenda was one of picking China in the eye and holding hostage an innocent independent, employee-owned company" (Osawa and Gorman 2012).

In a surprising move, Ren Zhengfei granted his first ever interview during a visit to New Zealand in 2013. The event happened shortly after he was called the "world's most controversial businessman" by Michael Schuman in a *TIME* magazine article about the 100 most influential people in the world. Ren's first interview is a milestone in the company's global communications strategy, as previously he had always remained absent and out of the spotlight. Huawei has experienced a business-friendly reception in New Zealand, and Ren took the opportunity to assure media outlets that Huawei had never had any connection to the cyber-security issues the US had encountered, nor would it in the future (Olsen 2013).

Moving Forward

Hall (2013) claims that if Huawei decided to decentralize its operations from China and be listed on an international stock exchange, it might help the company overcome some of the security concerns associated with it. Others, such as Mark Anderson of Strategic News Service, argue that such decentralization efforts would never be enough to satisfy some countries' security agencies. Huawei has made attempts to decentralize its communications efforts and change its strategy to a more regional approach in order to localize its public relations efforts and overcome these challenges. Cybersecurity-focused SANS Institute research director Alan Paller suggests that Huawei should invest in testing and defending its hardware and software in order to alleviate security concerns in the United States and abroad (Greenberg 2012).

The future of Huawei in the United States is unclear, as reports claim the corporation has withdrawn from the US market for the time being, though it plans to return in the future (Tiezzi 2013). The corporation's public relations efforts in the United States have proven to have little effect on its corporate reputation, and Huawei's global communications strategy will continue to evolve and change as it seeks to promote transparency and confront claims against itself and its home base, China.

Discussion Questions

1 What are some other communications strategies Huawei could implement to promote transparency and openness with regard to its products?

2 Describe the misalignment in Huawei's corporate reputation and identify its source(s).

3 Has Huawei's own corporate identity influenced the uncertainty and distrust of other countries? If so, in what ways?

4 How would Huawei benefit from switching to a regional public relations approach?

Class Activity

Volkswagen and Daimler AG, a multinational automotive corporation based in Germany, collectively recalled 1.5 million vehicles in the United States as a result of potential airbag malfunctions. Students should discuss the details and scope of this crisis and determine how it affected both host (the United States) and home (Germany) stakeholders. They might also determine whether this crisis affected any other potential host countries in which both Daimler and VW operate. In addition, students should discuss how US and German news outlets, as well as outlets elsewhere in the world, reported on this crisis.

Note

1 Taylor (2000) and Freitag (2001) did not base their research on propositions, but their work has always been cited and used to inform and develop the theory.

References

Bartlett, C.A. and Ghoshal, S. (2002). *Managing Across Borders: The Transnational Solution*. Boston, MA: Harvard Business School Press.

Bogdanich, W. and Koster, R.M. (2007). "The everyman who exposed tainted toothpaste." The *New York Times*, October 1. Retrieved January 10, 2019 from https://www.nytimes.com/2007/10/01/world/americas/01panama.html.

Bravo, V., Molleda, J.C., Giraldo, A.F., and Botero, L.H. (2013). Testing the theory of cross-national conflict shifting: a quantitative content analysis and a case study of the Chiquita brands' transnational crisis originated in Colombia. *Public Relations Review* 39: 57–59.

Calgary Sun. (2004). "Wal-Mart opens amid pyramids." *Calgary Sun*, p. 40.

Clark, A. (2009). "Pfizer drug breach ends in biggest US crime fine." The *Guardian*, September 2. Retrieved January 10, 2019 from https://www.theguardian.com/business/2009/sep/02/pfizer-drugs-us-criminal-fine.

CorpWatch. (2009). "Our history." Retrieved January 10, 2019 from http://www.corpwatch.org/article.php?id=11314.

Dean, J. (2011). "Huawei's PR strategy: Everything but the boss." *The Wall Street Journal*, February 25. Retrieved January 10, 2019 from https://blogs.wsj.com/chinarealtime/2011/02/25/huawei%E2%80%99s-pr-strategy-everything-but-the-boss/.

DeMers, J. (2013). "How social media is supporting a fundamental shift in journalism." *Huffington Post*, May 8. Retrieved January 10, 2019 from https://www.huffingtonpost.com/jayson-demers/how-social-media-is-suppo_b_3239076.html.

Economist. (2004). "Pyramid schemes: A Mexican shopping scandal." Retrieved January 10, 2019 from https://www.economist.com/the-americas/2004/11/11/pyramid-schemes.

Economist. (2011). "Huawei: The long march of the invisible Mr Ren." Retrieved January 10, 2019 from http://www.economist.com/node/18771640.

Economist. (2012). "Huawei: The company that spooked the world." Retrieved January 10, 2019 from http://www.economist.com/node/21559929.

Engleman, E. and Salant, J.D. (2012). "Huawei expands lobbying amid national security probe by Congress." *Washington Post*, August 26. Retrieved January 10, 2019 from https://www.washingtonpost.com/ business/economy/huawei-expands-lobbying-amid-national-security-probe-by-congress/2012/08/26/4b2d06f6-ecb5-11e1-b09d-07d971dee30a_ story.html?noredirect=on&utm_term=.b4434e2fd845.

Freitag, A. (2001). International media coverage of the firestone tyre recall. *Journal of Communication Management* 6 (3): 239–256.

Gainesville Sun. (2004). "A supercenter among the ruins: protesters, shoppers clash over Mexico store." The *Gainesville Sun*, p. 13A.

Gorman, S. and Osawa, J. (2012). "Huawei fires back at the US." *Wall Street Journal*, October 8. Retrieved January 10, 2019 from https://www.wsj. com/articles/SB10000872396390443982904578044190738613734.

Greenberg, A. (2012). "A better approach to Huawei, ZTE and Chinese cyberspying? Distrust and verify." Forbes, October 9. Retrieved January 10, 2019 from http://www.forbes.com/sites/andygreenberg/2012/10/ 09/a-better-approach-to-huawei-zte-and-china-distrust-and-verify.

Grunig, L.A. (1992). Strategic public relations constituencies on a global scale. *Public Relations Review* 18 (2): 127–136.

Hall, M. (2013). "Huawei in push to ease concerns over national security." The *Sydney Morning Herald*, August 13. Retrieved January 10, 2019 from http://www.smh.com.au/it-pro/business-it/huawei-in-push-to-ease-concerns-over-national-security-20130812-hv1cn.html.

Hong, L. (2009). "Changes in media – and in the practice of communications." FleishmanHillard-Public Affairs, March 17. Retrieved January 10, 2019 from http://fleishmanhillard.com/2009/03/public-affairs/changes-in-media-and-in-the-practice-of-communications.

Hooi, J. (2009). "Pfizer swallows a bitter US$2.3b pill." Retrieved January 10, 2019 from http://acctcollections101.blogspot.com/.

Kim, J.R., and Molleda, J.C. (2005). "Cross-national conflict shifting and crisis management: An analysis of Halliburton's bribery probe case in Nigeria." Paper presented at the 8th International Public Relations Research Conference, Miami, Florida.

Lee, Y. and Carsten, P. (2016). "Huawei posts strongest revenue growth in seven years." *Reuters.* Retrieved January 10, 2019 from https://www. reuters.com/article/us-huawei-tech-results/huawei-posts-strongest-revenue-growth-in-seven-years-idUSKCN0WY3D5.

Lim, J.S. (2010). Global integration or local responsiveness? Multinational corporations' public relations strategies and cases. In: *International*

Media Communication in a Global Age (ed. G.J. Golan, T.J. Johnson, and W. Wanta), 299–318. New York: Routledge.

Lim, J.S. and Molleda, J.C. (2009). "The influence of a cross-national conflict shift on a transnational corporation's host customers." Paper presented at the International Communication Association 59th Annual Conference, Division of Public Relations, Chicago, IL.

Luker, S. (2011). "Chinese telecoms giant Huawei calls in Fleishman-Hillard for mobile launch." *PRWeek*, October 14. Retrieved January 10, 2019 from http://www.prweek.com/article/1098820/chinese-telecoms-giant-huawei-calls-fleishman-hillard-mobile-launch.

Malkin, E. (2004). "Mexico: More sales than its 3 top competitors combined." The *New York Times*, December 6. Retrieved January 10, 2019 from https://www.nytimes.com/2004/12/06/business/businessspecial2/mexico-more-sales-than-its-3-top-competitors.html?mtrref=www.google.com&gwh=1EB7665BD2E53D2C88FED48C265F0F15&gwt=pay.

Mishra, P. (2012). "Asia knows how to get along with a bigger China." BloombergView, October 14. Retrieved January 10, 2019 from http://www.bloombergview.com/articles/2012-10-14/asia-knows-how-to-get-along-with-a-bigger-china.

Molleda, J.C. (2010). Cross-national conflict shifting: a transnational crisis perspective in global public relations. In: *Handbook of Public Relations*, 2e (ed. R. Heath), 679–690. Thousand Oaks, CA: Sage Publications.

Molleda, J.C. (2011). Advancing the theory of cross-national conflict shifting: a case discussion and quantitative content analysis of a transnational crisis' newswire coverage. *International Journal of Strategic Communication* 5: 49–70.

Molleda, J.C. and Laskin, A. (2010). Coordination and control of global public relations to manage cross-national conflict shifts: a multidisciplinary perspective for research and practice. In: *International Media Communication in a Global Age* (ed. G.J. Golan, T.J. Johnson, and W. Wanta), 319–344. New York: Routledge.

Molleda, J.C. and Quinn, C. (2004). Cross-national conflict shifting: a global public relations dynamic. *Public Relations Review* 30: 1–9.

Molleda, J.C., Connolly-Ahern, C., and Quinn, C. (2005). Cross national conflict shifting: expanding a theory of global public relations management through quantitative content analysis. *Journalism Studies* 6 (1): 87–102.

Molleda, J.C., Solaun, L., and Parmelee, K. (2008). "Advancing the theory of cross-national conflict shifting: An analysis of international news agencies' coverage of lead-tainted toys from China." Paper presented at the InterAmericas Council Congress of the Americas II, co-sponsored by ICA, Mexico City, Mexico.

New York Times. (2015). "How VW's scandal unfolded." Retrieved January 10, 2019 from http://www.nytimes.com/interactive/2015/10/23/business/international/vw-scandal-timeline.html?_r=0#/#time389_11292.

NOTIMEX. (2009). "Pagará Pfizer multa récord de 2.3 mil mdd por promoción ilegal." Retrieved January 10, 2019 from http://www.zocalo.com.mx/new_site/articulo/pagara-pfizer-multa-record-de-2.3-mil-mdd-por-promocion-ilegal.

Oliveira, T.M. and Molleda, J.C. (2008). Withdrawal of Vioxx in Brazil: Aligning the global mandate and local actions. In: *The Evolution of Public Relations: Case Studies from Countries in Transition*, 3e (ed. J.V. Turk and L. Scalan), 181–194. Gainseville, FL: Institute for Public Relations.

Olsen, R. (2013). "Huawei's CEO Ren Zhengfei speaks to media for first time." Forbes, May 9. Retrieved January 10, 2019 from https://www.forbes.com/sites/robertolsen/2013/05/09/huaweis-ceo-ren-zhengfei-speaks-to-media-for-first-time/#70fcdc063455.

Osawa, J. and Gorman, S. (2012). "Huawei fires back at the US." The *Wall Street Journal*, October 8. Retrieved January 10, 2019 from https://www.wsj.com/articles/SB10000872396390443982904578044190738613734.

Pang, A., Cropp, F., and Cameron, G.T. (2006). Corporate crisis planning: tensions, issues, and contradictions. *Journal of Communication Management* 10 (4): 371–389.

Pfizer Mexico. (n.d.). "Sala de Prensa." Retrieved January 10, 2019 from https://www.pfizer.com.mx/content/sala-de-prensa-0#.XDkG8lVKgdU.

Pfizer USA. (2009). "Recent Pfizer press releases." Retrieved January 10, 2019 from http://pfizer.com/news/press_releases/pfizer_press_releases.jsp#

Poling, G. (2012). "Who's afraid of Huawei?" The *Diplomat*, April 10. Retrieved January 10, 2019 from http://thediplomat.com/2012/04/whos-afraid-of-huawei.

Prasso, S. (2011). "What makes China telecom Huawei so scary?" *CNNMoney*, July 28. Retrieved January 10, 2019 from http://tech.fortune.cnn.com/2011/07/28/what-makes-china-telecom-huawei-so-scary.

Qin, S. and Yongqing, J. (2012). "Huawei transgenic." *China Entrepreneur*, August 6. Retrieved January 10, 2019 from http://finance.ifeng.com/news/corporate/20120806/6875129.shtml.

Schmidt, M.S., Bradsher, K., and Hauser, C. (2012). "US panel cites risks in Chinese equipment." The *New York Times*, October 8. Retrieved January 10, 2019 from https://www.nytimes.com/2012/10/09/us/us-panel-calls-huawei-and-zte-national-security-threat.html.

Taylor, M. (2000). Cultural variance as a challenge to global public relations: a case study of the Coca-Cola scare in Europe. *Public Relations Review* 26: 277–293.

Tiezzi, S. (2013). "Huawei official gives up on the US market." The *Diplomat*, December 5. Retrieved January 10, 2019 from http://thediplomat. com/2013/12/huawei-officially-gives-up-on-the-us-market.

Vance, A. and Eihorn, B. (2011). "At Huawei, Matt Bross tries to ease US security fears." Bloomberg Businessweek, September 15. Retrieved January 10, 2019 from http://www.businessweek.com/magazine/ at-huawei-matt-bross-tries-to-ease-us-security-fears-09152011.html.

Vincent, J. (2013). "Huawei, who are they? Explaining the Chinese firm with a billion pound investment in Britain." *Independent*, October 2013. Retrieved January 10, 2019 from http://www.independent.co.uk/life-style/ gadgets-and-tech/features/huawei-who-are-they-explaining-the-chinese- firm-with-a-billion-pound-investment-in-britain-8884463.html.

Wang, Y. (2005). "Cross-national conflict shifting: A case study of the DuPont Teflon crisis." Unpublished master's thesis, University of Florida, Gainesville, FL.

9

Corporate Social Responsibility, Sustainability, and Multisector Partnerships

Central Themes

- In today's global marketplace, corporations are members of the worldwide community rather than merely members of their city, town, or state.
- Corporate social responsibility (CSR) practices are essential and present an easy way for multinational corporations (MNCs) to use corporate power as a catalyst for social intervention and change.
- Joint interventions of organizations and professionals from multiple sectors, utilizing their joint resources and expertise, are required to accomplish common goals and make an impact on a large scale.
- There are three stages of collaboration in partnership building, which define the process: philanthropic, transactional, and integrative.
- A multipronged approach is used to conceptualize the concept of strategic participatory communications for social change and development.

Keywords *corporate social responsibility; sustainability; community building; multisector partnerships; multinational corporations; multilatinas; strategy; participatory communications*

Introduction

Founded in 1960, the Chilean CENCOSUD is the third-largest publicly-traded retail conglomerate in Latin America, with more than 140 000 employees in Argentina, Brazil, Chile, Colombia, and Peru. Since the opening of its first grocery store in Santiago, Chile in 1976, the Latin American multinational corporation (MNC), or **multilatina**, has developed different lines of business, such as supermarkets, home

Global and Multicultural Public Relations, First Edition. Juan-Carlos Molleda and Sarab Kochhar.

improvement stores, department stores, shopping centers, and financial services. Several companies under this multilatina went public in 2004 and accelerated their international expansion in 2007. CENCOSUD guides its actions and activities through its unifying mission:

> Our mission is to work day by day to become the most profitable and prestigious retailer in Latin America, based on excellence in our quality of service, respect for the communities where we live and commitment of our team of collaborators. All this, through the cornerstones of our company: vision, challenge, entrepreneurship and perseverance. (CENCOSUD n.d.-a, para. 1)

The conglomerate's long-term **corporate social responsibility (CSR)** program focuses on two sustainability pillars: economic performance (e.g. cost effectiveness) and the generation of social and environmental value for the societies in which it operates, including interest groups. For instance, the department store Paris, one of the multilatina's companies, develops programs and advocates for the wellbeing of women, who represent 60% of its customers and 70% of its employees (CENCOSUD n.d.-b). Another of CENCOSUD's main CSR initiatives is achieving energy efficiency through innovation and new technologies in its facilities in the five countries where it operates.

CENCOSUD's grocery store company in Peru, Wong, collects spare change from customers and donates to Caritas, a Roman Catholic charity that carries out programs for the poor. In Colombia, the conglomerate's leading company, the department store Jumbo, concentrates its CSR efforts in education, workplace inclusion, productive development, and environmental protection. The multilatina guides CSR multinational programs by following its core values and principles, as well as attending to the pressing needs of its host countries.

This chapter focuses on CSR programs in multinational organizations (MNOs), with an emphasis on balancing economic, social, and natural environments. The mechanics and illustrations of multisector partnering will be an important part of the chapter, because of the pressing challenges societies face worldwide when demanding collaboration among various economic, social, and political sectors of nations and localities.

Scope of CSR Across Borders

In today's global marketplace, corporations are members of the worldwide community rather than merely of the city, town, or state in which they are based. This change in the global scenario has made CSR all the more important. According to McDonald and Rundle-Thiele (2007), organizations have begun to invest millions in CSR initiatives, with end goals of refining their reputation and improving connections with organizational stakeholders and other organizations. Interest in CSR has been promoted by increased sensitivity to ethical issues among individuals and organizations.

There has been a change in the view of corporations by their enemies and ungrateful beneficiaries of their development initiatives, in response to efforts by change agents in managing the issues of human development and environmental sustainability, especially in developing countries (Bendell 2005; Visser 2007). CSR has come to be viewed as an opportunity and competitive advantage, with organizations basing their investment decisions on social responsibility and a clear focus on sustainability; in other words, there is a correlation among social, environmental, and financial performance. Ismail (2009) states that the real purpose of CSR is to provide a positive impact in communities – socially, environmentally, and economically.

Moir (2001, p. 18) defines CSR as "continuing commitment by business to behave ethically and contribute to economic development while improving the quality of workforce and their families as well as of the local community and society at large." A common theme of this definition and others is that business and society are not distinct, but interdependent.

CSR has been described as having three dimensions: economic, environmental, and social. According to Waddock and Bodwell (2004, p. 25), these dimensions help determine "the way in which a company's operating practices – policies, processes, and procedures – affects its stakeholders and the natural environment." Through their CSR initiatives, organizations are proving themselves valuable partners in delivering sustainable development.

Welford (2005) finds that other aspects of CSR include commitment to local community protection, protection of human rights in the company's operations, development of a code of ethics, and support for sustainable development. The role of MNCs in society has been understood as central, if not paramount, in achieving the economic, social, and environmental aspirations of governments and peoples worldwide. Therefore, CSR practices are essential, presenting an easy way for MNCs to use their corporate power as a catalyst for social intervention and change. This chapter will look at the pertinent issues taken up by MNCs, in collaboration with other public and civic organizations. The initiatives on common issues with partner organizations form an integrative approach to environmental, economic, and social goals as a collective vision for the community.

What are Multisector Partnerships?

The immense and complex educational, environmental, health, infrastructural, nutritional, agricultural, and social challenges faced by communities worldwide can no longer be limited to just one segment of society, to one sector, or to one region of the world. To take on these challenges, joint interventions of organizations and professionals from multiple sectors are required, leveraging their joint resources and expertise to accomplish common goals and make an impact on a much greater scale. The need for such strategic partnerships is not a new one. The United Nations Office for Partnerships (UNOPs) was founded as a clearinghouse for collaboration among the private sector, foundations, and UN agencies in 1998. UNOP "promotes new partnerships and alliances in furtherance of the Millennium Development Goals and provides support to new initiatives of the Secretary-General" (United Nations 2010, para. 1).

Multisector partnerships (MSPs) like UNOP started as an answer to the multitude of social issues that required government intervention. More specifically, Miller (2010, para. 1) states, for "development practitioners and nonprofit organizations looking to work in the burgeoning arena of food security, the private sector opens an alternative – and often quicker – avenue to success."

Increased insistence by the media and a more aware civil society have forced organizations to be more responsive and accountable to the communities they influence, engage with, and affect. Based on business requirements, organizations are exploring innovative opportunities to work closely with organizations from other sectors. Consequently, more and more organizations acknowledge the commitment to be good corporate citizens. Based on a comparison of corporate sales and country GDPs by the World Bank Institute, of the 100 largest economies in the world, 51 are corporations and only 49 are countries. The interests of development agencies and the expanding power of MNCs lead to added pressure on businesses to address the issues most relevant to their society. Also, public-sector development agencies have observed the challenges involved in effectively solving societal issues in a unilateral manner and are thus focusing on determining and prioritizing sectors where development challenges are intersecting with business opportunities and so form strategic alliance opportunities where partnerships can deliver substantial outcomes.

Challenges facing society are demanding the intervention and collaboration of business, government, nonprofit, and civic organizations. Interorganizations and MSPs combine resources and expertise to create synergy for social change. They are often commissioned to seek solutions to problems that impact partner organizations and broader society. CSR, philanthropy, strategic planning, and sustainability are often factors influencing this dynamic.

Because of the importance of MSPs for organizations and communities globally, this chapter aims to explore the typology and orientation of MSPs – or strategic public–private alliances among MNCs – headquartered in developed and emergent economies, and of governmental, nongovernmental, and multilateral organizations (i.e. UN agencies).

Average CSR programs by MNCs often address issues such as human rights, public health, the environment, education, and occupational health and safety. These are often areas which concern development agencies around the world, making this an ideal area for these agencies to engage with MNCs. The same goes for MNCs striving to be effective change catalysts in the community and hence organize multiple sectors to conduct programs and create partnerships for long-term mutual goals. This section of the chapter looks at how MNCs are adopting partnership strategies as a means of contributing to community development, building a mutually beneficial relationship with local communities, and reinventing themselves as a force for good in their home and host communities. Case studies have been reported to detail the benefits arising from MSPs primarily in developed countries. However, there is a need to document the growing role MSPs can play in emerging nations. The study of these best practices cannot be applied universally, and thus should be analyzed in a local context.

MSPs often call for a competent global and multicultural public relations strategist to assume an extended responsibility: to function as a clearinghouse of interorganizational communication processes beyond organizational boundaries. This view is consistent with the communitarian perspective of public relations. It suggests that in order to achieve broader solutions and improved quality of life, it is necessary to capture the experiences of community members, work together toward common goals, and facilitate participation by diverse groups (Hallahan 2004; Kruckeberg and Starck 1988; Martinez and Kiousis 2005; Starck and Kruckeberg 2001, 2003). Molleda (2001) states that public relations professionals are called to be agents of "social transformation" and part of the "social conscience" of an organization.

This chapter adopts the following definition from a global public relations perspective: MSPs are mutually beneficial strategic relationships between and among public institutions, private organizations, and nonprofit organizations that are based on a shared vision regarding objectives and the purpose of work.

The Process of Building MSPs

According to Austin (2000, p. 14), MSPs are difficult to build and maintain because members are "likely to have noticeably different performance measures, competitive dynamics, organizational cultures, decision-making styles, personnel competencies, professional languages, incentive and motivational structures, and emotional content." This requires that an MSP adopt a common set of goals and values.

There are three stages of collaboration in partnership building, which define the process: philanthropic, transactional, and integrative (Austin et al. 2004a). The **philanthropic stage** entails facilitating corporate donations to nonprofits. The **transactional stage** is characterized by a focus on activities between private and nonprofit organizations, with a significant two-way value exchange. Lastly, the **integrative stage** includes strategic alliances that involve a combination of missions, a synchronization of strategies, and a compatibility of values.

The partnering process has five main dimensions (Austin et al. 2004b). The first is **building cross-sector bridges** – identifying motivations to collaborate (i.e. altruism versus utilitarianism), overcoming barriers, searching for an interlocutor or spokesperson, capitalizing on pre-existing relations, acknowledging different institutional capabilities and organizational cultures, and valuing effective communications. The second dimension is **building alignment** – articulating a shared set of expectations, which each partner considers by analyzing how it fits into their organizational reality. Third is **value generation** for companies and communities through the combination of key resources. Fourth is **managing the relationship** – institutionalizing the partnership within member organizations and their stakeholders; this also entails promoting the role of internal and external communications and resources in order to build trust among partners. Finally, the fifth dimension, **growth and innovation**, consists in shared learning and knowledge to improve future interventions.

The Strategy Behind Participatory Communications

A multipronged approach is used to conceptualize strategic participatory communications for social change and development. Concepts from public relations and communications for development fields are combined. Smith (2005, p. 3) defines strategic communications as "intentional communication undertaken by a business or non-profit organization … It has a purpose and a plan … is based on research and subject to eventual evaluation."

Participatory communication involves the full participation of all partners in communications processes, giving them access to communications channels and enabling them to participate freely and equally in dialogue and debate. This concept can also be defined as participatory development communications, because of its close association with nation-building and social marketing initiatives. According to Molleda et al. (2008), regarding the media, participatory communications "no longer puts the emphasis on source and media, but on meaning and audiences." This new view of communications represents a clear departure from the modernity view, which emphasized asymmetrical communications and assumed a passive audience. Instead, it recognizes the need for a more inclusive and symmetrical communications approach that is also introspective and reflexive (Holström 2003; Holtzhausen 2000, 2002).

The notion of strategic communications is used in this chapter to refer to interorganizational communications efforts that target key audiences to achieve shared goals and objectives. Participatory communications provides members of a partnership with the communications mechanisms necessary to partake in the decision-making process. Therefore, MSPs, according to a strategic participatory communications perspective, are the product of effective research, introspection, transparency, interaction, and creativity.

The Role of a Strategic Participatory Communication Process in Facilitating the Dimensions of MSP

The role that strategic participatory communication plays in building and developing an MSP is crucial. Clear implications are important for the five dimensions of the partnering process. This process of multi-sector partnering would be more difficult without a systematic communications component that incorporates transparency, consistency, permanency, and openness. These are qualities that can be achieved as a result of the identification of common goals and interests and the acceptance of individual interests by the various partners. Emphasis on common mechanisms of communications, abiding policies and procedures, and trust in the leadership of the larger organizational partner leads to desired results.

The expected results encourage the use of strategic participatory communications at two distinct levels. First, emphasis on direct (i.e. interpersonal and group) communications is most valuable during the first three dimensions of the partnering process – building bridges, alignment, and generating value for each partner. Second, it seems controlled and mediated communications becomes essential as the partnership is established and begins operations. However, at both communications levels, an active involvement of the partners is necessary.

Strategic, participatory communications strategies are used by the MSP to build cross-sector bridges. Research efforts that aim to identify common needs, knowledge gaps, socialization of goals, and values and benefits for partners individually and collectively are representative of such strategies. Additionally, the use of multiple direct and mediated communications mechanisms (i.e. member correspondence, oral presentations, meetings, and open forums) to reach various members is an example of the strategic and participatory character of this dimension of MSP formation.

The very purpose of MSPs would prevent a powerful organization from taking center stage in the decision-making process. However, with a decentralized and participatory decision-making process, each of the partners is responsible for its own planning, with a leading organization playing a supportive and collaborative role.

Building Effective Relationships and Partnerships

At the beginning of the partnering process, there tends to be low involvement by various actors due to a lack of knowledge about the goals of the alliance (Molleda et al. 2008). Also, a lack of commitment by the actors threatens the effectiveness of the partnership initiation. Bridging the knowledge gap among partners requires time and consistent communication. Therefore, the strategy should entail gathering feedback from potential partners and using it to create a more inclusive strategic communications plan. Incorporating tactics like oral presentations and individual meetings involving each party is recommended.

Building partnerships also involves a great degree of strategy and participatory behavior on the part of the member organizations and their corresponding leaders. Emphasis in this dimension is mostly on exposing the different partners to their common and diverse needs. First-hand exposure to the issues facing the involved partners and communities will create a shared experience among the leadership, and a concerted effort will emerge.

Having collective meetings is an effective way of achieving a greater understanding of the motivations of each potential partner, addressing and overcoming obstacles for collaboration, taking advantage of pre-existing relationships, and encouraging select members to be active agents in the partnership. At meetings, leading organizations can be introduced as the headquarters for the MSP, and its communications director as the main spokesperson. Additionally, the first communications policies and norms can be clearly spelled out, and the differences among partners in terms of organizational culture and available resources can be openly discussed as an advantage rather than a barrier.

Partners are encouraged to share the contents of individual and collective meetings with their top administrators. Partners are also asked to assess the level of compatibility between the goals of the MSP and those of their organizations. Interpersonal communications is essential to keeping directors informed about the internal discussions of each partner. Also, leading partners should visit one another to facilitate discussions about the overall goal of the proposed MSP and to develop strategies to maximize the return on their effort.

Generating Value in Collaborations

Value generation relies on strategic, participatory communications in the form of "non-binding" agreements to institutionalize individual and aggregate benefits from the MSP. Generation of value for all parties culminates with the collaborative effort to create an MSP's visual identity, depicting their mutual goals and benefits. The process should be transparent, open, and inclusive.

To generate value in the partnership, the leading partners and the communications director of the MSP can host a meeting to announce the official installation of the partnership. Symbolic, non-binding agreements can be prepared and signed by each partner. Leading partners and representatives of each organization involved should also highlight the benefits they expect from the collaborative effort. A special event should be hosted, video-recorded, and distributed among the partners. Subsequently, the partners should agree to develop a visualization to identify the MSP. For example, a graphic designer could help in capturing the essence of the MSP. Members are usually convinced that being part of a solid interorganizational body requires a clear visual identity, which brings added value to their resource investment and participation.

Managing Relationships

Perhaps the dimension that requires most participation is managing relationships between partners. Interpersonal, group, and mediated communications tactics can be utilized to manage the relationships for the early stages of the enterprise. Despite the heavy reliance on public relations outputs to inform members and the community as a whole about MSP activities, much energy must be invested into meetings, discussions, and workshops to ensure that two-way communication exists between the communities and the partners.

A larger component of the communications plan should be devoted to managing relationships. The partners, including representatives of each organization and of community groups, should provide input for the planning and production of communications strategies and tactics. The approval of communications materials, such as news kits and online newsletters, may be cumbersome. However, it is possible to achieve the active involvement of all partners with strategic, participatory communications effort.

Consistency of message and action by the communications director and leading partners encourages members to trust the communications process. Additionally, assurances by leading partners and the communications director, coupled with tangible outcomes resulting from the strategic and participatory communications process, aid in galvanizing support among the remaining partners for the communications policies and procedures outlined in the plan.

The leading partners, communications director, and team must keep full records of the MSP and its communications outputs and outcomes (e.g. qualitative and quantitative research). These should be available to all partners for review. The leading organization serves as the repository for the documents and communications materials used during the building stages of the MSP.

Growth and Innovation

Finally, growth and innovation are also incorporated through an informed, targeted, and deliberative process. The information gathered, strategies and tactics developed, critical communications policies implemented, and plans put in place are disseminated to all partners. Meetings, workshops, websites, social media activities, and newsletters, among other tactics, serve to open the communications process for all.

In summary, the interlocking of organizational missions, strategy synchronization, and value compatibility is achieved as a key component of the integrative stage of the collaboration continuum.

A greater understanding of the roles that strategic participatory communications play in MSP formation enriches global public relations practice. The typology of indicators as predictors of success or effectiveness must be validated and tested in various contexts and situations, and for various types of MSP in multinational environments.

Factors Impacting the Development, Implementation, and Evaluation of MSP Communications Policies and Plans

In MSP communications, the factors that have the greatest effect on the development stages are member agenda and characteristics, partnership communications, and environmental threats.

Member Agenda and Characteristics

Members bring unique individual/organizational agendas to the partnership. Viewpoints may vary based on the organization or leader's sector, socioeconomic level, and geographic location within the scope of the partnership. Unique interests on the part of some organizations may serve both as a catalyst for the formation and a challenge to the maintenance of the MSP.

Partnership Communications

Strategic and participatory communications is used to ensure equal participation and integration of all parties in the building and maintenance of the partnership. Participative communications strategies can turn the community as a whole into the protagonist in this process, rather than giving center stage to other members, such as government officials or the business community. Threats to the partnership are avoided through clear, collaborative, and transparent communications processes. By providing a collaborative decision-making process, a strategic impasse can be trumped – the partnership is then perceived as a supra-organizational entity, greater than the issues and needs of any individual organization. A heightened level of co-responsibility also results from the communicative process, encouraging main players to transcend local laws and engage with issues and problems in conjunction as a team.

The visual identity design is also symbolic of the collaborative nature of partnership communications. Most partners are likely to attribute the success of the logo, the design, and other visual identity materials to the transparency of the communications process. The design should capture the priorities set for the partnership, without linking these to any particular organizational members.

The idea of a shared vision is another element that is considered by participants as a centerpiece of the success of a partnership. The diffusion of the plan, its strategies, and desired outcomes – as elaborated within a framework of the entire partnership – provides participants with a shared vision and language that allows communications about the initiative as one that is owned by all partners. However, institutional pride and agendas often get in the way of further developing the partnership. While participants may fear losing control of their resources, transparency and inclusiveness make it possible to see the benefit of putting aside individual organizational pride and culture in favor of common goals.

Environmental Threats

Environmental factors that may threaten a forming partnership during the early and mid stages are cultural and socioeconomic differences among members, a lack of previous experience with partnership building, and the supremacy of one member over the others.

Making Inferences from Real-World International MSPs

The authors of this textbook conducted a study of international MSPs. We used CSR reports as a way to benchmark various approaches to partnerships for MNCs. Organizational websites were evaluated for all CSR-related information. The CSR reports were studied in order to get a better understanding of the MNCs' approaches to working with development agencies internationally.

Our study selected leading oil and gas companies from five countries from the Fortune Global 500 List of 2011 as a representative sample of global organizations. The selection of countries was based on the 2011 rankings of the world's largest economies by World Economy Watch. We therefore looked at companies from the United States and the four BRIC (Brazil, Russia, India, and China) nations.

The Fortune List was sorted according to country and then by industry type. Each oil and gas company that was second from top-ranked (i.e. Chevron, CNPC, Lukoil, Petrobras, and Reliance) was included in the study. As cited in Onishi (2002), the importance of MSPs in the oil industry has been highlighted by David O'Reilly, chief executive of Chevron, who feels that although the oil companies understand their social responsibilities, the needs of home and host communities are growing and, hence, difficult to satisfy. Health, safety, and environmental issues have risen in the oil and gas industry's agenda, reflecting both increased public pressure and more complex operational challenges.

The analysis of the selected organizations revealed that MNCs are increasing their collaboration with a range of partners on a variety of issues and problems faced by the communities in which they operate.

Their CSR reports showcase the kind of work they undertake to make a difference to the world. The main aim of this analysis was to develop a typology of MSPs in order to apprehend how organizations share roles, responsibilities, and accountabilities. In order to develop the typology, the locations, partners, common issues, and modes of practice were classified for each organization.

The results show that the different types of partners ranged from government agencies to nongovernmental organizations (NGOs), community-based organizations, business entities, and academic research institutes.

Prominent Issues

The issues tackled by the organizations were diverse, including health, environment, education, charity, children, disability, support of the arts, sports, infrastructure development, women's empowerment, and poverty and disaster relief.

The most common themes (partner organizations, issues addressed, partnership location, and forms or resources) were combined to come up with coherent propositions. The most prominent categories were classified as the three Ps of strategic partnerships: problem-based, priority-based, and project-based. These three Ps define how MSPs are built and how partners work together for a common purpose and mutual benefit.

The **problem-based** category highlights partnerships that are formed based on specific problems in the community. These problems can be influenced by political, social, economic, or environmental factors. Examples include poverty alleviation, women's empowerment, public health concerns, the environment, and infrastructure development, among many others. For example, Chevron started an Alternative Livelihood program in partnership with an NGO to assist families in Bangladesh with training and assets to start new businesses. Chevron's partnerships with local nonprofits and NGOs, as well as its donations in various countries (e.g. Brazil, Kazakhstan, United States, and Vietnam), have provided business development assistance, construction skills training, management and professional training, and job placement to women.

Chevron's University Partnership Programs provides learning centers at underserved primary schools in Angola, Brazil, Nigeria, South Africa, and Venezuela. CNPC has established partnerships with primary and middle schools in numerous regions across China and sent trained teachers to demonstrate advanced teaching methods or provide training to local teachers, making great efforts to support education in those regions.

Challenges such as public health are prevalent in rural areas in India, which is why Chevron established an Early Intervention and Rehabilitation Center in partnership with a local NGO, to support mentally challenged children. Chevron's partnership with the Global Fund to Fight AIDS,

Tuberculosis, and Malaria has helped improve the health and wellbeing of millions of people in Africa and Asia.

The **priority-based** category refers to partnerships founded on time- and need-based priorities, which might plague any country at any time. These include issues such as natural disasters and the spread of epidemics. For example, Chevron partnered with the Angola Ministry of Health and the United Nations International Children's Education Fund (UNICEF) to address the needs of people in regions damaged by war and to provide vaccinations against wild poliovirus. Similarly, the Chinese CNPC has come forward to provide relief and aid in times of disaster both locally and globally. During calamities such as the Wenchuan and Yushu earthquakes and flood disaster, CNPC works to safeguard the supply of oil products for disaster relief and participates in rescue efforts. In November 2010, central Venezuela was hit by a severe flood, affecting around 500 000 people directly or indirectly. CNPC partnered with the Venezuelan government to organize disaster relief efforts and provide help and support in a variety of other ways. Local tie-ups with NGOs have helped Reliance adopt state highways in India in order to provide relief services during emergencies. Chevron's partnership with the Global Fund to Fight AIDS, Tuberculosis, and Malaria also belongs under this category.

Finally, partnerships in the **project-based** category are collaborations that happen on a project-by-project basis and utilize the capacity, resources, or expertise of one or all of the partners. Examples include marine biodiversity, providing books to schoolchildren, and building libraries, hospitals, and other infrastructure – all of which could be a major contribution to the involved community. A great example is Chevron's innovative model of MSPs, which established a US$50 million fund to support a foundation in the Niger Delta over a five-year period from 2010 to 2014. The goal of the project was to achieve a 1:1 match with donor partner funding, resulting in a project portfolio of US$100 million. The resources were utilized to focus on economic development, capacity-building, peace-building, analysis, and advocacy.

Reliance's partnerships with State Government AIDS Control Society and Primary Health Centers at several rural locations across India have helped launch an Integrated Counseling and Testing Center for HIV/AIDS and monitor the health of the increasing number of migrant workers in the regions. Reliance has collaborated on new projects with several agricultural institutes to help farmers increase their agricultural yields and grow high-quality produce for export business. For example, as a part of the Chinese government's Eight-Seven National Poverty Reduction Project, CNPC was assigned to assist 11 counties in the Xinjiang province. In 2010 alone, CNPC spent RMB12.36 million in eight poverty-alleviation programs and provided natural gas to Xinjiang, focusing on local infrastructure-building.

These themes represent how MNCs and other partners are actively pooling their resources and competencies to build synergies, scale-up projects, and reach out to more beneficiaries. This participative approach is increasing the impact of their initiatives on the lives of ordinary people.

Methods of Commitment and Engagement by MNCs

The most common forms of commitment shown by these MNCs were through philanthropy, funds, and sponsorship in the partnership. Philanthropic foundations, for example, were used by every MNC to support a number of causes. Another common form of commitment was volunteerism by employees, as reported by the Indian MNC.

In general, the results of this analysis brought out the possibilities and positive, far-reaching changes strategic MSPs can bring to home and host communities. The forms of private- and public-sector engagements the study explored have the potential to contribute to myriad problems and public concerns. These MSPs can bring together core competencies in a fundamental and long-term manner and tackle issues innovatively and efficiently.

The results define the rationale behind such partnerships amid the rapid changes in the world economy, which pose too great a challenge for one single sector to tackle. Additionally, the ideal situation for MNCs is to be a change catalyst and coordinate multiple sectors to assess, conduct programs, and create partnerships for long-term community change. The evaluation looked at how MNCs are adopting partnership strategies as a means of contributing to community development, building a mutually beneficial relationship with local communities, and reinventing themselves as a force for good in their home and host communities. The analysis identified emerging themes and relevant issues that can influence the genesis and development of partnerships.

We found that typical programs by MNCs often address issues such as public health, environment, education, infrastructure development, and poverty and disaster relief. These are often areas that concern development agencies, so such agencies might view these types of programs as potential opportunities to engage with MNCs over mutual goals. One of the reasons for this could be the growing attention given to particular issues around the world. As a part of the Millennium Development Goals, the United Nations provided a roadmap outlining what was needed to meet the goals by the agreed deadline of 2015. The goals documented empowering women and girls, promoting sustainable development, and protecting the most vulnerable from the devastating effects of multiple crises, such as conflict, natural disaster, and volatility in the prices of food and energy. Health, education, and the environment were also a focus.

As mentioned earlier, the three common types of partnership encompass a variety of measures whereby organizations pool their resources with governmental, intergovernmental, and civil-society organizations.

Ideologies

As already discussed, the common problems identified by the United Nations relate to the issues and programs of the selected MNCs. The US Chevron believes business and society are interdependent, and its partnership initiatives are geared toward providing health, education, and economic development to the communities prevalent in the regions where it operates. The Indian Reliance believes in engaging in strategic long-term partnerships with several NGOs and trusts across the country, based on a thorough evaluation of their work and its potential for positive impact on communities. The Brazilian Petrobras believes social investments have a positive impact on its business, enabling permanent, qualified, and dynamic interactions between the company and society capable of creating links that produce long-term shared value. Its work in the social area consolidates a proposal that, in addition to transferring financial resources, drives and strengthens the social leadership role of the communities involved. The Chinese CNPC has always stayed committed to social progress and improving local socioeconomic development. At Russian Lukoil, social and charity programs are inherent to the company's corporate strategy and help promote constructive cooperation with governmental authorities, the business community, and the public.

Partners and Locations of Partnerships

The results show that the actual combination of partners in an MSP will depend on the objectives of the partnership. The main partner categories are private enterprise, public sector, and civil society. The role of each partner, its contribution, and its reasons for joining the partnership vary depending on the problem, project, or priority. For example, a private enterprise might join a partnership because it is a good corporate citizen and wants to enhance its social legitimacy and, ultimately, its corporate reputation. The public sector has to ensure a sustainable framework for economic, political, and social development, and needs partnerships with MNCs to achieve its goals. Civil society may have interests in areas like social cohesion, environmental protection, and human rights, which can be improved by the large resources of an MSP in terms of expertise, technology, and financial capital. The members involved in an MSP are usually public institutions, private organizations, and non-profit organizations. In this context, where different sectors of society are voluntarily working together, having a **common vision** and **common purpose** is necessary to address a specific societal or communitarian need.

The locations of the MSPs were also seen to vary according to the partnership objective and the countries of operation. For example, Chevron has strategic partnerships with various communities as investments in the long-term success of the company's business; these strategic partnerships are prevalent in the regions where Chevron operates. Internationally, it focuses its involvement in the locations of its strategic operations, including Indonesia, Western Australia, Kazakhstan, Thailand, Brazil, and the United Kingdom. Similarly, Lukoil implements its strategic charity and social investment programs in such a way that there is always a link between social problems and the MNC's strategic goals and operations worldwide. Organizations have made CSR an intrinsic component of their overall business strategy, along with other functions like marketing, branding, research and development, talent management, and operations.

Based out of the necessity to find innovative ways to meet business needs, the private sector is discovering that partnering with organizations from other sectors opens up an infinite number of opportunities for collaboration and growth. The common areas in which partners collaborate are summarized as the three Ps, as already mentioned. The modes used in the partnerships differed depending on the projects undertaken and the country of origin. For instance, volunteering by employees was mentioned only by the Indian MNC. The differences in CSR modes between countries – philanthropy, sponsorship, volunteering, etc. – could be due to cultural attributes such as inherent modesty in Asian cultures, which works against touting one's success in activities such as CSR. Therefore, some activities may not be as readily discerned by outside observers. Also, the voluntary social activities on which companies report and the emphasis on presenting a socially responsible image vary significantly based on the country in which a business is based.

Foundations were the most used mode by the MNCs studied. Foundations help organizations team up with partners and work with them on world problems. The support shown by organizations when they build foundations is not limited to donations and charity. It can come in the form of resources, technology, or even the ability to influence decisions. MNCs can help the public sector improve the effectiveness of government through practical ideas. MNCs can also make contributions to help define the likely trajectory of development in developing countries. The organizational foundations are typically aligned to the organizational mission and vision or the economic issues that the country is facing. Given the importance of setting up foundations, the case study looks at the Tata Foundation and how it is advancing the culture and traditions of Indian philanthropy.

Case Study   The Tata Foundation – A Look at a Tradition of Corporate Social Responsibility

The Tata Group: Background

In 1868, 29-year-old Indian visionary, Jamsetji Nusserwanji Tata, pioneered industrialization and modernization of the East by founding a trading company in Bombay (now Mumbai), India (Tata Group 2014a). From various trips to England, it became apparent to Tata that the Industrial Revolution, which had thrust other countries on to the global market-place, had circumvented India, especially in the textile and steel industries (Tata Group 2014a). Thus, in 1869, the first venture of what would become a giant of global trade was born.

Today, Tata Group is a global competitor in over 80 countries in a range of sectors, including automobiles, steel, chemicals, hospitality management, software, and consulting (*Economist* 2011). Tata's origins gave way to the realization of a modernization of the East, and Tata Group is at the forefront of that modernization. Tata Consultancy Services is the largest software corporation in Asia (*Economic Times* 2013). Tata Steel has risen to number 11 on the list of the top steel-producing companies throughout the world (World Steel Association n.d.). Tata Global Beverages has become the second-largest producer of branded tea in the world (*Economist* 2011). These are just a few of the accolades Tata Group boasts.

Establishing the Tata Foundation

As a second-generation businessman coming from a long line of priests, Tata recognized the need to bring higher standards for worker welfare to a country plagued by poverty and foreign occupation (Tata Group 2014a). It was Tata's idea that for India to overcome the oppression of poverty and occupation by foreign forces, Indians must harness a foundation of schol-ars for the country to stand upon. The JN Tata Endowment was raised in 1892 to enable Indian students of all socioeconomic statuses to pursue higher education in England. Within just 32 years, 40% of the Indians going into the Indian Civil Service were Tata scholars (Tata Group 2014a). Jamsetji Tata passed down an idea from his forefathers:

> There is one kind of charity common among us. It is that patchwork philanthropy which clothes the ragged, feeds the poor, and heals the sick … What advances a nation or a community is not so much to prop up its weakest and most helpless members, but to lift up the best and most gifted, so as to make them of the greatest service to this country. (Tata Group 2014d, para. 8)

Today, the Tata Trusts, growing from the philanthropic sentiment of their original foundation, are avenues for the founder and his sons to bequeath large portions of their personal wealth to promote the advancement of the more than 1.2 billion people who call India home (Philanthropy Age 2014). The trusts control 66% of the shares of Tata Sons, the company in control of the Tata Group (Tata Group 2014d).

The Sir Dorabji Tata Trust and Allied Trusts (SDTT) allocate funds to natural resource management, urban poverty, education, health, civil society, governance and human rights, media, art, and culture. The Allied Trusts include nine other Tata Trusts bequeathed by members of the Tata family, including the original JN Tata Endowment, which provides educational opportunities outside of India (Tata Group 2014d).

The Tata Group is devoted to promoting the value of leadership, global communications, and trust. By returning earnings to the communities in which Tata Group operates, a great deal of trust is generated among internal and external publics, such as employees, shareholders, consumers, and community members (Tata Group 2014e). Tata is committed to five core values, which drive day-to-day activities: integrity, understanding, excellence, unity, and responsibility. Tata Group is committed to transparency and honesty, which are their first line of defense against negative public attention. Employees of the corporation are shown respect and compassion so that they can achieve the highest possible quality and thus keep up the standards of the goods and services provided (Tata Group 2014e). Tata Group is very interested in coordinating not only with members of the conglomeration, but with partners around the world to promote strong relationships standing on foundations of tolerance and understanding.

Tata Group will always uphold its sensitivity to the countries and environments in which each sector works, so that it can "always ensure what comes from the people goes back to the people many times over" (Tata Group 2014e). According to Ratan Tata, Tata Group still places CSR among its top priorities, spending 4% of its net profits annually on CSR activities. Another US$800 million was disbursed on similar activities from the two largest trusts during Ratan Tata's 20 years as chairman of the group and trusts (Philanthropy Age 2014).

The 2011 Hunger and Malnutrition survey found that 42% of children in India under the age of five were underweight and 59% were "stunted," or chronically malnourished. The prevalence of underweight children in India was double that in sub-Saharan Africa (Philanthropy Age 2014). Britain's Save the Children found that 42% of the Indian population was impoverished – estimated at one-third of the world's poor (Parliament of UK Session 2011).

According to Tata, the Indian population grows by 17 million each year. Given the increasing infirmity of the upcoming generations, the cost of healthcare will soon become an unmanageable problem for the country (Philanthropy Age 2014). Philanthropy among the younger generations must be embedded in order to lift up the impoverished and infirm. Tata Group and the allied trusts together face a country that does not share their values and vision.

Tata Trust in the Face of Global Public Relations

The Tata Group culture has been molded for generations to reflect core values of returning wealth to society and being innovators in business ethics worldwide (Tata Group 2014c). The Tata Trusts have grown an aura of trust and respect around all of their subsectors, which are situated in countries worldwide. One trust in particular, the JN Tata Endowment, was set up in 1892 by the founder of Tata Group, Jamsetji Tata, and is dedicated to offering educational opportunities to Indian students at top universities around the world (Tata Group 2014b). The endowment is described as a series of loan scholarships offered to about 120 scholars in the amount of Rs. 60 000–4 000 000 (Sir Dorabji Tata Trust 2014; Tata Group 2014b). A loan scholarship is awarded to students based on the stipulation that they fulfill an obligation to the granter (College Foundation Inc. 2014). In the case of the JN Tata Endowment, the condition of scholarship stipulates that students agree to participate in courses relevant to the country, which must be short-term training programs or part of a full-fledged master's or doctoral program (Sir Dorabji Tata Trust 2014). The loan scholarship amount is dependent upon the purpose of the study and the qualifications of the scholar, and does not cover the full cost of studies (Sir Dorabji Tata Trust 2014).

Although the scholarship does not discriminate based on caste, creed, gender, or socioeconomic status, the scholarship fund requires students to be under 45 years of age and be of Indian nationality (Sir Dorabji Tata Trust 2014). Additionally, they must be graduates from a recognized Indian university with good academic standing (Sir Dorabji Tata Trust 2014). Students may apply to the scholarship only once, at the beginning of the course of study (Sir Dorabji Tata Trust 2014).

The loan scholarship provides an opportunity for Indian students to gain a greater understanding of their studies in foreign countries, so that they can bring knowledge back to India to be used for the greater good. The students will contribute to the workforce and economy of India upon their return.

Currently, the JN Tata Endowment scholarship programs are not communicated specifically through any forms of social media. Of the top

15 social media sites, the Tata Group and its conglomerates are mentioned or have a professional page on only eight: Twitter, LinkedIn, Google+, Tumblr, Pinterest, Instagram, Flickr, and Meetup (Ebiz 2014). However, only Twitter mentions Tata Foundation scholarships. More specifically, the Tata Group official Twitter account under the handle @TataCompanies mentions the application process and provides a link to information about the JN Tata Endowment scholarship program. This post received only one retweet and one favorite from the more than 140 000 followers the Tata Group boasts on Twitter.

The JN Tata Endowment is not mentioned on Facebook, one of the largest social networking sites, which attracts users within the age range of the requirements for application to the scholarship program. The expansiveness of membership of such a massive social networking site could prove to be a very worthwhile channel for the JN Tata Endowment scholarship program to communicate to publics in its target demographic.

Another large social networking site that does not mention the JN Tata Endowment scholarship program is VK, a European-based social network-ing site boasting more than 100 million users. Like Facebook, VK allows users to share photos and videos, connect with people locally and inter-nationally, and listen to music and play games. The JN Tata Endowment scholarship program seeks to send students of Indian nationality to coun-tries abroad, especially in Europe, to pursue higher-education study. VK presents a unique opportunity for the Tata Foundation to connect with users in areas relevant to the program. The foundation could provide rel-evant materials for students in Europe so that they can learn more about the opportunities available through the program. The myriad channels available on VK alone would allow the Tata Foundation to share photos, videos, documents, and links to the scholarship program website.

In addition to social media, the JN Tata Endowment does have a pres-ence on various websites linked to students seeking scholarships, includ-ing but not limited to scholarshipneeds.com, topuniversities.com, scholarshipportal.eu, and nesoindia.org. These websites are hosted in the United States, Canada, India, the United Kingdom, and other European countries. However, a student would have to be aware of the scholarship program in order to use a search engine to find one of these websites, which would then lead the student to the official website of the Tata Group. Although the mention of the scholarship program on these sites may prove helpful for informational purposes, a trail of websites is hardly ideal for such an advanced corporation.

On October 3, 2014, author P.R. Sanjai wrote an article on the tradition of philanthropy and scholarship represented by the Tata Group, and more specifically the J.N. Tata Endowment: "Jamsetji Tata was considered on a par with the UK's Joseph Rowntree and Scottish American industrialist Andrew Carnegie in pioneering the concept of building wealth for the public good" (LiveMint 2014, para. 15). His article touches on the history of the J.N. Tata Endowment and how it affects Indian society, but does not show the ramifications of the scholarship fund in the global sector. The Tata Foundation could use authors such as Sanjai to show how the scholarship program promotes relationships internationally.

Discussion Questions

1 What is corporate social responsibility (CSR)? Why must companies implement CSR in their business model today?

2 What attributes and values are necessary for successful multisector partnerships (MSPs)?

3 How has participatory communication shifted from the modernity view? Why did participatory communication evolve?

4 Provide an example of each of the five dimensions of an MSP. How would an MSP implement the five dimensions in its strategy?

5 What factors most impact the development stages in MSPs, and how?

6 Define the three Ps of strategic partnership and provide an example of each.

7 Through the Tata Foundation's scholarship endeavors, what types of publics are affected by the exchange of knowledge coming from studies abroad?

8 How can a brand create a culture of trust and CSR through the use of national scholarships?

9 How do the scholarship programs offered by the Tata Trusts impact the public's perception of the brand?

10 What steps could the Tata Group take to improve the relationship of its stakeholders with other global corporations?

11 What can the Tata Group improve upon when it comes to getting the word out about its scholarship program?

12 Which social media sites do you deem to be most potentially beneficial to the Tata Foundation in regard to disseminating information about the scholarship program and its application process? Could the process be interactive?

Class Activity

An imaginary company wants to implement MSPs on a global scale in order to improve its CSR. It wants to find three NGOs to partner with. Students should write a report on planning, developing, and implementing the partnership, incorporating the dimensions and stages discussed in this chapter, including the three Ps of strategic partnership.

References

Austin, J., Reficco, E., and SEKN Research Team (2004a). The key collaboration questions. In: *Social Partnering in Latin America; Lessons Drawn from Collaborations of Businesses and Civic Society Organizations* (ed. J. Austin, E. Reficco, G. Berger, et al.) the Social Enterprise Knowledge Networks (SEKN) Team, 3–28. Cambridge, MA: Harvard University Press.

Austin, J., Reficco, E., and SEKN Research Team (2004b). Building cross-sector bridges. In: *Social Partnering in Latin America; Lessons Drawn from Collaborations of Businesses and Civic Society Organizations* (ed. J. Austin, E. Reficco, G. Berger, et al.) the Social Enterprise Knowledge Networks (SEKN) Team, 29–74. Cambridge, MA: Harvard University Press.

Austin, J.E. (2000). *The Collaboration Challenge: How Nonprofits and Businesses Succeed Through Strategic Alliances.* San Francisco, CA: Jossey-Bass Publishers.

Bendell, J. (2005). In whose name? The accountability of corporate social responsibility. *Development in Practice* 15 (3,4): 362–374.

CENCOSUD. (n.d.-a). "Nuestra misión." Retrieved from: https://www. cencosud.com/nuestra-mision/cencosud/2016-01-19/180703.html.

CENCOSUD. (n.d.-b). "Responsabilidad social empresarial." Retrieved from: https://www.cencosud.com/cencosud/site/tax/port/all/taxport_3___1. html.

College Foundation Inc. (2014). "Scholarships-loans defined" Retrieved January 10, 2019 from https://www.cfnc.org/paying/schol/schols_loans_defined.html.

Ebiz. (2014). "Top 15 most popular social networking sites." Retrieved January 10, 2019 from http://www.ebizmba.com/articles/social-networking-websites.

Economic Times. (2013). "Tata Consultancy Services Ltd." Retrieved January 10, 2019 from http://economictimes.indiatimes.com/tata-consultancy-services-ltd/infocompanyhistory/companyid-8345.cms.

Economist. (2011). "Out of India." Retrieved January 10, 2019 from http://www.economist.com/node/18285497.

Hallahan, K. (2004). 'Community' as a foundation for public relations theory and practice. *Communication Yearbook* 28: 233–279.

Holström, S. (2003). "The reflective paradigm of organizational legitimation." Paper presented at the conference Legitimacy in a Changing World, September 27–30, 2007. Roskilde University/Lund University.

Holtzhausen, D. (2000). Postmodern values in public relations. *Journal of Public Relations Research* 12 (1): 93–114.

Holtzhausen, D.R. (2002). Towards a postmodern research agenda for public relations. *Public Relations Review* 28: 251–264.

Ismail, M. (2009). Corporate social responsibility and its role in community development and international perspective. *The Journal of International Social Research* 2. Retrieved January 10, 2019 from http://www.sosyalarastirmalar.com/cilt2/sayi9pdf/ismail_maimunah.pdf.

Kruckeberg, D. and Starck, K. (1988). *Public Relations and Community: A Reconstructed Theory*. New York: Praeger.

LiveMint. (2014). "Philanthropy in India, an age-old tradition." Retrieved January 10, 2019 from http://www.livemint.com/Specials/91k22CWjd0CU36or3ezHoN/Philanthropy-in-India-an-ageold-tradition.html.

McDonald, L.M. and Rundle-Thiele, S. (2007). Corporate social responsibility and bank customer satisfaction. *International Journal of Bank Marketing* 26 (3): 170–182.

Martinez, B. and Kiousis, K. (2005). A theoretical approach for developing effective public relations media strategies: Empowering citizens in emerging democracies. *Studier I Politisk Kommunication [Political Communication Studies]* 3: 4–20.

Miller, J. (2010). "Private sector emerges as key partner in food aid." Devex. Retrieved January 10, 2019 from http://www.devex.com/en/news/private-sector-emerges-as-key-partner-in-food-aid/70759.

Moir, L. (2001). What do we mean by corporate social responsibility? *Corporate Governance* 1 (2): 16–22.

Molleda, J.C., Martinez, B., and Suarez, A.M. (2008). Building multi-sector partnerships for progress with strategic, participatory communication: A case study from Colombia. *Anagramas* 6 (12): 105–125.

Molleda, J.C. (2001). International paradigms: The Latin American school of public relations. *Journalism Studies* 2 (4): 513–530.

Onishi, N. (2002). "Left behind; As oil riches flow, poor village cries out." The *New York Times*, December 22. Retrieved January 10, 2019 from https://www.nytimes.com/2002/12/22/world/left-behind-as-oil-riches-flow-poor-village-cries-out.html.

Parliament of UK Session. (2011). "The future of DFID's programme in India." Retrieved January 10, 2019 from http://www.publications. parliament.uk/pa/cm201011/cmselect/cmintdev/writev/616/m15.htm.

Philanthropy Age. (2014). "Ratan Tata: India's icon." Retrieved January 10, 2019 from http://www.philanthropyage.org/2014/02/06/indias-icon/

Smith, R.D. (2005). *Strategic Planning for Public Relations*, 2e. Mahwah, NJ: Lawrence Earlbaum Associates.

Starck, K. and Kruckeberg, D. (2003). Ethical obligations of public relations in an era of globalisation. *Journal of Communication Management* 8 (1): 29–40.

Starck, K. and Kruckeberg, D. (2001). Public relations and community: A reconstructed theory revised. In: *Handbook of Public Relations* (ed. R.L. Heath and G. Vasquez), 51–59. Thousand Oaks, CA: Sage.

Sir Dorabji Tata Trust. (2014). "J. N. Tata endowment for the higher education of Indians." Retrieved January 10, 2019 from http://www. jntataendowment.org/.

Tata Group. (2014a). "The giant who touched tomorrow." Retrieved January 10, 2019 from http://www.tata.com/aboutus/articlesinside/ AapOEYsYNwI=/TLYVr3YPkMU=.

Tata Group. (2014b). "JN Tata endowment." Retrieved January 10, 2019 from http://www.tata.com/aboutus/articlesinside/ JN-Tata-Endowment.

Tata Group. (2014c). "Tata group profile." Retrieved January 10, 2019 from http://www.tata.com/aboutus/sub_index/Leadership-with-trust.

Tata Group. (2014d). "A tradition of trust." Retrieved January 10, 2019 from http://www.tata.com/aboutus/articlesinside/A-tradition-of-trust.

Tata Group. (2014e). "Values and purpose." Retrieved January 10, 2019 from http://www.tata.com/aboutus/articlesinside/Values-and-purpose.

United Nations. (2010). "About the UN." Retrieved January 10, 2019 from http://www.un.org/en/about-un/index.html.

Visser, W. (2007). Corporate social responsibility in developing countries. In: *Oxford Handbook of Corporate Social Responsibility*, vol. 11, 473–499. Oxford: Oxford University Press.

Waddock, S. and Bodwell, C. (2004). Managing responsibility: What can be learned from the quality movement. *California Management Review* 47 (1): 25–37.

Welford, R. (2005). Corporate social responsibility in Europe, North America and Asia. *Journal of Corporate Citizenship* 17: 33–52.

World Steel Association. (n.d.). "Top steel-producing companies 2017." Retrieved January 10, 2019 from https://www.worldsteel.org/steel-by-topic/statistics/top-producers.html.

10

Employee Communication and Global Teams

Central Themes

- Employee communications, internal communications, and organizational communications all refer to the relationships and interactions within an organization.
- Three types of communications patterns are found in employee communications: vertical, horizontal, and diagonal.
- Trust, two-way engagement, and respect can help form and maintain effective employee communications.
- For successful employee communications, employees need to be engaged and feel a sense of belonging in the organization, in order to put valuable time and effort into their work.
- Globalization and advancements in technology have positively affected global teams' effectiveness and success.
- Cultural differences, language barriers, and low employee engagement are some of the challenges global teams inevitably face.
- Virtual communications tremendously improved how global teams work, making it easier to communicate and be time efficient

  Keywords   *virtual teams; leading office; virtual communications; cultural differences; employee communications; globalization; social distance*

Introduction

In general, organizations in the world have teams spread across multiple locations. With advancements in technology, businesses are now able to communicate with each team on a global scale in easy and cost-effective ways. What once would have required a plane ride can now be done over a video conference call. However, the technology is worthless if an organization's employees are not sufficiently trained and motivated to

Global and Multicultural Public Relations, First Edition. Juan-Carlos Molleda and Sarab Kochhar.
© 2019 John Wiley & Sons, Inc. Published 2019 by John Wiley & Sons, Inc.

communicate in an effective manner. In global teams, employee communications is crucial to advancing an organization's goals.

What Is Employee Communications?

Employee communications (or internal or organizational communications) refers to communications activities or interactions that take place inside of an organization and among organization members (Berger 2008). Employee communications are viewed as an indicator of management's ability to nurture relationships with various internal stakeholders (Welch and Jackson 2007).

Three types of communications patterns are found in employee communications: vertical, horizontal, and diagonal. **Vertical communications** usually takes place between supervisors and their subordinates. **Horizontal communications** happens among individuals who do not have any hierarchical relationships, normally same-level workers in different departments. **Diagonal communications** happens across both function and level, such as interactions between supervisors and employees from different departments (Williams pers. comm.).

Overall, excellent communication is about much more than disseminating information. Built on trust and respect, effective employee communications are multifaceted, two-way communications that strive for employee engagement (Tomasco 2017).

A poll conducted in the United States and United Kingdom shows that more than 80% of employees would take the quality of internal communications into account when thinking about staying in or leaving a position; almost 33% of respondents stated communications in the organization were a key influencer affecting their willingness to work for a company (Burton 2006). Companies recognize the importance of employee communications. Research demonstrates that companies with engaged employees are 50% more efficient than those that are not successful in engaging employees (Izzo and Withers 2000). Furthermore, the amount of time the top 200 "most admired" companies devote to employee communications is triple that for the 200 "least admired" (Seitel 2004).

Employee Engagement as the Biggest Challenge in Business

Establishing effective communications methods among employees is crucial in any organization as a way of maintaining employee engagement, a concept often seen as the biggest challenge in the business world. A 2012 Gallup poll studied the effect of high employee engagement in about 50 000 businesses, looking at 1.5 million employees in 34 countries. The study showed that organizations in the top half of employee engagement have twice the success rate of those in the bottom half (Gallup 2012).

Engagement begins in the culture embedded in the company. The company culture must foster enough trust to allow employees to make autonomous decisions. In doing so, employees will feel empowered in their ability to manage their own careers and will exhibit larger levels of engagement. However, this does not necessarily mean that employees should be left completely alone. Instituting mentors can prevent a remote employee from falling into the psychological traps that can accompany working alone. This is important because employees who report low feelings of engagement often experience little team support for their contributions. Short, frequent communications with purpose can help remote employees feel connected and included (Janove 2004).

Mentors can come in managerial roles that do not primarily focus on leading or ordering, but rather revolve around tailoring communications and goals to the individual employee (Snell 2009). This method is mutually beneficial, because managers are best able to interact with remote employees in a decentralized system. A manager should make a special point to acknowledge the contributions of remote employees. Informal feedback also becomes critical in engagement (Linkow 2008). Employees must know their work is being noticed and is critical to the group effort (Derven 2007). Managers must make time for personal interaction, especially if it's done virtually, to compensate for the impersonal means of communication.

Best Practice in Employee Communications

The Institute for Public Relations (IPR) studied 10 global organizations with outstanding internal communications programs in order to build a greater understanding in building efficacy and adopting the best practices in employee communications (Debreceny and Learch 2014). The study showed that perceived efficacy in internal communications is limited, with employees who participated in the survey reporting they were reluctant to say they contributed to the success of their organization. This shows both modesty and reflection among the interviewees, who believed they could be more effective or fell short on goals.

Furthermore, the study showed that efficacy in employee communications can be recognized through: tools and resources, like periodic assessments and internal social media platforms; an organizational structure, with internal communications team leaders; specific practices, like keeping employees informed of current issues in a timely manner; and a strong internal communications mindset that illustrates the organization's purpose and values for future success and future employees. Respondents appreciated emerging tools and resources, but their usage was limited. The two most important tools, according to the respondents, were a periodic assessment of employee perceptions and a way of listening to employees across the organization, such as via so-called "listening posts" (Debreceny and Learch 2014).

Overall, effectiveness can be built in an organization's structure, but it is crucial to put the structure, tools and resources, and mindset into action. It is also important to use feedback from employees in improving an organization's structure. Both team leaders and employees can benefit from this exchange, and therefore so too will the organization.

How Do Global Teams Work?

A team can be conceptualized as a group of people working toward a common goal, where everyone is accountable for the actions, decisions, and outcomes of the collective effort. One of the effects of globalization is the advent of cross-cultural opportunities and collaboration needs across geographical borders. **Globalization** has influenced an upward trend in the need for global interactions and communications, aided by the advent of the Internet and of communications technology. The concept of the **team** was initially used in the United States in the 1960s. With the transformation of economic globalization, many US companies expanded their businesses to foreign countries and set up offices worldwide, spreading the teamwork concept to Asia, Europe, and Latin America. Meanwhile, the burgeoning growth of communications technologies like the Internet made virtual communications and distant teamwork achievable and cost-efficient (Ale Ebrahim et al. 2009).

Language Barriers in Global Teams

Global teams can benefit from multiculturalism and diversity, but these can also create disorganization, including language barriers. A Rosetta Stone survey found that 90% of organizations struggle with day-to-day work as a result of language barriers, and while 71% of business leaders plan to expand into non-English-speaking regions, only 30% of companies invest in foreign-language skills training (Association for Talent Development n.d.). Unrestricted multilingualism can create inefficiency by causing friction in cross-border interactions, lost sales, and other problems that jeopardize competitiveness (Kaplan and Neeley 2014). To prevent this, companies often implement a common language, or lingua franca. A common language can noticeably improve how employees collaborate across borders, but it can also cause tensions, with, for example, employees struggling to express themselves due to lack of fluency.

To diminish language barriers, global leaders should directly manage these issues and promote productive global cooperation. Meetings and calls should be facilitated to ensure native and non-native speakers get equal time to have their say. Also, setting up clear agendas, establishing effective modes of communication, and choreographing meetings in advance can help include all employees, regardless of their primary language.

Moreover, having global teams adopt global mindsets, as opposed to limiting themselves with a local mindset, can help establish broad and multiple perspectives, teamwork, diversity, open-mindedness, and an eagerness to change and create new opportunities (Heller 2010). To adopt a global mindset, some important competencies should be prioritized, such as cross-cultural leadership, cultural intelligence, communications, and interpersonal skills. Furthermore, international assignments, cross-boundary teams, and cultural adaptation training can help overcome challenges and establish effective global teams, though a globally minded manager will be necessary to maximize this effort. Management can help balance the skills of the team and amplify each individual's capabilities while making sure no one is overshadowed. In this way, language barriers and other obstacles will be less likely to interfere in the success of global teams.

Challenges for Global Team Leaders

Five challenges global team leaders should be prepared to confront in virtual communications are: (i) building trust relationships among team members; (ii) increasing process gains and reducing process losses; (iii) eliminating team members' feelings of isolation and detachment; (iv) treating interpersonal skills as importantly as task-related skills; and (v) evaluating and rewarding team members (Kirkman et al. 2002).

Managing a group of people who work at the same location is fairly complicated – to say nothing of coordinating employees who are both geographically diffused and ethnically distinct. **Social distance**, the degree of emotional connection among team members, is a discriminator of the success of a global team. Normally, people working at the same location have relatively low social distance. They have many opportunities to interact in daily life, communicate face-to-face, and eliminate misunderstandings. In contrast, team members who work remotely feel less engaged and more disconnected. They experience high degrees of social distance and face many challenges when trying to build trust with their coworkers (Neeley 2015).

Another obstacle to building an excellent global team is balancing team members' perceptions of power. Usually, the group with the most employees or working at the same site as the team leaders feels it is in the dominant position and undervalues other groups' contributions. Meanwhile, minority groups far from the headquarters or distant from the leaders feel they are ignored and have little voice in the global team. In these circumstances, it is extremely important for the leader to balance the imbalanced power distribution and unite all team members. To prevent this imbalance, managers can remind all members that the team is a single entity, focus on corporate goals and business objectives, and pay attention to every individual (Neeley 2015).

Cultural differences are also salient problems in managing global teams. In order to better motivate employees, managers need to be careful and sensitive to each person's cultural background. For example, in the United States, if an employee says, "I can do it" when presented with a task, it means they are confident in their ability to complete it. In India, such a response may suggest that they will do their best, but they are not self-assured in their ability to do so (Neeley 2015).

Another example is that Americans and Thais take different attitudes toward participating in discussion. When attending a meeting together, Americans are active and talk most of the time, while Thais are relatively quiet. The Americans may feel their Thai colleague are introverts and do not have many thoughts to share. However, in Thai culture, people think it is polite to wait until for another person to finish talking before having your own say, and they prefer to think discreetly before speaking (Rizk 2014).

Managing a global team is always challenging. In order to unite a team spread over several locations, team members must be motivated by the same goals, and remote employees must feel connected and appreciated. Moreover, everyone should be treated fairly, and every employee's cultural background should be respected and properly handled.

Virtual Communications in Global Teams

Virtual teams are groups of people who use modern technologies to communicate and work independently, while striving for common goals (Kirkman et al. 2002). Adopting virtual teams allows companies to hire the most suitable talent around the world at the lowest cost, and also to cut down on real-estate and business-travel expenses. For example, research shows that, on average, a Chinese engineer only makes one-tenth to one-sixth of a US engineer's salary. For the purpose of controlling the cost of human resources, many companies have moved their research and development departments to China. As early as 2005, Motorola opened 19 research labs in China, which develop products for the Chinese and global markets (Fishman 2005).

Virtual communications is a computer-mediated form of communication that transcends the barriers of time, space, and distance. However,

Zaugg et al. (2015) state that initiating cross-cultural collaborations via Internet-based technologies is not as simple as we probably assume. According to Scott (2013, p. 301), "When team members are separated by distance, time, and culture, they often experience difficulties in developing trusting relationships and negotiating conflict." Further, sub-teams may become divisive due to geographical location barriers. Global virtual teams come with their challenges, but the structural setup can enhance their effectiveness nonetheless (Scott 2013).

A global virtual team is a team of people who are physically dispersed by geographical barriers of time, distance, and space, committed to a common goal, but assemble together through mediated communications technologies powered by the Internet. Usually, virtual teams are set up for long- or short-term projects.

Virtual communications in global teams requires a degree of intercultural competence in order to best understand how to build relationships across different cultural values. In other words, the ability to manage intercultural communications is important to the success and effectiveness of global teamwork. This requires a depth of respect for others' culture, understanding, and trust-building, and for the richness of diversity. Kiesler and Cummings (2002) explain that face-to-face communication has the richest potential for successful teamwork and effective collaboration, because the closer the proximity of the communicators, the greater their level of cooperation, conformity to norms, commitment, and trust. This does not suggest that face-to-face team communications are devoid of challenges, but they are less challenging than virtual team communications.

Virtual communications have become a crucial part of the professional's life. Emails, phone calls, and video conferences are critical tools for effective teamwork. Newly emerging technologies, which can significantly boost teamwork productivity and communication efficiency, provide further options. For instance, G Suite, which includes Google Docs, Google Calendar, and Gmail, is embraced by small team leaders as a means of sharing documents and scheduling meetings. Basecamp, an online project-management tool, is also perfect for small virtual teams. It allows team leaders to create to-do lists and projects for workers and to monitor their progress. Dropbox is favored by teams of every size, because it helps members access their group and personal files from any PC or smartphone with an Internet connection (Grey 2011).

Challenges in Global Virtual Teams

According to Scott (2013), conflicts within virtual teams last longer due to reduced sharing of information, prolonged decision-making as a result of slow response times (an effect of distance and time zone differences), and reduced interpersonal relationships between members. Computer-mediated communications in global teams requires a higher level of trust, especially because identities are shrouded behind the technology itself. As already noted, geographical barriers often lead to the formation of divisive sub-teams that engage in unhealthy competition.

Virtual communications noticeably lacks certain nonverbal cues that convey intended meanings, such as oculesics, proxemics, haptics, chronemics, facial expressions, vocal cues, physiological cues, gestures or body movements, and action cues. In lieu of these, it is important to "substitute the expression of impression bearing and relational messages into the cues available through the CMC [computer-mediated communication]" (Walther and Parks 2002, p. 535).

Another common misunderstanding when it comes to virtual communications in global teams is the idea that interpersonal skills are not important, and technical skills should be the major concern when recruiting team members. In interviews with virtual team leaders and members, researchers have found they rank communication skills as the most significant factor of effective and sustainable teamwork (Kirkman et al. 2002). Thus, when selecting new team members, managers should try to find a balance interpersonal and task-related skills.

There are various best-practice approaches to the management of communications within virtual teams. Grosse (2002) explains that virtual communications in teams requires "understanding the advantages and limitations of technology and how to build relationships via technology." The literature points to some different approaches to successfully handling virtual team communications, including:

i) Identifying the ideal channel of communications (e.g. email, phone, Skype, fax, Adobe Connect, etc.). The more appropriate the members find the channel of communications, the more on-time, real-time response time will be enhanced.

ii) Building trust relationships between team members. This will improve the effectiveness of team communications, leading to optimal team performance. It is difficult to trust people who we think of as strangers, so it behooves the team leader to encourage a good networking of relationships between team members in order to boost their confidence in one another.

iii) Teaching team members that technology has both advantages and limitations. Technology enhances efficiency in terms of on-time response rate, cost-effectiveness, and ease of performing stipulated duties. However, it is prone to network failures and system malfunctions. This makes it unreliable to a considerable extent, and it does not guarantee the success and productivity of the team. Besides, more often than not, the use of technology requires training, and problems can occur when a team member is yet to be completely familiarized with the type of communication technology used by the team (Grosse 2002).

iv) Appreciating cultural diversity in terms of the richness of values and insights. For instance, a person from a low power distance culture will expect a different pattern of behavior from his or her subordinates than a person from a high power distance culture (Hofstede 1991). So, while a team leader from a high power distance culture like Africa will expect his or subordinates to take directives without question, a team member from a low power distance culture might innocently make contributions during meetings, which the leader will perceive as an act of insubordination or disrespect.

Virtual team communications requires a deep understanding of and tolerance for the social systems, attitudes, and cultures that come into play as intervening communications variables. It is important that team members understand that computer-mediated communications is more challenging than face-to-face communications processes.

Virtual Leadership

Virtual leadership is exemplified by the situation where an individual manages and coordinates the activities of a work group or team that is geographically dispersed in terms of time, distance, and space. This coordination is done electronically through computer-mediated communications technology. Virtual leadership is also termed e-leadership by some scholars. Avolio and Kahai (2010, p. 239) define virtual leadership as "a process of social influence that takes place in an organizational context where a significant amount of work, including communication, is supported by IT [information technology]."

In teamwork, there is a need for a successful collaboration through proper coordination and control. The task of coordination and control of team activities toward a mutual goal is vested on a group of individuals or, in some cases, a single individual. The task assignment is usually dependent on the hierarchical position of the team members. In some circumstances, the team leadership is not hierarchical, but circumstantial. For instance, a group of students working on a project for an online class will most likely have a focal person as their team leader, and this position is not based on any hierarchical positioning. Leadership, according to Kahai et al. (2013), "provides structures that facilitate social interactions for achieving group goals" by giving instructions and enhancing group participation.

Leadership is necessary to tackle the problems that arise due to the lack of physical presence of team members. Two broad categories of virtual leadership have been identified: transformational and transactional (Bass 1985). Kahai et al. (2013, p. 971) explain **transactional leadership** as "an influence process that motivates individual effort by engaging the follower." A transactional leader employs extrinsic motivations in the form of bonus pay, pay raises, and other types of reward for exceptional effort and performance. A transactional leader is more task-oriented and focuses more on directing given tasks through instructions and guidelines. **Transformational leadership** employs intrinsic motivations to influence individual commitments and the efforts of team members. This can be explained as a leadership approach that does not simply reward effort, but grooms team members toward intellectual self-development and self-actualization beyond the assigned tasks. A transformational leader focuses more on building relationships with team members and acting as a mentor. Kahai et al. (2013) explains this as an approach that uses inspirational motivations by giving personalized considerations to team members' specific work-related needs. A transformational leader is considered more productive in terms of effectiveness and reaching developmental goals.

A synthesis of different scholarly opinions on best practice in virtual leadership suggests there are certain principles that should be followed by a virtual team leader, irrespective of the type of leadership (transformational or transactional). It is especially important for virtual team leaders to build trust relationships in order to enhance team cohesion and efficiency. Cowan (2014) explains that a virtual team leader needs to establish a social presence within the team. This should not be confused with being authoritative. It simply means the virtual team leader needs to exert some subtle influence, enabling other members to perceive a sense of leadership and control. Malhotra et al. (2007) suggest leaders of successful virtual teams should "establish and maintain trust." Team leaders in virtual workspaces should also ensure that distributed diversity is understood and appreciated. This is important because, more often than not, virtual teams are composed of individuals with different cultural orientations and experiences. These differences should be appreciated and maximized to the advantage of the team, rather than being differentiated. Having team members from different cultures pair together on small projects and giving an ear to diversified opinions helps ensure diversity is maximized. This also encourages members to show their expertise in different cognitive areas. Team progress monitoring is essential (Hirschy 2011). This can be done through an assessment of team discussions and exchanges online, and of participations in virtual meetings. In the same vein, it is important to establish team values and norms; these should be well articulated and communicated to avoid ambiguity of meanings. Timeliness of responses, feedback, and recognition for deserving performances will also help promote a healthy team.

Another important skill for a virtual team leader is conflict management. This is especially sensitive because of the culturally diverse nature of a typical virtual team. This means a virtual team leader is expected to be particularly sensitive to the cultural norms of the diverse team members. It is not uncommon for conflicts to occur among team members due to cultural incongruencies and clashes. This is why it is important for a virtual team leader to be able to recognize emotional indicators of impending or existing conflict, and manage such situations properly.

Recommendations for Improving Global Teams and Employee Communications

In terms of designing an efficient and productive global team, a strong commanding office is essential. Even if every office had similar expertise and experience, the absence of a reliable commander would increase conflicts and slow progress. Every office would look at a problem from its own perspective. This makes the existence of a leading office critical. The ultimate goal of a **leading office** is to ensure the project will be completed on time and on budget. It achieves this goal by coordinating resources to offices that have urgent needs and shortening unnecessary internal processes (Wilson and Doz 2012).

Other rules for successful global team management are to give timely feedback and to reward team members fairly. Communication is difficult in a geographically dispersed team, so it is extremely important for managers to give timely feedback, contact team members regularly, keep messages consistent, and appropriately reward team members to motivate employees. In the global team setting, remote workers feel they are less close to managers than employees working at the same office as them. Thus, leaders should pay extra attention to the organization's rewarding mechanism, making sure everyone's work is valued and rewarded equally (Mind Tools Editorial Team n.d.).

Since face-to-face communication is rare in virtual teams, the way leaders cultivate trust relationships among remote workers is different from past experiences. To be specific, because virtual team members have very few personal interactions outside of work, their trust is based on coworkers' consistency, reliability, and responsiveness. Thus, managers should take a positive approach to emphasize the importance of these three attributes in virtual teamwork.

Generating synergy without regular face-to-face communication is another problem virtual team managers have to deal with. However, diversity research also shows that the influence of visual factors, such as race/ethnicity and gender, is weakened in virtual communication. With telecommunications, minorities are more likely to speak and participate in interactions. Providing training on decision-making and project management, creating business plans, and stressing common goals can help to eliminate process losses and keep the entire team on the same page.

Avoiding the situation where some employees feel isolated is crucial in virtual communications in global teams. The absence of physical interactions hinders informal communications among team members. In the office, employees having lunch together or chatting during breaks can strengthen their social bonds. However, some team members who are located in different time zones and come from distinct cultural backgrounds might feel disconnected and ignored by others. Paying extra attention to employees' social needs and identifying individuals who require more engagement can help global teams to overcome this challenge.

Lastly, establishing a comprehensive performance measurement system to reward every team member equally is key to retaining employees and improving team productivity. Through a reliable evaluation system, all employees can be assessed and rewarded under the same criteria. Moreover, when evaluating a team member, team leaders should gather feedback from both his or her direct reports and his or her peer group.

Case Study   Embraer Soars with Strong Internal Communications

In 1969, Empresa Brasileira de Aeronáutica, later abbreviated to Embraer, was formed to jumpstart the aviation industry in Brazil. In the 1940s, through the Smith-Montenegro Plan, the government of Brazil began a process to develop the country's aerospace design and production capability. In 1946, an engineering school and research institute, the Aeronautical Technical Center (CTA), was created in São José dos Campos, which later became Embraer's hometown (Rodengen 2009). Programs designed to develop experimental aircraft began in 1965, and went on to become the foundation for the August 19, 1969 implementation of Embraer-manufactured planes.

Financing Embraer in the late 1960s was no easy task. The military had only come into power in 1964, following the overthrow of an extremely leftist president. The government, along with the country's top investors, was not interested in the risk. However, a few Brazilian influentials believed a domestic aviation industry could create higher-level employment opportunities and a boost in the upper levels of the economy, to the tune of tens of millions of dollars.

In May 1969, the military president of Brazil, Arthur da Costa e Silva, found he could not fly out of Rio de Janeiro because the airport was closed by extreme fog. Embraer's first chief executive officer (CEO), Air Force Major Ozires Silva, offered to fly the president using aircrafts manufactured by Embraer. Ozires then convinced the military president to allocate government funds to the company, creating the Brazilian aeronautical industry. Despite the country depending heavily on flight for transportation, up until that point Brazil had been unable to produce even one part of its own aviation needs, according to Ozires.

Although the government supported Embraer, private investors had to be encouraged to participate in public ownership of the company, by converting 1% of their income taxes into Embraer shares. In 1970, the third Embraer portfolio project, Ipanema, a small crop duster, took flight as the first Embraer plane to achieve CTA (the Brazilian equivalent of the US Federal Aviation Administration, FAA) certification. Since then, Embraer has produced thousands of this model, and it is still in use well into the twenty-first century.

By 2016, Embraer was one of the top airplane manufacturers in the world, encompassing design, development, manufacturing, sales, and technical support for commercial, defense, agricultural, and executive aviation. The company has produced more than 5000 aircraft, operating in 80 countries on 5 continents. It employs more than 19000 people around the world, 75% based out of its Brazil office, and the majority of the rest in various US offices, as well as Portugal, the Netherlands, France, Singapore, and China.

Despite a lack of resources in the 1970s, Embraer reached high standards in design and construction by strictly adhering to FAA standards before presenting plans to the CTA. The company still maintains the same high quality through 30 jobs grouped in 5 different areas of the company – aircraft maintenance, logistics/material, customer support, commercial, and support functions.

Employee Relations

Embraer demonstrates respect for its employees by offering a "flight plan" for new hires that includes mentorship and induction programs, ensuring they acclimatize to the company's environment and values. It holds all employees and stakeholders to a high standard, as outlined in its compliance program, demanding commitment to laws, regulations, and its own company policies (Embraer n.d.-a).

Embraer upholds six key corporate values:

- our people are what makes us fly;
- we are here to serve our customers;
- we strive for company excellence;
- boldness and innovation are our hallmarks;
- global presence is our frontier;
- and we build a sustainable future. (Embraer 2016)

The compliance program promotes a culture of integrity based on the company values and code of ethics and conduct, while addressing any issues pertaining to risk management and the prevention of misconduct and compliance issues. This program aims to uphold Embraer's values and principles through prevention, implementation of best practices according to Embraer's excellence program (P3E), and consolidation of all compliance initiatives – in particular, its anti-corruption and export control programs.

The compliance program is based on five elements: leadership and organizational structure; risk management; policies, procedures and controls; training and communication; and monitoring, auditing, and reporting, through the company's helpline. The program's cycle has four divisions: enhancement, prevention, detection, and remediation. In the enhancement division, existing processes are reviewed and improved as necessary. The prevention division prevents misconduct through risk assessment, policies and procedures, internal controls, training, and communication; it also provides guidance and advice to employees. The detection division assesses compliance issues, through monitoring, auditing, and a whistleblower allegation channel. Finally, the remediation division investigates issues, resolves problems, and takes appropriate actions (Embraer n.d.-a).

Other programs Embraer offers its employees include the Programa Innova and the Good Idea Program. The Programa Innova offers channels and opportunities for the development and consolidation of innovative ideas from any employee worldwide. Within this program is a team dedicated to studying and enabling new technologies and processes with the intention of adding value to the company. On average, 40 to 50 projects are developed from the Programa Innova each year. Due to this program, Embraer is recognized as being fertile ground for cutting-edge technology (Embraer n.d.-b).

The Good Idea Program promotes innovation within the company by encouraging its employees to contribute suggestions. This program has been running for 25 years. Embraer employees can contribute suggestions on absolutely anything from process simplification to cost reduction, occupational health and safety, ergonomics, and the environment. Embraer's chief executive officer (CEO), Artur Coutinho, said the success of the Good Idea Program is synonymous with the company's own success. Over 60 000 ideas originating with this program have been implemented in the last 15 years, resulting in $32.3 million in benefits, at a cost of just $3.2 million.

With a company of this magnitude, clear communication is both imperative and challenging. In previous years, Embraer strove to improve communications across its offices by developing various activities such as offering lectures by renowned professionals to its managers and organizing group activities for employees. Additionally, it gave a presentation on the 6 Embraer Values to a crowd of 20 000 of its employees' relatives (Embraer 2012). According to annual reports, the main focus of the company's 2013 communications plan was to create spaces and moments for reflection and practice of values among its employees. The company's transparency with its team is in part due to its efforts to incorporate local adaptation to each of its offices while still respecting cultural context. Spotlighted in Embraer's 2014 annual report was its Excellence in Communications Program, which seeks to instill the habits of continuous and high-quality internal communication and leverage modern electronic internal media. The Internal Communications Department at Embraer is said to provide major support to all of the programs being carried out in other divisions of the company and in its business units, aiding with awareness-raising and informational campaigns as developments of the organizational culture.

International Internal Communications

As new technology emerges, new network communications technologies come into play. This enables a greater rate of exchange of data and information between global offices, giving companies like Embraer a competitive edge (Figueiredo et al. 2007). According to culture and internal communications senior analyst Teresa Cepinho, Embraer has an internal communications structure that broadcasts information to employees across the globe through various vehicles. The structure comprises global and local channels, including intranet, blogs, internal TV, and newsletters for leaders and employees, alongside its robust communications process and the efforts of its integrated communications team. Embraer's CEO, Frederico Curado, contributes to the communications efforts by working closely with his team and writing his own company blog.

In addition to these channels, Embraer's goals also rely on different communications networks, including global and local leaders, global and local communications teams, and a variety of focal-point groups organized by theme. The focal-point groups contain experts on each theme for each office. The Brazil office passes key messages to each of these experts, which they can then share with their unit, allowing all Embraer employees worldwide access to the same message and the ability to create local dialog among peers.

In an attempt to remain consistent with the company's internal communications efforts, new employees and leaders are required to complete a variety of training exercises. In addition to training, a senior analyst at

Embraer is dedicated to creating and implementing new strategies to help management improve their communications skills. Despite all these communications efforts, Embraer is always looking for ways to improve. The company is currently in the beta phase of implementing an internal social media platform, and experimenting with networks around the globe (Cepinho 2016).

Discussion Questions

1 Name some communications patterns in employee communications. Provide an example of each.

2 Name some vital elements of effective employee communications.

3 How can employee engagement in employee communications be improved? Why is this necessary for effective employee communications?

4 How are companies implementing globalization in their businesses? How can the use of global teams benefit companies today?

5 Identify three challenges in global teams and provide a recommendation for improving each.

6 What is virtual communications? State three advantages and three disadvantages in global virtual communications.

7 Name some skills necessary for a position in virtual leadership.

8 How can employee communications in global teams be improved? Give three suggestions.

9 How can the Embraer compliance program improve global employee relations with upper management?

10 How can involvement in various Embraer programs be mutually beneficial for the company and its employees?

11 Do you agree with Embraer's past communications efforts? Why, or why not?

12 What is the significance of the company presenting its corporate values to the relatives of its employees?

13 What internal social media channels are best suited for Embraer? How should they be grouped?

14 What other actions do you suggest Embraer take to improve its internal communications with employees across the globe?

Class Activity

Company XYZ is a global beverage company that has its headquarters in the United States and three regional corporate offices in China, Italy, and Brazil. The CEO wants help in designing a strategic plan that can improve its employee communications. The company is currently struggling with language barriers and internal employee motivation. Students should consider some strategies to recommend to the CEO, bearing in mind the cultures in the four countries in which it is based and the languages spoken in each. They should find two real-world companies that have offices in the same or similar countries, and use them as examples to show Company XYZ effective employee communications in global teams.

References

Ale Ebrahim, N., Ahmed, S., and Taha, Z. (2009). Virtual teams: a literature review. *Australian Journal of Basic and Applied Sciences* 3 (3): 2653–2669.

Association for Talent Development. (n.d.). "Language barriers in the workplace." Retrieved January 10, 2019 from https://www.td.org/magazines/td-magazine/language-barriers-in-the-workplace.

Avolio, B. and Kahai, S. (2010). E-leadership. In: *Leading Organizations. Perspectives for a New Era*, 2e (ed. G.R. Hickman). Thousand Oaks, CA: SAGE Publications, Inc.

Bass, B.M. (1985). *Leadership and Performance Beyond Expectations.* New York: Free Press.

Berger, B. (2008). "Employee/organizational communications." Retrieved January 10, 2019 from http://www.instituteforpr.org/employee-organizational-communications.

Burton, S.K. (2006). Without trust, you have nobody: Effective employee communications for today and tomorrow. *The Strategist* 12 (2): 32–36.

Cepinho, T. (2016). "Embraer internal communication efforts." Email interview. 20 January.

Cowan, L.D. (2014). e-Leadership: Leading in a virtual environment – guiding principles for nurse leaders. *Nursing Economics* 32 (6): 312–319.

Debreceny, P. and Learch, C. (2014). "What does good look like? A quantitative perspective on best-in-class practices in employee communication." Retrieved January 10, 2019 from https://instituteforpr. org/good-look-like-quantitative-perspective-best-class-practices-employee-communication/.

Derven, M. (2007). The remote connection: Leading others from a distance requires set expectations, trust, and unique methods of evaluation. *HR Magazine* 52 (3): 111–115.

Embraer. (n.d.-a). "The compliance program." Retrieved January 10, 2019 from http://compliance.embraer.com.br/en/SitePages/Home.aspx

Embraer. (n.d.-b). "Corporate philosophy." Retrieved January 10, 2019 from https://www.relatoweb.com.br/embraer/12/en/corporate-philosophy#. XDPHSVVKgdU.

Embraer. (2012). "Relatório anual (2012)." Retrieved January 10, 2019 from http://www.relatoweb.com.br/embraer/12/pt-br/nossa-gente-e-o-que-nos-faz-voar/comunicacao-interna.

Embraer. (2016). "Annual report (2016)." Retrieved January 10, 2019 from https://www.embraer.com/relatorio_anual2016/en/download/Embraer-RA16.pdf.

Figueiredo, P., Gutenberg, S., and Sbragia, R. (2007). Risk-sharing partnerships with suppliers: The case of Embraer. *Management of Technology Challenges in the Management of New Technologies* 3 (1): 241–262.

Fishman, T. (2005). "How China will change your business." Retrieved January 10, 2019 from http://www.inc.com/magazine/20050301/china.html.

Gallup. (2012). "The engaged workplace." Retrieved January 10, 2019 from https://www.gallup.com/services/190118/engaged-workplace.aspx.

Grey, J. (2011). "7 effective tools for managing a virtual team." Retrieved January 10, 2019 from https://www.americanexpress.com/us/small-business/openforum/articles/7-effective-tools-for-managing-a-virtual-team.

Grosse, C.U. (2002). Managing communication within virtual intercultural teams. *Business Communication Quarterly* 65 (4): 22–38.

Heller, R. (2010). "Global teams: Trends, challenges and solutions." Retrieved January 10, 2019 from https://est05.esalestrack.com/eSalesTrack/Content/Content.ashx?file=4578f59e-21b3-4a2c-bbfe-63e53af3f5dc.pdf.

Hirschy, M.J. (2011). Virtual team leadership: A case study in Christian higher education. *Christian Higher Education* 10 (2): 97–111.

Hofstede, G.H. (1991). *Cultures and Organizations: Software of the Mind*. New York: McGraw Hill.

Izzo, J.B. and Withers, P. (2000). *Values Shift: The New Work Ethic and What it Means for Business*. Upper Saddle River, NJ: Prentice Hall.

Janove, J.W. (2004). Management by remote control. *HR Magazine* 49 (4): 119–124.

Kahai, S., Jestire, R., and Huang, R. (2013). Effects of transformational and transactional leadership on cognitive effort and outcomes during collaborative learning within a virtual world. *British Journal of Educational Technology* 44 (6): 969–985.

Kaplan, R.S. and Neeley, T. (2014). "What's your language strategy?" Retrieved January 10, 2019 from https://hbr.org/2014/09/whats-your-language-strategy.

Kiesler, S. and Cummings, J.N. (2002). What do we know about proximity and distance in workgroups? A legacy of research. In: *Distributed Work* (ed. P.J. Hinds and S. Kiesler). Cambridge, MA: MIT Press.

Kirkman, B.L., Rosen, B., Gibson, C.B., et al. (2002). Five challenges to virtual team success: lessons from Sabre, Inc. *The Academy of Management Executive* 16 (3): 67–79.

Linkow, P. R. (2008). "Managing across language, culture, time, and location: Meeting the challenges of a dispersed workforce." The Conference Board, Inc. Retrieved January 10, 2019 from https://www.conferenceboard.ca/(X(1)S(ds3l5xuvmpxwzgoyi3m2jmvw))/e-library/abstract.aspx?did=2784.

Malhotra, A., Majchrzak, A., and Rosen, B. (2007). Leading virtual teams. *Academy of Management Perspective* 21 (1): 60–70.

Mind Tools Editorial Team. (n.d.). "Managing a geographically dispersed team." Retrieved January 10, 2019 from https://www.mindtools.com/pages/article/newTMM_40.htm.

Neeley, T. (2015). "Global teams that work." Retrieved January 10, 2019 from https://hbr.org/2015/10/global-teams-that-work.

Rizk, C. (2014). "Erin Meyer can make your global team work." Retrieved January 10, 2019 from http://www.strategy-business.com/article/00282?gko=38b19.

Rodengen, J.L. (2009). *The History of Embraer*. Fort Lauderdale, FL: Write Stuff Enterprises, Inc.

Scott, M.E. (2013). Communicate through the roof: A case study analysis of the communicative rules and resources of an effective global virtual team. *Communication Quarterly* 61 (3): 301–318.

Seitel, F.P. (2004). *The Practice of Public Relations*, 9e. Upper Saddle River, NJ: Pearson Prentice Hall.

Snell, A. (2009). Tackling the challenges of employee engagement. *Strategic HR Review* 8 (2): 37–38.

Tomasco, K. (2017). "The philosophy of effective business communication." Retrieved January 10, 2019 from http://www.ehow.com/info_7818674_employee-communication-strategies.html.

Walther, J.B. and Parks, M.R. (2002). Cues filtered out, cues filtered in: computer mediated communication and relationships. In: *Handbook of Interpersonal Communication*, 3e (ed. M.L. Knapp and J.A. Daly). Thousand Oaks, CA: Sage.

Welch, M. and Jackson, P.R. (2007). Rethinking internal communication: a stakeholder approach. *Corporate Communications* 12 (2): 177–198.

Wilson, K. and Doz, Y. (2012). "Structure your global team for innovation." Retrieved January 10, 2019 from https://hbr.org/2012/10/structure-your-global-team-for-innovation.

Zaugg, H., Davies, R., Parkinson, A., and Magleby, S. (2015). Best practices for using global virtual team. *TechTrends: Linking Research & Practice to Improve Learning* 59 (4): 87–95.

11

Technology, Social Media, and Big Data

Central Themes

- Emergent communication technologies and social media have signifi-cant implications for public relations.
- The Internet has created the possibility of reaching publics that previ-ously could not be easily accessed.
- Social media has changed how people communicate, as well as when they communicate, where they communicate, and who they communi-cate with.
- Organizations are exploring how large-volume data can usefully be deployed to create and capture value for individuals, businesses, communities, and governments.
- Big data enables businesses to execute trend analysis, stakeholder map-ping, market analysis, and consumer and public behaviors.

Keywords *Big Data; analytics; social media; digital world; technology; rise of the Internet*

Introduction

The Internet has created the possibility of reaching publics that previously could not be easily accessed. As markets expand and organizations enter new territories, the daunting task of creating and maintaining culture-tailored communications strategies frequently falls to public relations professionals. This process is labor-, resource-, and time-intensive, and entails the initiation of baseline data and cumbersome processing tasks. Before the birth of the Internet, physical transportation of information was a common practice, and the cost of both labor and time was expensive. The results were often not worth the investment. While the Internet has

Global and Multicultural Public Relations, First Edition. Juan-Carlos Molleda and Sarab Kochhar.

created the possibility of defying space and time, social media has created the possibility of reaching publics much more conveniently. Organizations are closer to their publics than ever before. Connecting to the Internet with a computer, smartphone, or other device is enough to defy space limits – it does not matter where you are in the world.

Social media has become a convenient space for people who live anywhere in the world to find common ground on matters that cross borders. The violent and nonviolent anti-government protests in the Middle East and Northern Africa, referred to as the "Arab Spring," show how social media has become a powerful platform for civic engagement. As another example, different hashtags were created for the terror attacks in France and Belgium; this is an example of mass mobilization for a cause run by people from different corners of the globe. This, again, is a possibility created by social media.

Let's look at the 2016 US election campaigns and how they were unique in terms of the peculiarities they brought. One particular theme that drew enormous public attention was the candidates' use of technology. Current US President Donald Trump consistently accused Secretary Hilary Clinton, his opponent in the race for the presidency, of deleting emails from a private server. His accusations were based on the inference that she exchanged official and work-related confidential emails from a private server, compromising national security. On the other hand, President Trump's frequent tweets sparked controversies and were provocative in many ways. Throughout the campaign, he tweeted his opinions on a number of sensitive issues, which many thought was inappropriate from an aspiring president. He announced a number of major decisions and plans for his time in office via his Twitter account, leading many to question his adequacy to lead the nation.

Even since winning the election and becoming the 45th President of the United States, President Trump has continued to announce major official decisions via Twitter. Within the first week of setting foot in the White House, he had signed an executive order to move forward with building a wall along the US–Mexico border – one of his campaign promises, which had stirred controversy before the election date. In the same week, President Trump tweeted that Mexico should pay for the wall; if not, he suggested that planned visits with the President of Mexico be cancelled. As he sent out the tweets, his senior advisor was holding discussions with top Mexican officials. Following the tweets, Mexico's president (2012-18), Enrique Peña Nieto, canceled a visit to the White House planned for January 31, 2017. Peña Nieto announced the cancellation through his own Twitter account.

These examples show how enormously government-exchanged official communications have changed with the growth of emergent communications technology. Social media in particular has radically altered how humans communicate. It has changed peoples' way of life, the nature of organizational communications, how nation states communicate, and how information is shared on a global scale. The past decade has shown an amazingly accelerated growth of technology, in terms of both innovativeness and expansion. Whether for good or bad, technology has changed how the world interacts.

Until a few years ago, the public had to wait for scheduled, traditional mainstream media to tell them what was happening in the campaign process. Now, election and campaign updates are in the palm of your hand. This is only one reflection of the growth of technology we are currently witnessing. According to the Pew Research Center (2014, p. 3), 59% of employed adults say that they "take their jobs outside of the physical boundaries of the workplace at least occasionally." Moreover, the Internet, email, and mobile devices have caused changes in the work environment, with 51% of employees saying that they have expanded the number of people who can communicate with them outside of work (Pew Research Center 2014). This demonstrates that the use of technology dissolves the boundaries of time and space, allowing people to do nearly anything they desire, anywhere, at any time.

The Rise of the Internet: From Dial-Up to Broadband

The rise of the Internet is a key component in the technological revolution. The Internet makes it possible to connect person-to-person or even world-to-world. The Internet, as stated by Leiner et al. (2009, p. 22), is "a world-wide broadcasting capability, a mechanism for information dissemination, and a medium for collaboration and interaction between individuals and their computers without regard for geographic location."

The dissemination of broadband, a revolutionary Internet transmission technology that provides much greater speeds than conversational narrow-band telephone lines, influences individuals' lives from their social relationships to the way they work and learn. According to the Pew Research Center (2016), the number of people who access the Internet at home via high-speed broadband gradually increased from 3% in 2000 to 70% in 2013. With the widespread and rapid adoption of Internet browsers (e.g. Internet Explorer, Google Chrome, Safari, and Firefox) and search engines (e.g., Google, Yahoo!), people can access a multitude of information from across the world. Thus, the Internet is a "commodity" service, and much of the latest technology aims at providing sophisticated information services based upon it (Leiner et al. 2009). For instance, mobile devices with broadband capability (e.g. smartphones, tablet computers) provide users with quick and easy browsing services that allow them to search for information from anywhere.

According to the Pew Research Center (Smith 2015), the use of mobile devices, including cellphones, smartphones, and tablet computers, is growing rapidly – as compared to other technologies, which have declined or stayed flat in the past few years. In 2015, 92% of adults in the United States were using a cellphone, compared to 65% in 2004. Smartphone users have grown to 68%, compared to 35% in 2011. Tablet computer users have grown to 45%, compared to just 3% in 2010. Additionally, the number of people who own a smartphone, a desktop or laptop computer, *and* a tablet has more than doubled since 2012, from 15 to 36% of US adults (with 66% using at least two) (Smith 2015). The growth of smartphone use is seen in other countries, too. According to the Ericsson Mobility Report (Ericsson 2015), smartphone subscriptions will reach 6.1 billion worldwide by 2020, which means that 70% of the world's population will own a smartphone. The report also anticipates that over 90% of the world will be covered by mobile broadband networks.

As the Internet brings about change in the ways people communicate, work, and learn, so mobile technology changes when, where, and how people obtain information and entertainment. People increasingly use smartphones not only to make calls, but also to get directions (90%), listen to online radio/music services (67%), participate in video calls or chats (47%), and watch movies or streaming TV (33%) (Pew Research Center 2016).

The Growth of Social Media

The use of social media has grown rapidly; as of 2015, 65% of people used social media, compared to only 7% in 2005 (Pew Research Center 2016). The generation aged between 18 and 29 still leads the charge, with 90% using social media, compared to 12% in 2005 – a 78% increase. The use of social media among people between the ages of 30 and 49 has also consistently increased, from 8% in 2005 to 77% in 2015. Interestingly, usage among people aged 65 and older is also rapidly growing, from 2% in 2005 to 35% in 2015. This research shows social media is pervasive across many different age groups.

According to the Pew Research Center (2016), 82% of Internet users around the world use social network sites such as Facebook and Twitter to communicate with their family and friends. According to the Global Web Index (2015), people spend 1.77 hours per day on social media – more than a quarter of the total amount of time they spend online.

The growth of social media has influenced our lives; it allows people to stay in touch and to obtain and share news and information in real time with ease. Research shows that 50% of users are consuming news via Facebook and 50% of social media users are sharing and reposting news stories (Pew Research Center 2014). People can even send money to other users or buy items via payment services in social media applications (e.g. the "Send Money" button in a Facebook message) (*Time* 2014). Social media integrates most online activities into a single web service, allowing users to consume news and information, participate in conversations, buy products, and exchange money.

Brands are discussed on social media, whether or not they are present in the conversation. Businesses that are late to make needed changes to their customer service, policy, or beliefs – or that refuse to change – are left behind, distancing themselves from their clients. Businesses must step up to become their own media gatekeepers, as controlling and filtering what brand message is being passed along is crucial. Thriving companies that lack a long-term vision for adapting to an online identity lose business.

For example, most Netflix subscribers were once customers at video-rental company Blockbuster. In 2010, Blockbuster went bankrupt, while Netflix has grown to be worth almost $30 billion dollars. In 2000, Netflix's founder met with Blockbuster's chief executive officer (CEO) to propose merging the two companies – Netflix would run Blockbuster's online brand, while Blockbuster would advertise Netflix in-store. The proposition was immediately denied. Six years later, as Blockbuster started to see Netflix as a threat, it tried to invest in its own online network. Profitability failed, and the company was soon in over its head. Within a few years, Blockbuster went bankrupt. Its inability to adapt to the online network changes struck it twice – first in the failure to see Netflix's niche as a viral success, and second in the failure to design a digital presence stable enough to support its original business platform.

In another example, in August 2016, Delta Airlines canceled 2300 flights due to glitches in its computer systems resulting from a fire. The problem went on for days, and customers were stranded in airports for extended periods. Delta was again forced to cancel 280 flights in January 2017 due to similar glitches, which again lasted for several days. Meanwhile, in January 2017, United Airlines had to ground all domestic flights for several hours due to computer system issues, and in July 2016, Southwest Airlines had to do the same thing. In January 2017, Air Canada had a computer system glitch that created delays and missed flights nationwide. During this chaos, the airlines' teams sent out updates through different social media platforms advising customers on the flight issues. The updates not only reached customers instantaneously, preventing confusion that could have left thousands in limbo, but also helped the airline teams instantly receive feedback and concerns from their customer base. This shows how businesses can use social media to easily and instantaneously reach their publics and address emergencies.

Public relations professionals must adapt to a two-way communications system. Starbucks has one of the strongest brand presences on social media, building off its original business model as an "affordable luxury" for working professionals. Dachis Group's Social Media Index ranked Starbucks as the 36th most effective company on social media in the United States in 2014 (Poirier 2014). Starbucks was one of the earliest adopters of social media. Its brand style of comfort, rather than convenience like competitors Dunkin Donuts and McDonalds, made way for a unique positioning in the coffee marketplace. The company website, its primary social presence, is accompanied by five platforms: Facebook, Twitter, YouTube, Pinterest, and Google+. Starbucks' content is fairly uniform between accounts; it does not produce content specifically for one site. Because of its cross-platform posts, Starbucks is able to reach practically any customer. Each network provides the opportunity to reach a different audience. But quantity of viewers does not establish a quality relationship, so how has Starbucks succeeded with emergent digital marketing?

Starbucks values its consumer relationships. Rather than targeting new customers, it embraces its current ones and aims to strengthen its bonds with them. According to inbound marketing and sales company HubSpot, "Social media is not about farming followers, it's a way of cultivating relationships" (QA Graphics n.d.). Starbucks acquires most of its followers organically. Current customers are inclined to share its posts. As its fan/customer base grows, it continues to foster existing brand advocates, producing more engagement while creating a positive customer experience.

Starbucks knows its consumers and how to tie coffee into trending topics. It is a holiday staple, with its pumpkin spice lattes and red holiday cups. Reflecting this image via social media keeps its product relevant in practically any conversation. Ensuring that its content is both timely and consistent encourages a two-way conversation with its consumers. Oddly enough, one piece of recurring negative feedback regarding Starbucks' social media presence is over its lack of updates. Critics believe the company should be posting more content, more often.

Perhaps more than anything, Starbucks customizes its user experience. Its Facebook page gives customers all the information they might need – store locations, how to send/win/reload Starbucks gift cards, customer polls, employment opportunities, and more. This information benefits both the audience and the business, without forcing a transaction. Starbucks also keeps posts attractive and visual. Using images enhances content sharing. The company has even launched an online rewards program that allows customers to create and name their own drinks. Users can share the drink with friends and see its nutritional value. Giving consumers a chance to feel like they're part of the behind-the-scenes production only strengthens the business–consumer relationship.

Social media will only show worthwhile results when it is used correctly. Establishing a mission and maintaining an online identity sounds easy, but you cannot force your business on social media users. It is a fragile relationship that requires research and planning on your part, and trust and support from your customers. When done correctly, you'll receive loyalty, referrals, and word-of-mouth marketing. When done poorly, you'll be speaking to an audience that simply isn't listening.

The Reach of Social Media

Imagine the number of people an airline or coffee company reaches with a single tweet, Facebook post, or other social media message. Unlike traditional mainstream media, social media is a means of reaching a mass audience regardless of space and time. Public relations professionals can communicate with larger audiences than at any time in the past. Other than social media itself, the major enabler for this is the fact that so many people are connected to the Internet and thus have access to these new technologies.

It is important to note that even though businesses can reach such large audiences through social media, this does not mean that social media is replacing traditional mainstream media; there is still a significant number of people who do not regularly use the Internet. It is better to say that social media has become an integral part of organizational communications strategies, not a replacement for all traditional communications strategies.

For example, in protest over President Trump's announcement of his plans to build a wall along the US–Mexico border, for which he expected Mexico to pay, Mexicans vowed to boycott US companies, including Starbucks. Starbucks was swift to respond. Chairman and CEO Howard Schultz took to social media, tweeting that his company resisted the new executive order and would hire 10 000 refugees in the coming five years.

Regarding the airline emergencies already discussed, as the airlines were sending out updates, their customers and other affected people were interacting with the airline teams. Unlike with traditional mainstream media, social media gives publics an enormous possibility for interactivity. The sharing of information, especially in the lens of public relations, is no longer a one-way affair. Publics are now part of any message that an organization crafts, and they are present in the flow of it. This interactivity elevates the position of the public in the information-sharing process, and at the same time enables organizations to discern public reactions. This two-way flow greatly increases public engagement. Once again, interactivity is not limited by space and time and is comparatively free, or at least comes with very minimal cost.

Big Data and Analytics in Public Relations

Big data, usually defined in terms of its size, is at the heart of nearly every digital transformation (Gandomi and Haider 2015). The world produces around 2.5 quintillion bytes of data every day, 90% of which is unstructured data (Dobre and Xhafa 2014). The amount of data generated and consumed is estimated to reach over 40 zettabytes (or 40 trillion gigabytes) by 2020 (Gantz and Reinsel 2012). What is an organization to do with all these data? There are many questions around what is important, how to manage it, how to make sense of it, and how to mine it in order to draw insights. Organizations are exploring how large-volume data can be usefully deployed to create and capture value for individuals, businesses, communities, and governments (McKinsey Global Institute 2011). Whether to predict individual action, consumer choice, search behavior, traffic patterns, or disease outbreaks, Big data is fast becoming a tool that not only analyzes patterns but can provide the predictive likelihood of an event occurring (Editors 2014).

The term big data is used to describe "the overwhelming volume of information produced by and about human activity, made possible by the growing ubiquity of mobile devices, tracking tools, always-on sensors, and cheap computing storage" (Lewis et al. 2013, p. 2). Big data is often defined by the "four Vs": volume, velocity, variety, and value. Volume can vary from tens of terabytes to hundreds of petabytes. Velocity indicates the rate at which an organization receives Big data and needs to act upon it. Variety (unstructured, structured, or semi-structured) impacts how an organization might summarize and analyze the data. Finally, the data's value helps organizations derive meaning from it, recognize patterns, and make informed assumptions in their decision-making.

The terminology might change in the coming years, but the need to strategize, collect, and analyze data will remain a top priority for organizations (Marr 2015). In its early stages, organizations focus on the amount of data they collect, but in time, they need to look at its importance and the value that can be derived from it.

Challenges

Given the nature of big data, organizations and professionals face multiple challenges in dealing with it. In a conceptual classification, Sivarajah et al. (2017) define big data challenges as those related to the characteristics of the data itself, including volume, velocity, variety, variability, veracity, visualization, and value. Process challenges revolve around issues encountered while processing the data, such as data acquisition and warehousing, data mining and cleaning, data aggregation, and analysis and modeling. Management challenges revolve around privacy, security, governance, data ownership, and the skills related to understanding and analyzing the data.

Some of the challenges of big data lie in its complexity and scale, but other issues include heterogeneity, timeliness, and privacy concerns, all of which can make it difficult to derive value from the data. The huge volume collected is represented by heterogeneous and varied dimensionalities; with them, the complexity and relationships underpinning the data also increase. The complexity and the disparate origins of the data often lead to gaps or errors. It is important to understand how structured and unstructured data work, and the challenges associated with the two.

Wiesenberg et al. (2017) studied the use of big data and automation, and how they are especially challenging for strategic communications professionals. They surveyed respondents across more than 40 countries and found a large gap between the perceived importance of big data and current practices in its use, a lack of competencies and ethical reflection, and a limited utilization of opportunities. There are very few studies on the use of big data in communications and public relations, but all of them look at its risks and challenges (Holtzhausen 2016; Holtzhausen and Zerfass 2015; Weiner and Kochhar 2016).

Structured and Unstructured Data

Much of the challenge with big data comes from the integration of structured and unstructured data. According to Godika (2015), about 80% of the data held by an organization is unstructured data, comprising information from customer calls, emails, and social media feeds. Since data in communications and public relations is also increasingly generated in a digital format, there is a need to identify ways to link it and transform it for analysis. Unstructured data continue to grow, and organizations have to find ways to automate and improve their ability to understand their business.

The fundamental difference between structured data and unstructured data is that structured data is organized in a highly mechanized and manageable way. Structured data are ready for seamless integration into a database or well-structured file format such as XML. Unstructured data, by contrast, are raw and unorganized. Digging through unstructured data can be cumbersome and costly. One example of unstructured data is email. Although it is indexed by date, time, sender, recipient, and subject, the body of an email remains unstructured. Other examples include books, documents, medical records, and social media posts.

Spreadsheets, on the other hand, would be considered structured data, which can be quickly scanned for information because it is properly arranged in a relational database system. Unstructured data is data that does not follow a specified format for big data. If 20% of the data available to an enterprise are structured data, the other 80% is unstructured. The problem that unstructured data presents is one of volume; most business interactions are of this kind, requiring a huge investment of resources in order to sift through and extract the necessary elements, as in a web-based search engine. Because the pool of information is so large, current data-mining techniques often miss a substantial amount of what is out there, much of which could be game-changing if efficiently analyzed. Structured data have a high degree of organization and is readily searchable by simple algorithms. Unstructured data lack organization, making it time-consuming to analyze.

Unstructured data are everywhere. In fact, most individuals and organizations conduct their lives around it. Just as with structured data, unstructured data are either machine-generated or human-generated. An example of machine-generated unstructured data is satellite images, which include weather data, scientific data, meteorological data, vehicular data, and traffic data – think about Google Earth. Examples of human-generated unstructured data include email, text, mobile data, data generated from social media platforms (tweets, likes, posts, shares), and any website content.

Unstructured data are so important for organizations that it is imperative to find ways to tease meanings, connections, and patterns out of it. Analyzing unstructured data requires analytical tools and machine-based learning techniques. Machine learning can help analyze large, complex volumes of data, both structured and unstructured, using multiple variables to make accurate predictions. The question is not whether data should be unstructured or structured. There is an internal value to data and it needs to be put to good use.

Big data, while considered the future of business, marketing, and public relations, still has its challenges. One is the level of expertise required to correctly analyze it. When analyzed properly, big data enables businesses to execute trend analysis, stakeholder mapping, market analysis, and consumer and public behavior analysis. Sectors such as banking, the stock market, retail, insurance, and other businesses that rely on behavioral analysis of consumers can make use of continuously generated and stored big data. One of the authors of this book wrote a white paper on the use of big data in public relations and communications, on which the following sections are based (Weiner and Kochhar 2016).

Sources

As big data are generally characterized by a collection of data sets too large for common business software tools to capture, manage, and process, sources tend to deliver sets that are large, dynamic, and diverse. At the same time, big data comprises many "Small Data" streams, of which public relations is one example.

For business overall, external data sets may represent economic, financial, and societal/lifestyles data. Internal data sets represent organizational documents and business archives, including production, costs, pricing, staffing, and other statistics, as well as shared data sources, including the weather, census data, organizational websites, and secondary sources from industry groups and more.

Public Relations Data Streams

Much of the data generated for, by, and about public relations comes through research based on the measurement of factors categorized as outputs, outtakes, or outcomes (Figure 11.1). Stacks and Bowen (2013) define these factors as follows:

> **Output.** What is generated as a result of a public relations program or campaign that may be received and processed by members of a target audience, and may have cognitive impact on outtakes: the way a target audience or public feels, thinks, knows, or believes; the final stage of a communications product, production, or process resulting in the production and dissemination of a communications product (brochure, media release, website, speech, etc.); the number of communications products or services resulting from a communications production process; the number distributed and/or the number reaching a targeted audience; sometimes used as an outcome serving as a dependent variable in research.

> **Outtake.** Measurement of what audiences have understood and/ or heeded and/or responded to a communications product's call to seek further information from public relations messages prior to measuring an outcome; audience reaction to the receipt of a communications product, including favorability of the product, recall

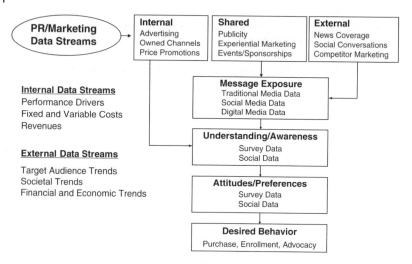

Figure 11.1 Data sets concerning brand public relations and marketing in corporate communications.

and retention of the message embedded in the product, and whether the audience heeded or responded to a call for information or action within the message; sometimes used as an outcome serving as a dependent variable in research.

Outcomes. Quantifiable changes in awareness, knowledge, attitude, opinion, and behavior levels that occur as a result of a public relations program or campaign; an effect, consequence, or impact of a set or program of communications activities or products, and may be either short-term (immediate) or long term.

Questions Every Data-Driven Public Relations Person Should Answer

- What do you want to achieve through your data-driven communications?
- How does your organization apply big data in its business applications now?
- In what ways will your data applications interact/interrelate with others?
- What can you do now to ensure that your data align well with theirs?
- In the area of talent, does your team have big data skills for critical thinking and statistical analysis?
- Do you have the tools you need to capture relevant content to produce accurate data?
- What can you do to create an environment that encourages discovery and learning through data (rather than "data as a scorecard")?

Big data has a lot to give to the future of public relations. Given how public relations practices are changing as technology advances, organizations need to – and certainly will – strategize on how to best make use of such large data sets. Big data will also become a key growth factor in the business world, if it is not one already. Organizations will shift to focus on restructuring their public relations departments to focus more on digital analytics and technology-oriented and digitally interactive units. The traditional data analytics and the strategies used for such a capacity do not transfer to Big Data analysis; hence, businesses will need new methodologies and a sharp turn in thinking to match the magnitude of what is coming. This will bring huge transformations in global public relations strategies. The case study on Procter & Gamble is a perfect example of how organizations plan, execute, and manage campaigns using digital and social platforms.

Case Study   Procter & Gamble – "Like A Girl"

The US multinational corporation Procter & Gamble Co. (P&G) was not always considered a leader in the feminine hygiene market. The company's first feminine protection product, Rely, launched in 1979, but failed within a year after being linked to a potentially fatal disease (Vitale 1997). Several years later, P&G learned from its mistakes when it successfully launched its Always line. Always' mission is to help "women embrace womanhood positively – from the beginning of puberty through their adult lives" (Procter & Gamble n.d.). Today, Always plays a commanding role in the world of feminine products.

The Campaign

As the Always brand grew, it sought to lay roots deeper than product functionality. But how can a brand that represents a topic so unpopular – feminine hygiene – successfully spread a conversation about itself? In 2013, Always discovered that younger girls didn't know or care about Always, or what it stood for. When they thought about Always, they associated it with a brand their mothers would use. The company was losing these girls' attention. So, instead of targeting heads, Always chose to target hearts.

Marketing to Millennials has become an obstacle for many successful businesses. This generation's population, at 76 million, surpasses that of the Baby Boomers. When a company doesn't understand, engage, or relate to Millennials, it fails to win over its largest market audience. Purpose-driven brands succeed because they make emotional connections with their customers. CEB Iconoculture Consumer Strategist Katie Elfering says most brands believe connecting with Millennials is extremely difficult, when in reality it comes down to a few straightforward strategies (Spenner 2014). Brands must speak to the values that drive

Millennials – happiness, passion, diversity, and discovery. Understanding their lifestyles will help brands amplify day-to-day experiences. It is important to inform and involve Millennials so that they feel like individuals, instead of transactions.

Always sought to create a campaign to build on the brand's mission of supporting girls while at the same time reinforcing why its products are relevant to them, underscoring the issues that today's girls face during puberty. It established three objectives. First, increase emotional connection and improve overall equity scores; that is, rather than improve its reputation as a product, Always wanted to improve customers' perceptions of its brand as a whole. Second, drive brand popularity through top-of-mind awareness; when a woman thinks of feminine hygiene products, Always wants to be the first brand to come to mind. Third, progress brand growth by measuring purchase intent pre- and post-exposure to the campaign: How likely is Always' audience to buy its product? How much more likely will it be once it has seen the campaign (Campaign Submission 2015)?

Details

Research conducted for the campaign showed more than 50% of women claimed they experienced a decline in confidence during puberty, dropping to two times less than boys. Even more discouraging, this confidence didn't seem to return until much later in life, if at all. In these findings, Always found an opportunity. Young girls are first introduced to Always at an awkward, uncomfortable time in their lives; a time when they have a great need for self-confidence, yet can't seem to evoke it in themselves.

Always pinpointed one moment: the common schoolyard insult, "You throw like a girl." The campaign was built around a social experiment to show the phrase's impact on society and attempt to change it. A long-format online video was the centerpiece of its efforts. Adolescent adults – male and female – were asked to run, throw, and fight like a girl. Participants giggled as they clumsily performed each action. Transition to young girls, who ran, threw, and fought "like a girl" with unwavering passion and purpose. These girls clearly had no conception that doing something like a girl was an insult. The authenticity of the responses pricelessly captured the essence of the campaign.

The video was released to YouTube with limited paid support, meaning earned media was crucial to campaign success. The hashtag #LikeAGirl was created as a call to action to reverse the negative meaning. It allowed Always to magnify the conversation throughout social media. Facebook, having the most users, was the ideal platform for Always. With the use of #LikeAGirl, Always could encourage viewers to help change the meaning of the phrase. Because of Facebook users' frequent use and high engagement level, Always could reach out and respond to consumers to build the deeper connections it was seeking. Always' team maintained a heavy social media presence throughout the launch to ensure real-time responses.

Results

Within a year, the #LikeAGirl video had accrued more than 85 million views from more than 150 countries. Always initiated post-release research, which found that 76% of 16–24-year-olds had a positive association with the phrase "like a girl." Two out of three men who watched the video said they would now think twice before using "like a girl" as an insult. Always launched two additional campaign pieces. The first, a 60-second television ad aired during the 2015 Super Bowl, was the most talked about Super Bowl commercial according to Adobe Marketing Cloud analysis (Adobe 2015). The second, a follow-up video released on International Women's Day, discussed how the meaning of "like a girl" had already begun to change.

Through social media, #LikeAGirl was able to reach 53% of 13–24-year-old women in the United States. The video became the most watched in P&G's history, boasting 3.4 billion global impressions. The #LikeAGirl hashtage was used 133 000 times, more than 150 000 comments were posted on Facebook, nearly 350 000 people shared the video via Facebook, and more than 40 000 tweets were made. Always' Twitter followers increased by 195%. All objectives were achieved, with hard-number benchmarks being met or surpassed. Always' brand equity boasted a sturdy increase, even while its competitors saw a slight decline.

Conclusion
The campaign had multiple elements that contributed to its overall success. Using Facebook was key to spreading awareness. Because Facebook is the home base of social media users around the world, it was the best choice as the campaign's main platform. Encouraging the use of the hashtag #LikeAGirl unified users across various social media sites. People could post opinions, share the video, and explore reactions regardless of platform. The video was creatively designed and resonated well with viewers. A simple production paired with a powerful meaning was the perfect formula for a viral video. Its genuine, effective messaging convinced viewers to watch it in its entirety, and it appropriately encouraged conversation about its movement. Paid YouTube promotions and the Super Bowl TV spot helped land the awareness and exposure the campaign needed. Perhaps best of all, the real-time support of Always team members was able to organize and strengthen the community of people affected by the campaign.

Discussion Questions

1 Discuss some of the unintended consequences of changing technology for the practice of global public relations.

2 Think of some effective ways to design messages for an emergent medium, or digital, networked media environment.

3 Do you think the power dynamics between organizations and their publics has changed in this emergent digital world? How, and why?

4 What are the implications of emergent technology and the changing media landscape for the agenda-setting process and how the media frame news coverage?

Class Activity

Students should create a marketing plan driven by social media tools for a global organization of their choice. Within the plan, students should decide which social media platform should be used and what types of content should be shared. What will the posting format be? What sort of interaction with users is intended? Students should present their plans to the class, including specific business and communication objectives they hope to achieve.

References

Adobe. (2015). "See which brands made the most of the second screen." Retrieved January 10, 2019 from http://admeter.usatoday. com/2015/02/02/adobe-second-screen-top-10/?adbid=562268782853230 592&adbpl=tw&adbpr=15151711&scid=social39782577.

Dobre, C. and Xhafa, F. (2014). Intelligent services for Big Data science. *Future Generation Computer Systems* 37: 267–281.

Editors (2014). From the editors: Big Data and management. *Academy of Management Journal* 57 (2): 321–326.

Ericsson. (2015). "Ericsson mobility report: On the pulse of the Networked Society." Retrieved January 10, 2019 from https://www.ericsson.com/ assets/local/news/2013/6/ericsson-mobility-report-june-2013.pdf.

Gandomi, A. and Haider, M. (2015). Beyond the hype: Big Data concepts, methods, and analytics. *International Journal of Information Management* 35 (2): 137–144.

Gantz, J. and Reinsel, D. (2012). "The digital universe in 2020: Big Data, bigger digital shadows, and biggest growth in the Far East." Retrieved January 10, 2019 from https://www.emc.com/collateral/analyst-reports/ idc-digital-universe-united-states.pdf.

Godika, S. (2015). "Big Data: 9 steps to extract insight from unstructured data." *Datamation*. Retrieved January 10, 2019 from https://www. datamation.com/applications/big-data-9-steps-to-extract-insight-from- unstructured-data.html.

Holtzhausen, D.R. (2016). Datafication: threat or opportunity for communi cation in the public sphere? *Journal of Communication Management* 20 (1): 21–36.

Holtzhausen, D.R. and Zerfass, A. (2015). Strategic communication: opportunities and challenges of the research area. In: *The Routledge Handbook of Strategic Communication* (ed. D.R. Holtzhausen and A. Zerfass), 3–17. New York: Routledge.

Leiner, B.M., Cerf, V.G., Clark, D.D., Kahn, R.E., Kleinrock, L., Lynch, D.C., et al. (2009). "Brief history of the Internet." Retrieved January 10, 2019 from https://www.internetsociety.org/internet/history-internet/ brief-history-internet/.

Lewis, S.C., Zamith, R., and Hermida, A. (2013). Content analysis in an era of Big Data: a hybrid approach to computational and manual methods. *Journal of Broadcasting & Electronic Media* 57 (1): 34–52.

Mander, J. (2015). "The latest social networking trends." Retrieved January 10, 2019 from https://www.globalwebindex.net/blog/gwi-social- q4-2014-the-latest-social-networking-trends.

Marr, B. (2015). "Why big data is just a fad." *Business Insider*. Retrieved January 10, 2019 from https://www.businessinsider.com/why-big-data- is-just-a-fad-2015-3.

McKinsey Global Institute. (2011). "Big data: The next frontier for innovation, competition, and productivity." Retrieved January 10, 2019 from https://www.mckinsey.com/business-functions/digital-mckinsey/ our-insights/big-data-the-next-frontier-for-innovation.

Pew Research Center. (2014). "How social media is reshaping news." Retrieved January 10, 2019 from http://www.pewresearch.org/ fact-tank/2014/09/24/how-social-media-is-reshaping-news/.

Pew Research Center. (2016). "More Americans using smartphones for getting directions, streaming TV." Retrieved January 10, 2019 from http://www.pewresearch.org/fact-tank/2016/01/29/ us-smartphone-use/.

Poirier, G. (2014). "Starbucks' killer social media strategy." Retrieved January 10, 2019 from https://www.linkedin.com/pulse/20141112163710- 200769548-starbucks-killer-social-media-strategy.

Procter & Gamble. (n.d.). "P&G's Always brand, the global leader in feminine care, launches revolutionary new Always Discreet for sensitive bladders." Retrieved January 10, 2019 from https://news.pg.com/press-release/pg-corporate-announcements/pgs-always-brand-global-leader-feminine-care-launches-revol.

QA Graphics. (n.d.). "Changing the social media game." Retrieved January 10, 2019 from https://www.qagraphics.com/changing-social-media-game/.

Sivarajah, U., Kamal, M.M., Irani, Z., and Weerakkody, V. (2017). Critical analysis of Big Data challenges and analytical methods. *Journal of Business Research* 70: 263–286.

Smith, A. (2015). "US smartphone use in 2015." Retrieved January 10, 2019 from http://www.pewinternet.org/2015/04/01/us-smartphone-use-in-2015/.

Spenner, P. (2014). "Inside the millennial mind: The do's & don'ts of marketing to this powerful generation." Retrieved January 10, 2019 from http://www.forbes.com/sites/patrickspenner/2014/04/16/inside-the-millennial-mind-the-dos-donts-of-marketing-to-this-powerful-generation-3/.

Stacks, D. and Bowen, S. (2013). *Dictionary of Public Relations Measurement and Research*. Gainesville, FL: Institute for Public Relations.

Vitale, S. (1997). "Toxic shock syndrome." Retrieved January 10, 2019 from http://web.archive.org/web/20060316030919/http://www.io.com/~wwwomen/menstruation/tss.html.

Weiner, M. and Kochhar, S. (2016). *Irreversible: The Public Relations Big Data Revolution* [IPR Whitepaper]. Gainesville, FL: Institute for Public Relations.

Wiesenberg, M., Zerfass, A., and Moreno, A. (2017). Big Data and automation in strategic communication. *International Journal of Strategic Communication* 11 (2): 95–114.

12

Public Diplomacy and Corporate Foreign Policy in Government Institutions and Agencies

Central Themes

- Public diplomacy is, to a significant extent, concerned with identity, reputation, and mutual relations between nations and individuals that require trust and build nations' brands.
- The variety of efforts of governments and corporations to build national, and even city, identities and to engage with people of foreign nations is evolving constantly.
- Factors such as people or human capital determine how the people of a nation are perceived by the rest of the world.
- Corporate diplomacy is not merely the participation of organizations in public diplomacy initiatives.

Keywords *public diplomacy; country reputation; national identity; corporate diplomacy*

Introduction

China paid for and helped build a stadium in Costa Rica at a cost of $105 million (Manfred 2011). Costa Rica's soccer federation also received a significant amount of cash from a Chinese company. The reasons for such a significant sponsorship may be related to a potential trade agreement to be signed between the two nations. Noteworthy is the fact that the tiny Central American country has historically been an ally of the also tiny island nation of Taiwan, which China considers a renegade province. Because it is not easy to determine how closely the company in question is related to the Chinese government, this case may be an example either of public diplomacy (a government- or state-led initiative) or of corporate

Global and Multicultural Public Relations, First Edition. Juan-Carlos Molleda and Sarab Kochhar.
© 2019 John Wiley & Sons, Inc. Published 2019 by John Wiley & Sons, Inc.

diplomacy (a non-state- or corporate-led initiative). This chapter will explain both international practices: public diplomacy and corporate diplomacy (or corporate foreign policy).

Voice of America and US-sponsored cultural and language centers, the British Council and the British Broadcasting Corporation (BBC), China Network Corporation (CNC) and Chinese Confucius Institutes, and France 24 and the Alliance Française are wholly government-owned media and institutions that expose foreign audiences to, and engage them with, the interests, values, traditions, and perspectives of their home nations. Extensions of these operations as cultural diplomacy practices are educational-exchange programs (people-to-people), such as the US Fulbright program, and the touring programs of certain cultural groups, such as the Simón Bolívar Youth Orchestra of Venezuela, directed by world-renowned conductor Gustavo Dudamel. Nations build relationships with the publics of other nations through music, theater, fine arts, news, language training, education exchanges, and communications campaigns and efforts that convey the essence of their national identities and national priorities.

Large nations, in particular, are increasingly competing for attention on the world stage and to cultivate relationships with regions and countries of geopolitical and economic relevance. For instance, Russia, China, Iran, and other large countries aggressively compete with the United States for the "hearts and minds" of people around the world (Dale et al. 2012). These countries are using the same international relations that the United States has used for decades. Emergent and developed countries are also innovating to engage foreign audiences with the ideas and ideals of their nations and native citizens. Emergent technologies and advanced transportation infrastructures are allowing countries and citizens to reach and encounter one another in multiple ways. The world, for the most part, is an open marketspace that allows multiple exchanges and creates interdependencies. Countries nurture direct human interactions, aiming to gain allies, attract investors, or captivate visitors. However, as organizations aiming to engage external publics, the house must be in order first. For instance, after the Arab Spring, Egypt deposed two presidents, in 2011 and 2013, leading to political and economic instability. In late 2015, it launched a global tourism campaign (#Thisisegypt) to attract much-needed visitors. Critics claimed that images in YouTube promotional videos did not reflect the reality on the ground, challenging Egypt's goal of rescuing one of its most important economic sectors: international tourism (Fadel 2015).

The variety of efforts of governments and corporations to build national and even city identities and to engage with people of foreign nations are constantly evolving, from cultural diplomacy to sports diplomacy.

International events such as Expo Milan or Milan's World Fair in Italy have been described as "food diplomacy" (Powell 2015). Centers and interest groups (e.g. the Public Diplomacy Council, UK Foreign & Commonwealth Office's Public Diplomacy Board, the University of Southern California (USC) Center on Public Diplomacy) that unite public diplomacy professionals and study and advocate for the ethical and effective exercise of the practice are blossoming.

This chapter focuses on the efforts of governments and multinational corporations (MNCs) to consolidate their home nations' identity and global reputation though nation-building programs and international relations practices with peoples of foreign nations; that is, on public and corporate diplomatic efforts.

Public Diplomacy and Corporate Diplomacy as Global Public Relations Practices

Today, more than ever before, the foreign-policy decisions and actions of nations and MNCs are scrutinized by the global community, organized in multilateral organizations or activist networks, among other global actors. The dawn of globalization has made it challenging for organizations and nations to gain acceptance and recognition among the community of nations. The challenge of global recognition demands that nations eliminate negative or inaccurate perceptions among their stakeholders, so that they gain legitimate power and a clear voice on the world stage.

Countries around the world have their own public diplomacy mechanisms, which shape and refine public attitudes overseas. There are many examples of issues and crises where the attitudes of overseas publics play a decisive role in a nation's ability to implement its foreign policies. There are also examples of countries branding themselves in an original way. "Iceland Wants to Be Your Friend" was a social media campaign aimed at humanizing the island nation, with the Icelandic Tourism Board calling on Internet users worldwide to become connected with the country through all sorts of digital platforms.

Dimensions of Public Diplomacy

Tufts University's Murrow Center defines public diplomacy as a practice that "deals with the influence of public attitudes on the formation and execution of foreign policies. It encompasses dimensions of international relations beyond traditional diplomacy; the cultivation by governments of public opinion in other countries; the interaction of private groups and interests in one country with those of another; the reporting of foreign affairs and its impact on policy; communication between those whose job is communication, as between diplomats and foreign correspondents; and the processes of inter-cultural communications" (Edward R. Murrow Center of Public Diplomacy 2015). In plain words, public diplomacy is the influence of a nation's institutions on foreign audiences (Ordeix-Rigo and Duarte 2009) through activities such as educational exchange programs for scholars and students at all levels, visitors programs and country tours, language training, cultural events and exchanges, radio and television broadcasting, and social media campaigns (USC Center on Public Diplomacy n.d.). A description of public diplomacy includes both state and non-state actors:

> Public diplomacy can be defined as an activity conducted by nations (stateless and otherwise), organizations, which operate globally (national sporting bodies, tourist bodies), global organizations (corporations such as Nike and nongovernmental organizations [NGOs] such as the International Olympic Committee, World Health Organization, and the Catholic Church), and international political organizations advocating change (Greenpeace). (L'Etang 2009)

According to Taylor (2008, p. 12), public diplomacy may also be defined as "direct communication with foreign peoples, with the aim of affecting their thinking and, ultimately, that of their governments." Hence, public diplomacy can be thought of as a process of a nation listening and understanding the needs of other countries and communicating its viewpoint in order to eventually build relationships.

Public diplomacy is based on a nation's identity (what it is and how it desires to be understood) and reputation (how it is perceived and understood by foreign people), as dictated by many factors: political, social, economic, and cultural. Payne (2009) states that achieving trust in a nation and its people is the most important factor necessary to initiate a conversation, sustain a dialog, and build relationships. The focus on developing relationships is also indicated in Sharp's (2007, p. 106) definition of public diplomacy as "the process by which direct relations are pursued with a country's people to advance the interests and extend the values of those being represented." According to Molleda (2011), active engagement and dialog are also key indicators of developing relationships in public diplomacy. Payne (2009, p. 582) explains, "Effective public diplomacy is a two-way street with reciprocal influence on both the source and receiver involved in the ongoing communication process."

The ongoing communications process leads to the development of lasting relationships with foreign audiences that bestows nations with soft power. Soft power is an advantage in world affairs and incites admiration and respect around the world.

In the context of international relations theory, the term "soft power" is defined by Nye (2004) as "an intangible attraction that persuades us to go along with others' purposes without any explicit threat or exchange taking place." A country's soft power is defined by three factors: its culture, its political values, and its foreign policies. These factors rest primarily on its ability to shape the preferences of others using strategic communications skills. But, for Nye (2010, p. 31), public diplomacy is not a public relations campaign; instead, it "involves building long-term relationships that create an enabling environment for government policies."

China provides an example of the benefits of a soft-power portfolio. With its focus on strengthening energy relationships in the Middle East, Africa, and Latin America, Chinese leaders aim to deepen relationships with nations in these regions and thereby increase their influence over them. China's strategy, as articulated by Hu Jintao (2012), President of the People's Republic of China (PRC), is in response to international hostile forces and the fact that the Asian giant is under assault by Western soft power.

Anholt (2000) states that public diplomacy is, to a significant extent, concerned with identity, reputation, and mutual relations between nations and individuals that require trust and build the nations' brands, or "the way the world sees the world." The Nation Brands Index, as developed by Anholt (2000), measures the power and appeal of a nation's brand. It is a reflection of global opinion and the effectiveness of public diplomacy efforts, as measured in six areas: exports, governance, culture and heritage, people, tourism, and investment and immigration. These dimensions provide a framework for nation-to-nation comparison against the key factors impacting a nation's reputation.

Factors such as people or human capital determine how the people of a nation are perceived by the rest of the world. For example, the Colombian government attempted to improve its reputation abroad by conducting national and international campaigns, such as Colombia is Passion and The Only Risk is Wanting to Stay, that communicated positive claims about the South American country and its people. Similarly, the Israeli Ministry of Public Diplomacy and Diaspora Affairs launched a website in 2010 in an effort to enable every single Israeli citizen to become an ambassador for the country. The website, Together, We Can Change the Picture, provides information on Israel's achievements and global contributions, and gives tips on how to practice public diplomacy while abroad. The efficacy of Israel's branding initiative is particularly interesting as research by Gallup (2012) indicates an increase in the United States' favorability toward Israel as a result of the campaign (71% in 2012 as compared to 68% in 2011). Corporate communications plays a role in a country's promotion of its national identity and in enhancing perceptions of its reputation among the citizens of other nations. Research from White and Kolesnicov (2015) supports the argument that increasingly, the role of social media in the co-creation of national identity through brands campaigns produces a positive national identity that may be an antecedent of a positive international reputation.

These examples of public diplomacy using social media, global citizen diplomacy, platforms for networked communications, and so on emphasize the need for nations to keep abreast of the challenges and demands of global interconnectedness – defined by an increasingly interdependent world, economically, environmentally, politically, and socially/demographically. It is also important to identify and acknowledge the growing impact of non-state actors on the practice of public diplomacy. Public diplomacy is no longer restricted to governmental efforts, but also incorporates non-state actors, including multilateral organizations, corporations, nongovernmental groups, and activists. As Zakaria (2011, p. 5) says:

> Functions that were once controlled by governments are now shared with international bodies like the World Trade Organization and the European Union. Nongovernmental groups are mushrooming every day on every issue in every country. Corporations and capital are moving from place to place, finding the best location in which to do business, rewarding some governments while punishing others ... Power is shifting away from nation-states, up, down, and sideways.

Corporations that operate in many world locations have enormous resources that they can put to work in public diplomatic efforts. Instead of directly engaging in public diplomacy, corporations are likely to support their home governments' communications with foreign publics in order to protect their economic self-interest (White 2015). This interplay between corporations and governments may be achieved through strategic coordination, where the heavy hand of business may exert significant influence.

The Shift of Influence: From Country Power to Corporate Power

The power and reach of transnational corporations (TNCs) is a reality that has drawn enhanced critical analysis from various non-state actors, including media and NGOs, worldwide. Globalization has promoted mutual reliance between countries and has given TNCs the ability to shape global trade, production, and financial transactions. Top companies on the Forbes 2015 Global 2000 list stack up against many countries around the globe (Murphy 2015). Examples range from HSBC Bank, which has 300 000 employees around the world (more than Germany has active military troops), to ExxonMobil, which produces 2.4 million barrels a day of crude oil and natural gas liquids (more than the 2.2 million barrels produced in the entire European Union). The ICBC Asia made profits of US$18.8 billion in 2011, which is more than Syria's annual budget expenditure. Citigroup does business in over 140 countries, more than Italy has embassies in. Corporate power has the ability to create and redefine the global perception of a nation. TNCs are progressively adopting a global perspective in order to survive in a complex environment shaped by dynamic political, economic, and social factors. A significant rise in the number of TNCs from emerging economies is projected in coming years. According to PricewaterhouseCoopers (PwC) (2010), India is expected to overtake China and become a world leader in the number of new TNCs. PwC (2010) reports more than 2200 Indian companies are projected to start operations worldwide from 2014 onward, owing to an increase in investment, government support, and trade policies.

Public diplomacy and corporate diplomacy are closely linked, as a nation's reputation helps organizations sell its products to the world over, while the organizations' products and services reinforce the nation's reputation and heritage. TNCs shape international relations and can enhance the national reputation of home nations in many ways. Globalization is one of the main reasons for a shift in power between government and organizations (Scherer and Palazzo 2007). For example, the Chinese-manufactured products quality crisis of 2007 gained extensive international notoriety, deeply affecting the nation's trade. This had long-term ramifications for its national brand and reputation. Corporate diplomacy is, therefore, crucial to the credibility of an organization in developing a unique position, voice, and influence in shaping public opinion and policies in a host country. Eskew (2006) states that organization and country are seen as dependent and integrated in everyday operations and specific objectives.

The concept of corporate diplomacy was originally suggested by Albert Herter, the former general manager of the government relations department at Socony Mobil Oil Company, in 1966. Herter emphasized the need for corporate diplomacy following World War II, due to the increased global competition and mistrust toward Western nations, as well as the fact that the majority of European corporations were state-owned (Molleda 2011). Corporate diplomacy is defined as "a complex process of commitment towards society, and in particular with its public institutions, whose main added value to the corporation is a greater degree of legitimacy or 'license-to-operate', which in turn, improves its power within a given social system" (Ordeix-Rigo and Duarte 2009, p. 549). This definition focuses on corporate legitimacy, by which an organization will gain better acceptance in a host country. However, the expectations of stakeholders are changing as organizations come to be evaluated more from a morally legitimate perspective than from a financially practical one. An enhanced and favorable corporate reputation is just as important to an organization as its financial performance. The foundation of success in effective corporate diplomacy lies in understanding the diverse agendas and alignments of home and host influencers.

Toyota provides a great example of the successful management of a non-market business environment and of corporate diplomacy. In California, Toyota has been successful in including its flagship Prius hybrid model in a program granting low-emissions vehicles access to the state's carpool lanes when they have only a single occupant. With minimum financial investment, Toyota has managed to give its product a decisive competitive advantage. Building on this success, the company won Prius owners the right to park for free at public meters in Los Angeles and other cities.

Support for the common goals of government, by communicating the nation's values and so strengthening understanding among home and host publics, underlies the purpose of corporate diplomacy (Wang 2006). The role of organizations as political actors can be analyzed through a deeper understanding of corporate social responsibility (CSR). A similar idea of social responsibility is included in Amann et al.'s (2007, p. 34) definition of corporate diplomacy as "the attempt to manage the business environment systematically and professionally, to ensure that business is done smoothly, with an unquestioned license to operate and an interaction that leads to mutual adaptation between corporations and society in a sense of coevolution."

Corporate diplomacy is not merely the participation of organizations in public diplomacy initiatives; rather, the challenge is for organizations to connect corporate diplomacy initiatives with public diplomacy initiatives (Ordeix-Rigo and Duarte 2009). The concept of building trust and long-term relationships is shared between public and corporate diplomacy. Conglomerates like Microsoft, Lexus, Samsung, Huawei, and Siemens are symbols of their home country – its people, its culture, and its legacy. Using corporate diplomacy, organizations can leverage their power and legitimacy across various stakeholders. A comprehensive communications strategy that embraces all stakeholders, facilitates dialog, and measures the reach and effectiveness of the message is necessary to ensure the effectiveness and success of corporate diplomacy campaigns.

Engaging Stakeholders in Corporate Diplomacy

Previous discussion on public and corporate diplomacy reiterated the importance of public perceptions about a nation or organization. Various definitions and examples indicated the need to establish legitimacy in the minds and hearts of foreign publics. The various stakeholders of an organization have been studied in the form of stakeholder theory, which describes the relationship an organization has to its various constituency groups, including customers, employees, community leaders, and shareholders and investors. According to Donaldson and Preston (1995), an organization must be receptive to various stakeholders in order to facilitate its long-term success.

Similarly, in corporate diplomacy, identifying stakeholders is important, as organizations need to ensure that their organizational decisions are globally accepted. According to Friedman and Miles (2006), an organization can be defined as a set of various stakeholders that have the prime aim of maintaining their respective varied interests and viewpoints. Maignan and Ferrell (2004) report stakeholders are those who are motivated to participate in organizational activities by various interests. Overall, stakeholder theory describes an organization "as an open and flexible system made up of diverse actors and active in a network or relationships with various other actors" (Maignan and Ferrell 2004, p. 5). An organization has interest in communicating with the stakeholders it serves, and its messages are expected to address topics of interest to those stakeholders. In corporate diplomacy, addressing stakeholders can be approached as a two-step process of "who" to engage and "how" to engage them.

In an extension to the discussion on stakeholders, Rawlins (2006) has developed a stakeholder prioritization model based on stakeholder theory, stakeholder management, and public relations. The four-step model outlines the process of classifying an organization's stakeholders, beginning with identification, followed by prioritization based on stakeholder importance, need, and communications strategy (Rawlins 2006).

Stakeholders can be defined based on their relationship to an organization, whereas a public can be defined based on its relationship to a message (Rawlins 2006). In corporate diplomacy, an organization has to address its stakeholders in order to ensure its financial success and has to approach publics for its acceptance in the host country. Hence, the stakeholder prioritization model can help organizations identify ways to develop a strategy to identify, address, engage, and build relationships with its stakeholders that are long-lasting and fulfilling.

Case Study   Hallyu – Public Diplomacy Surfs the Korean Wave

Hallyu (한류), or the Korean Wave, is a cultural phenomenon that began in the late 1990s when South Korea (hereafter Korea) initiated diplomatic relations with China (Korea.net n.d.). In that period, Korean popular culture – including television dramas, music, and movies – began spreading beyond Korea's borders, first to China and South East Asian countries, then to Japan and the Middle East (Hong-June 2015), and finally beyond Asia and into Latin America, North America, and Europe.

The Stages of Hallyu

After a series of political and cultural reforms in the 1980s, the Korean drama *What is Love* (사랑이 뭐길래) made its debut on Chinese CCTV in 1997 (Tuk 2012). *What is Love* conquered the Chinese audience through its "freewheeling attitudes" and its depictions of the "sophisticated life-styles of modern-day Koreans" (Tuk 2012, p. 12). Two years later, in 1999, the drama *Star in my Heart* (별은 내가슴에) became a hit on Phoenix TV in Hong Kong (Tuk 2012). However, the event that marked the true beginning of Hallyu as a cultural movement was the concert performance of Korean boyband H.O.T. at the Beijing Workers' Gymnasium in 2000 (Korea. net n.d.). It was then that Chinese reporters coined the term "Hallyu" (*Hanliu* in Chinese) (Korea.net n.d.). Although the word implies something temporary, Korea's success was anything but. Many K-pop artists, such as Baby V.O.X, Clon, and NRG, also made their way not only into China, but also into Taiwan, Singapore, and other South East Asian countries (Tuk 2012). Most scholars refer to the early successes of Korean popular culture in China and South East Asia as the First Hallyu.

The Second Hallyu began when the drama *Winter Sonata* (겨울연가) became a hit on NHK TV in Japan in 2003 (Tuk 2012). That same year, *Jewel in the Palace* (대장금), more commonly known by its Korean title, *Dae Jang Geum*, became the first Korean drama to go global (Tuk 2012). It was broadcast in China, Japan, Taiwan, and other South East Asian countries, and even reached the Middle East, including Iran, Jordan, Saudi Arabia, and Egypt (Tuk 2012). As of 2011, the drama had been seen all over Asia, Latin America, the United States, and much of Europe. It also helped increase the popularity of Korean food globally, as it heavily featured royal court cuisine. Following its airing, food like bibimbap (비빔밥) became popular in many countries.

The global success of *Dae Jang Geum* opened the doors for the third, most current age of Hallyu, also known as Hallyu 2.0, led by the rise of K-pop (Jang and Paik 2012). A number of Korean groups and singers achieved success not only in Asia, but across the globe. Girl group Girls'

Generation achieved platinum status in Japan, while girl group KARA's single, "Mister," made the TOP Five on Oricon's Daily Chart (Tuk 2012). In 2008, BoA became the first Korean female singer to debut in the United States, and she released an album in English in 2009 (Tuk 2012). Wonder Girls performed with the Jonas Brothers and were the first Korean group to make it on the US Billboard Hot 100 chart (Tuk 2012). Another milestone of Hallyu was the success of Psy's "Gangnam Style" in 2012. The song placed first on the British Official Singles Chart, then on the US Billboard Hot 100, and topped charts in 30 other countries, including Italy, Germany, France, Canada, and Australia (Korea.net n.d.). As of 2012, Hallyu had a fan base of over 6.7 million people worldwide, in over 80 different countries (Sam et al. 2012). Psy released a new song titled "Daddy" on November 30, 2015, whose video was viewed more than a million times in the first 10 hours after its release, and almost 60 million times (58 727 945) in the next two weeks.

Hallyu as a Gateway for Public Diplomacy

Hallyu provided the Korean government with a great launch pad for public diplomacy (Sam et al. 2012), exposing people worldwide to Korean culture through a nontraditional approach (Cheng 2008). A national image promotion committee was set up under the prime minister's office, and in 2003, President Roh Moo-Hyun established the Government Information Agency (Cheng 2008). One of the most recent bodies, the Korea Culture Agency (KOKKA), was set up in 2011 under the Ministry of Culture, Sports, and Tourism (MCST); it now has offices in Beijing, London, Tokyo, and Los Angeles. With the help of these institutions, the MCST started a campaign intended to turn aspects of Hallyu – including K-pop, movies, and dramas, as well as writing, clothing, and cuisine – into a global lifestyle. The government hoped this would help incorporate Korean culture into aspects of everyday life for global citizens (Cheng 2008). The country's effort did not end with government agencies, however. It mobilized NGOs, global companies, public figures, and even private individuals to spread positive information about Korea and help foreigners better understand the country (Sam et al. 2012).

Major tactics implemented involved special events (e.g. sporting events, food and culture festivals, and public diplomacy conferences), traditional media (e.g. TV channels and newspapers), and, most importantly, the Internet (e.g. government websites, blogs, and various digital platforms).

In 2008, the Korean government hosted a conference on country-image branding, inviting world-renowned experts on public diplomacy and branding such as Harvard professor Joseph Nye and French intellectual Guy Sorman (Cheng 2008). In 2010, during the first Korean Public Diplomacy Forum, Korea elected its first public diplomacy ambassador (Sam et al. 2012). Conferences and festivals have proved to be a successful tool of public diplomacy, engaging both Korean citizens and foreigners, and increasing tourism. Events such as the Busan International Film Festival, the Hampyeong Butterfly Festival, and the Hwacheon Sancheoneo (Mountain Trout) Festival – selected as one of the Seven Wonders of Winter by travel site CNNGo – have gained international recognition (Sam et al. 2012; Visit Korea n.d.). The K-pop Cover Dance Festival has been particularly successful; in 2011, it attracted participants from 38 different countries, gaining 16 million views during the first round alone (Tuk 2012).

Sporting events are also effective. In fact, one of the first attempts at rebranding was the Dynamic Korea campaign during the 2002 Korea–Japan World Cup. The Korean government hoped the slogan would give off an image of a new and more active Korea. In 2011, it became the first Asian country to host the IAAF World Championship in Athletics. It also hosted the 2014 Asian Games in Incheon and the 2018 Winter Olympics in Pyeongchang. Taekwondo, now an official Olympic discipline, is also increasing in popularity, with over 70 million professionals in 190 countries (Sam et al. 2012).

TV stations like KBS World and Arirang TV, which are broadcast worldwide, serve as ways for Hallyu to reach faraway audiences. TV dramas, K-pop, and Korean movies, through their portrait of a modern Korea, debunk stereotypes and help foreigners better understand the country.

However, the most successful tactics Korea has used to engage in public diplomacy through various aspects of Hallyu were implemented through the country's cutting-edge innovation technology. Korea has 100% Wi-Fi coverage, allowing Korean citizens, as well as foreigners, to access information and connect with others across the world (Sam et al. 2012). The Ministry of Foreign Affairs and Public Trade (MOFAT) has exploited this outstanding technology through podcasts and social media (Twitter and Facebook) accounts (Sam et al. 2012). MOFAT also makes government applications available to Korean citizens for free, which they can use to inform themselves and others about Korea.

MOFAT hosts online contests such as the 2012 essay contest on Korea's national image, Quiz on Korea, and the video contest, I love Korea Because (Sam et al. 2012). For the latter, MOFAT asked Hallyu fans worldwide to submit a 3-minute video explaining what they love most about Korea. The judges received around 1400 entries from 110 countries. All of the winners were awarded the honorary title "Friend of Korea" during a televised award ceremony featuring many K-pop acts.

The Internet also allows ordinary Korean citizens to act as ambassadors for their country. For instance, a web-based pen-pal system called Friendly Korea helps Koreans and foreigners connect through email, so that the "friends" can get to know the real Korea (Friendly Korea n.d.). Hallyu stars themselves have been serving as Korean ambassadors by giving interviews, participating in festivals, and generally interacting with their fans. Many, such as Amber from female group F(x), even feature as guests in videos made by YouTubers.

Finally, the Korean government has implemented programs involving foreign individuals and institutions. For instance, Pusan National University started a partnership with the University of Groningen allowing students from Groningen to intern in Korean companies and Korean students to study in the Netherlands (University of Groningen 2014). MOFAT also started the Honorary Ambassadors of Korea initiative, an overseas mission to elect foreign celebrities and artists to represent Korea to their home countries (Sam et al. 2012).

Evaluation

Overall, Hallyu has helped Korea's public diplomacy and country-branding efforts. Korean culture has now reached people all over the world, with visible effects. Tourism is on the rise. Many locations that appear in Korean dramas and movies become Korean Wave tourism destinations (Tuk 2012). A survey conducted in 2015 by Korea Focus showed that Seoul was the Asian city foreigners most wanted to visit (Sang-Hyeon and Sung-Tai 2015). Korea's official language, Hangul, is now taught at over 640 universities and 2,100 schools worldwide (Sam et al. 2012). Korean companies have a major international presence, with 13 listed in the Fortune Global 500 (Sam et al. 2012). In 2012, Vietnam awarded eight Korean companies social responsibility awards for making a "significant contribution to society" (Ngoc 2012, para. 1).

However, there have been some recent anti-Hallyu movements, particularly in Asia. In 2012, BBC, Le Monde, and other global publications expressed concern over potential human rights violations in the unjust contracts and excessive work hours of Korean stars (Kim and Lee 2014). Meanwhile, the Chinese government recently limited the total air time of foreign dramas and expressed its unease over Koreans' growing pride (Kim and Lee 2014). Most of the anti-Hallyu sentiment in Asia can be attributed to political tensions due to Korea's history with countries like Japan and China.

Corporate Foreign Policy: The Role of Corporations in Bilateral Trade Promotion

By Kamal I. Latham

Former Deputy Executive Director, US–China Aviation Cooperation Program and Former US Diplomat, US Embassy Beijing

MNCs have been actors in bilateral trade promotion activities between sovereign nations. Public–private partnerships such as the US–China Aviation Cooperation Program (ACP) have facilitated increased demand in the PRC for US aerospace goods and aviation services. ACP programs funded by corporate membership dues and US government grants have promoted PRC aviation safety and efficiency and facilitated billions of US dollars in exports to the PRC since 2004.

Bilateral trade negotiations in air services have featured the presence of corporations. The US government allowed publicly traded air carriers and the PRC government permitted state-owned airlines to be present during several rounds of government negotiations credited with brokering the 2007 US–China Air Transport Agreement (ATA). This trade deal was estimated to stimulate approximately US$5 billion in new economic activity for US air carriers over 5 years. It was a key outcome of the US–China Strategic Economic Dialogue (SED) launched by US President George W. Bush and PRC President Hu Jintao in 2006.

The participation and presence of corporate actors in trade promotion activities is an established practice between major nations such as the United States and China. Corporations seeking to influence foreign trade policy formulation or execution – which could lead to a desired increase in corporate sales or an undesired increase in market competition – should contact their respective overseas business associations and national governments and explore whether participation in public–private partnerships or government negotiations is possible.

Case Study   US–China Aviation Cooperation Program (ACP) – Public–Private Partnership

As a former deputy executive director of ACP, I saw first-hand how US companies collaborated with the US government to help improve PRC aviation safety and efficiency and increase their exports to the PRC. Launched in 2004 by the US government and corporations, the Wright Brothers Partnership US–China ACP was intended to support the fast-growing China market and counter subsidized competition.

ACP has both public and private members. Public members include the US Trade and Development Agency (USTDA), US Federal Aviation Administration, US Embassy Beijing, US Foreign Commercial Service at US Embassy Beijing, US Transportation Security Administration, and American Chamber of Commerce in China. There are over 40 corporate members, including companies such as Boeing, FedEx, GE Aviation, UTC, American Airlines, Textron, and UPS.

The President of Boeing China and the US Federal Aviation Administration Attaché at the US Embassy Beijing co-chair the ACP public–private partnership. The partnership is housed within the American Chamber of Commerce in China and has several Chinese national staff members, led by an American. ACP's public and private members work together to plan and execute aviation capacity-building programs in the PRC, funded by corporate membership dues and USTDA grants. Since the program's inception, USTDA has issued over US$7 million in ACP program grants, which have facilitated billions of US dollars in exports to the PRC.

ACP program examples include Executive Management Development Training, Air Traffic Flow Management, China General Aviation Development and Implement Support, and Civil Aviation Administration of China (CAAC) Flight Standards Inspector Training. CAAC is the PRC government agency responsible for regulating China's aviation industry. ACP staff and members work with CAAC and a cross-section of airlines, airports, think tanks, and other Chinese aviation stakeholders to tackle an array of safety, technical, and infrastructure issues affecting the growth of commercial and general aviation in China.

In the Executive Management Development Training program, more than two dozen managers from the PRC aviation industry are hosted by US aviation stakeholders (e.g. manufacturers, airports, universities, etc.) each year, spending several months learning about the US aviation and aerospace industry. These interfaces are important opportunities for US hosts to leave positive impressions on rising stars in the Chinese aviation industry, who may be future leaders with decision-making authority. They can help level the playing field for US companies competing in the PRC market against subsidized competition.

ACP membership meetings are held each month, and ACP's members belong to various committees tasked with delving into certain topics and developing collaborative programs enhancing US–China aviation cooperation and promoting increased US exports. The US–China Aviation Symposium, held every 2 years, is the capstone engagement, drawing aviation professionals from multiple countries who are interested in networking and hearing the latest in bilateral aviation cooperation between the United States and China. My consulting company, Diplomatic

Treatment, was contracted by a leading US trade association to organize logistics and manage vendors for the 2009 Symposium in Beijing, which had nearly 300 participants and featured remarks from leaders such as the United Airlines CEO and CAAC Minister. USTDA, which is a trade promotion agency, sponsored the event.

2007 US–China Air Transport Agreement (CATA): Bilateral Trade Negotiations Case Study

As a US diplomat assigned to the Economic Affairs Section at US Embassy Beijing, I was responsible for promoting expanded market access opportunities in China for US companies. I served on the US government delegation in multiple rounds of talks with China on liberalizing air services, a key US economic development goal. Travel and trade flows between the two countries were key air service demand drivers. Increasing the number of nonstop daily passenger flights – and relaxing restrictions on air cargo transport – would facilitate more economic growth and job creation on both sides of the Pacific Ocean.

Bilateral air services negotiations were headed on the US side by the Department of State and on the Chinese side by the CAAC. My role was to help design the negotiation strategy and participate in official talks in Washington, DC, Chengdu, and Beijing. Multiple passenger and cargo airlines from both countries were present in these negotiations, seated behind the government representatives. Although the corporate actors were just there as observers, their presence reminded both governments that negotiated outcomes could materially affect multiple employers and employees in a vital network industry.

In 2007, the US Secretary of Transportation and the Minister of CAAC agreed to further amend the original 1980 bilateral air services accord by more than doubling the number of nonstop daily passenger flights between the two countries and dropping restrictions on the number of cargo flights in 2011. The agreement was estimated to stimulate roughly US$5 billion in new economic activity by 2012 for US air carriers. It was deemed a key deliverable at the US SED, hosted by US Treasury Secretary Henry Paulson and involving over three dozen US cabinet secretaries and agency heads, PRC ministers, and other high-level PRC officials.

Conclusion

US foreign trade policy promotes expanded market access opportunities overseas for US companies. This is not dissimilar to the trade policies of other major economies, with domestic corporate actors pursuing new markets. Public–private partnerships and trade negotiations are two routes by which corporate actors can engage in foreign trade policy activities. MNCs seeking profit maximization should consider engaging in these activities with their sovereign governments, if the opportunity arises.

Discussion Questions

1 What are the factors that caused Hallyu to become such a worldwide phenomenon?

2 How did Hallyu serve as a tool of public diplomacy to help Korea improve its international reputation?

3 What kind of research would help the Korean government prevent the decline of Hallyu and the birth of new anti-Hallyu movements?

4 What are some areas the Korean government could exploit to further improve Korea's international reputation?

5 What are some of the downsides to Hallyu and Korea's increased influence in the international arena?

6 What could the Korean government do to tackle some of the concerns that are generating anti-Hallyu feelings?

7 What are some unexplored demographics Hallyu could aspire to reach?

Class Activity

Students should examine the concept of digital diplomacy, focusing on the use of digital media in the field of diplomacy and how countries are utilizing it. The Twiplomacy Study is an annual global survey of the presence and activity of heads of state and government, foreign ministers, and their institutions on Twitter, conducted by Burson Cohn & Wolfe. Students should look at the results of the study from the last few years to find trends in the most listed world leaders, most active world leaders, and most conversational world leaders.

References

Amann, W., Khan, S., Salzmann, O., et al. (2007). Managing external pressures through corporate diplomacy. *Journal of General Management* 33 (1): 33–49.

Anholt, S. (2000). "The good country." Retrieved January 10, 2019 from http://www.simonanholt.com/Research/research-introduction.aspx.

Cheng, L. (2008). "The Korea brand: The cultural dimension of South Korea's branding project in 2008." SAIS: US–Korea Yearbook, 1–14.

Dale, H.C., Cohen, A., and Smith, J.A. (2012). "Challenging America: How Russia, China, and other countries use public diplomacy to compete with the US Heritage Foundation website." Retrieved January 10, 2019 from http://www.heritage.org/research/reports/2012/06/challenging-america-how-russia-china-and-other-countries-use-public-diplomacy-to-compete-with-the-us.

Donaldson, T. and Preston, L. (1995). The stakeholder theory of the corporation: concepts, evidence, and implications. *The Academy of Management Review* 20 (1): 65–91.

Edward R. Murrow Center of Public Diplomacy. (2015). "What is public diplomacy?" Retrieved January 10, 2019 from https://www.uscpublicdiplomacy.org/page/what-is-pd.

Eskew, M. (2006). Corporate diplomacy. *Leadership Excellence* 23 (4): 5–6.

Fadel, L. (2015). "Egypt's tourism hashtag hijacked to show a repressive state." *NPR*. Retrieved January 10, 2019 from http://www.npr.org/2015/12/15/459788992/egypts-tourism-hashtag-hijacked-to-show-a-repressive-state.

Friedman, A.L. and Miles, S. (2006). *Stakeholders: Theory and Practice.* Oxford: Oxford University Press.

Friendly Korea. (n.d.). "About us." Retrieved January 10, 2019 from http://korea.prkorea.com/wordpress/english/about-us/.

Gallup. (2012). "Americans give record-high ratings to several US allies." Retrieved January 10, 2019 from http://www.gallup.com/poll/152735/americans-give-record-high-ratings-several-allies.aspx.

Hong-June, Y. (2015). "The origin and future of 'Hallyu." Retrieved January 10, 2019 from http://www.koreafocus.or.kr/design2/layout/content_print.asp?group_id=101213.

Jang, G. and Paik, W. (2012). Korean Wave as tool for Korea's new cultural diplomacy. *Advances in Applied Psychology* 2 (3): 1–7.

Jintao, H. (2012). "Why China is weak on soft power." *The New York Times.* Retrieved January 10, 2019 from https://www.nytimes.com/2012/01/18/opinion/why-china-is-weak-on-soft-power.html.

Kim, J. and Lee, J. (2014). Korean pop culture: A decade of ups and downs. *International Journal of Multimedia and Ubiquitous Engineering* 9 (3): 129–134.

Korea.net. (n.d.). "Hallyu (Korean Wave)." Retrieved January 10, 2019 from http://www.korea.net/AboutKorea/Culture-and-the-Arts/Hallyu.

L'Etang, J. (2009). Public relations and diplomacy in a globalized world: an issue of public communication. *American Behavioral Scientist* 53 (4): 607–626.

Maignan, I. and Ferrell, O.C. (2004). Corporate social responsibility and marketing: An integrative framework. *Journal of the Academy of Marketing Science* 32 (1): 3–19.

Manfred, T. (2011). "Here's why China gave Costa Rica a $105 million stadium and flooded its soccer federation with cash." *Business Insider*. Retrieved January 10, 2019 from http://www.businessinsider.com/costa-rica-china-soccer-2011-11.

Molleda, J.C. (2011). Global political public relations, public diplomacy, and corporate foreign policy. In: *Political Public Relations: Principles and Applications* (ed. S. Kiousis and J. Strömbäck), 274–292. New York: Routledge.

Murphy, A. (2015). "2015 Global 2000: Methodology." Forbes. Retrieved January 10, 2019 from http://www.forbes.com/sites/andreamurphy/2015/05/06/2015-global-2000-methodology.

Ngoc, B. (2012). "CSR is a way to give back." *Talk Vietnam*. Retrieved January 10, 2019 from https://www.talkvietnam.com/2012/11/csr-is-a-way-to-give-back/.

Nye, J.S. (2004). The decline of America's soft power. *Foreign Affairs* 83: 16–20.

Nye, J.S. (2010). "The new public diplomacy." Retrieved January 10, 2019 from https://foia.state.gov/searchapp/DOCUMENTS/HRCEmail_August_Web/IPS-0065/DOC_0C05767159/C05767159.pdf.

Ordeix-Rigo, E. and Duarte, J. (2009). From public diplomacy to corporate diplomacy: increasing corporation's legitimacy and influence. *American Behavioral Scientist* 53 (4): 549–564.

Payne, G.J. (2009). Trends in global public relations and grassroots diplomacy. *American Behavioral Scientist* 53 (4): 487–492.

Powell, A. (2015). "US food diplomacy wins fans at Milan's World Fair. USC Annenberg Center of Communication Leadership and Policy." Retrieved January 10, 2019 from https://communicationleadership.usc.edu/uncategorized/u-s-food-diplomacy-wins-fans-at-milan-worlds-fair.

PricewaterhouseCoopers. (2010). "India to produce 2219 new multinational companies between 2010–2024." Retrieved January 10, 2019 from http://www.pwc.com/in/en/press-releases/press-releases-2010.jhtml.

Rawlins, B.L. (2006). "Prioritizing stakeholders for public relations." Retrieved January 10, 2019 from https://instituteforpr.org/prioritizing-stakeholders/.

Sam, M., Jung-He, S., and Moore, D. (2012). Korea's public diplomacy: A new initiative for the future. *ISSUE Brief* 29: 1–25.

Sang-Hyeon, J. and Sung-Tai, H. (2015). "Korea, Koreans and Korean products as seen by foreigners." Retrieved January 10, 2019 from http://www.koreafocus.or.kr/design2/layout/content_print. asp?group_id=105095.

Scherer, A.G. and Palazzo, G. (2007). Toward a political conception of corporate responsibility: Business and society seen from a Habermasian perspective. *Academy of Management Review* 32 (4): 1096–1120.

Sharp, P. (2007). Revolutionary states, outlaw regimes and the techniques of public diplomacy. In: *The New Public Diplomacy: Soft Power in International Relations* (ed. J. Melissen), 106–123. London: Palgrave MacMillan.

Taylor, M. (2008). "Toward a relational theory of public diplomacy." Paper presented at the annual meeting of the 94th Annual National Communication Association, San Diego, CA.

Tuk, W. (2012). "The Korean Wave: Who are behind the success of Korean popular culture?" Leiden University. Retrieved January 10, 2019 from https://openaccess.leidenuniv.nl/handle/1887/20142.

University of Groningen. (2014). "UB Korea Corner officially opened." Retrieved January 10, 2019 from https://www.rug.nl/news/2014/12/korea-corner-in-ub-officieel-geopend?lang=en.

USC Center on Public Diplomacy. (n.d.). "Defining public diplomacy." Retrieved January 10, 2019 from http://uscpublicdiplomacy.org/page/what-pd.

Visit Korea. (n.d.). "Embrace the cold at Hwacheon Sancheoneo Ice Festival." Retrieved January 10, 2019 from http://english.visitkorea.or.kr/enu/SI/SI_EN_3_6.jsp?cid=1547131.

Wang, J. (2006). Public diplomacy and global business. *Journal of Business Strategy* 27 (3): 41–49.

White, C.L. (2015). Exploring the role of private-sector corporations in public diplomacy. *Public Relations Inquiry* 4 (3): 305–321.

White, C. and Kolesnicov, I. (2015). Nation branding in a transitional democracy: The role of corporate diplomacy in promoting national identity. *Place Branding and Public Diplomacy* 11: 324–337.

Zakaria, F. (2011). *The Post-American World: Release 2.0*. New York: W. W. Norton & Company.

Index

Global and Multicultural Public Relations, First Edition. Juan-Carlos Molleda
and Sarab Kochhar.
© 2019 John Wiley & Sons, Inc. Published 2019 by John Wiley & Sons, Inc.